GOING FOR

55

GOING FOR

55

RANGERS' JOURNEY BACK TO
THE TOP OF SCOTTISH FOOTBALL

CHRISTOPHER JACK

POLARIS
PUBLISHING

POLARIS PUBLISHING LTD
c/o Aberdein Considine
2nd Floor, Elder House
Multrees Walk
Edinburgh
EH1 3DX

Distributed by Birlinn Limited

www.polarispublishing.com

ISBN: 9781913538606
eBook ISBN: 9781913538613

British Library Cataloguing-in-Publication Data
A catalogue record for this book is available on request from the British Library.

Designed and typeset by Polaris Publishing, Edinburgh
Printed and bound by CPI Group (UK) Ltd, Croydon CR0 4YY

In loving memory of my grandparents Archibald and Isabel Hall.
I hope I have made you both proud.

FOREWORD

BY DAVE KING

WHAT A GREAT time to be a Rangers fan following the terrible moments we have endured for so many years.

Every single Rangers supporter has suffered and every single supporter will be aware of what it has taken to restore our club to the pinnacle of Scottish football. We can all rejoice at this significant moment in our history – not only for winning the title but for the resilience that we have all shown to get to this point. Many feared it would never happen.

From my personal perspective, I cannot adequately express my joy at securing our 55th league title. What a pleasure to be able to look ahead to our 150th anniversary celebrations next year as champions of Scotland. It is truly fitting and extremely well deserved.

Winning the title is the fulfilment of a dream and the end of an era for me and Chris has asked me to touch on my recollections of the past few years in this foreword. I have also been interviewed for comment in some of the chapters.

Supporters already know that I was initially unwilling to get involved when the club was at its lowest ebb in that darkest of times. I believed that the local Scottish business community was best able to take on that responsibility and my understanding at the time was that a number of local consortiums were being put together for that very purpose. Without an intervention by Rangers-minded people we were consigned to perpetual failure under the control of the Easdale/Ashley axis.

It was only when I realised that the Scottish community had been unable to marshal the necessary resources that I stepped in as lead investor. It was a huge decision for me at the time to take on the responsibility of further funding of the club given that I had already lost £20million. But, equally daunting, was the realisation that I would have to devote much of my time and business expertise to the double challenge of removing the Ashley virus while simultaneously making progress on the pitch. It was quite a hurdle and ultimately involved much more of my time than I had envisaged or hoped, which also negatively affected my other business interests. But, like every supporter, we all do what we can and I felt an obligation to the present and past generations to do everything in my power to reverse the downward trend and to then restore the club to again being number one in Scotland.

At the end of 2014 I asked the supporters to back me to try to remove the previous regime and, together, we managed to achieve this in 2015. From that time on, despite the numerous obstacles put in our way, everything was geared towards returning Rangers to being number one. I will never forget how hollowed out and derelict the club was when John Gilligan, Paul Murray and I first walked through the doors of Ibrox after we took over in 2015.

For me, title 55 is the culmination of the recovery project that my fellow investors and I commenced, but I hope that for Steven Gerrard and the team it is the continuation of their journey. We must keep improving or we still stand still. The board has demonstrated that it will continue to invest and improve the squad and support Steven to build on this Premiership win.

I have had the prime seat to witness the drama unfolding over the recent years and must pay tribute to every board member for the financial and emotional backing that I was given when making tough decisions – including the appointment of a young, unproven manager. I am absolutely convinced that the inspired appointment of Steven and his support team was vital to where we are today. Steven may not have had top flight managerial experience but he is a winner and winners find a way to win in any situation.

But, ultimately, this is all about the supporters because without them none of this would have been possible. The energy I had to devote to it and the money that I and my fellow investors had to put into it could not have happened without the belief and backing of the supporters. The energy that I drew for everything I have done for the club was because of the supporters and I thank you all for the opportunity to have been chairman of our great club during this critical time in its history.

Onwards and upwards – going for 56.

ONE

THIS ONE IS for the fans. It is a reward for your loyalty and your passion, your time and your money. It is justification of your faith, a validation of your service to a cause and your club.

It is for those that didn't do walking away, those that followed near and far and that feared no foe to keep the blue flag flying. You could have fallen divided, but it is united you stand.

What Ally McCoist started, Steven Gerrard has completed. History has been made, wounds have been healed and a club, an institution, that could have been condemned to mediocrity stands tall, proud and victorious as champions of Scotland once again.

It is an achievement that wouldn't have been possible without the influence of so many individuals, yet none are as significant as the power of the collective. No support has been through as much and no support deserves these joyous moments more.

The past decade will never be forgotten, and nor should it be. History is written not chosen and the scars will remain on

Rangers forevermore. The past shouldn't be airbrushed, but instead serve as a reminder and an inspiration. Now, Rangers are going for 56.

Every fan will have their own tales to tell and those memories will be shared in times of celebration, reflection and emotion. The message to them is simple yet evocative.

"To every one of them, every one of them, I personally would just say 'thank you' and I really mean that," McCoist said. "That is all I can say, really. It is 'thank you' for your support.

"I remember being at Ibrox and there was 50,000 there for a game against Stranraer and I turned to Kenny and Durranty and said 'this is the reason that we will be back, this is why we will be back winning titles again and back in the Champions League'. There was an element of madness about it all but that was the Rangers support and their backing of the club has been incredible. Nothing would have been possible without them. So I can only say 'thank you'."

The instruction of 'Go with Gerrard' has been central to the success. It would put a deal in place, make headlines far beyond Govan and change the course of Scottish football.

When Rangers celebrate their 150th anniversary in 2022, they will do so as champions, with a 55th league flag adorning the Trophy Room wall and the most sought-after silverware in the club's illustrious history glistening in the cabinet, once again draped in red, white and blue ribbons.

It was in that very room on 4 May 2018, that Gerrard stood with the scarf hanging around his neck and held above his head. Three seasons on, he would strike similar poses on the pitch as the scarf was replaced by a medal and a trophy. It signified the end of a journey for Rangers and the achievement marks a moment at which a line in the sand can be drawn. For Gerrard, it is only the beginning as the man that made himself a legend in Liverpool has earned god-like status in Glasgow.

Gerrard has achieved what many considered impossible, what his doubters and detractors believed he was incapable of. That makes this success all the sweeter. As Gerrard has overcome his own trials and tribulations, Rangers have emerged through the ultimate adversity. The Rangers story is not merely one of sporting achievement, but one of loyalty and of belief, of loss and of sacrifice. In the end, it was one of emotion and celebration.

The fall and rise of Rangers is incomparable in sport and those two numbers – 55 and 150 – carry a unique significance for supporters whose lives have been dominated by the events of the last decade. Some will think of friends and family who sadly passed away before their club returned to the top, while others will cherish a first success with a generation who have only known defeat and discord. Those outside of Ibrox will say this is the season that Rangers stopped Celtic winning ten-in-a-row but that has never been the most pertinent focus for fans. Their club is one which succeeds for itself and its people, not because it prevents a rival from an achievement that many in Scottish football assumed was a fait accompli.

When Rangers were playing Challenge Cup ties in front of the hedge at Brechin, losing to Alloa in the same competition and being beaten by a Stirling Albion side whose manager missed the game to get married, days like those experienced this season, albeit in unique and Covid-impacted circumstances, could barely have been dreamt of. Those years traipsing around the country, ticking off the lower league grounds out of a sense of duty rather than desire, have shaped the Rangers support and given them memories, more bad ones than good, than they would ever have expected whilst they were winning leagues and cups and reaching European finals just a few years before. It was christened as 'The Journey'.

It is only now that Rangers have completed it as the Premiership has been added to the Third Division, League One and Championship titles. The script couldn't have been written, but the story will forever be told by those who lived through it, endured it and now savour it as the most important triumph of all for an institution that can again beam with pride at its tagline of the 'the world's most successful club'.

"I remember saying that to the boys down south," McCoist said. "Andy Townsend phoned me after the game at Brechin and said 'did I just see that ball getting stuck in a hedge?' and I said 'aye, it did, it got stuck in the hedge'. He phoned me three weeks later and said 'did I just see 50,000 at your home game against Stranraer?' and I said 'aye, you did'. He laughed and said 'what is going on up there?' and I said 'I don't know, Andy, but I have got myself strapped in for the ride anyway. I am sure there is plenty more to come'. And there was!

"But to those supporters, I would just say 'thanks' and urge them to enjoy this moment of celebration with each other when they can. It has been phenomenal and they deserve as much credit, if not all the credit, for the achievement of this season."

There would have been moments when even the most diehard and determined of Rangers supporters may have feared that these times would never come, but those days are what make these achievements all the more romantic and the way in which they are savoured is the essence of sport. Two occassions in particular – the Extraordinary General Meeting in March 2015 and the appointment of Gerrard three years later – proved to be defining as Rangers were saved and then restored. The mistakes made along the way are countless, but the anguish and the anger are now enveloped by sheer joy and relief as those tumultuous days, while they will never be forgotten, are finally put to the back of minds.

It was the standards and philosophy of Bill Struth that shaped Rangers as a club from the 1920s through the next two decades. Today, his words still resonate strongly with those associated with Rangers and in these times of celebration and achievement, they are as apt as ever. They act as a reminder of where Rangers have come from, but also of what the club stands for and the bond between Rangers and its supporters is stronger now than ever before.

"Our very success, gained you will agree by skill, will draw more people than ever to see it," Struth said as he was presented with the portrait that now watches over the medals and mementos and observes all those that enter the Trophy Room at Ibrox. "And that will benefit many more clubs than Rangers. Let the others come after us. We welcome the chase. It is healthy for us. We will never hide from it.

"Never fear, inevitably we shall have our years of failure, and when they arrive, we must reveal tolerance and sanity. No matter the days of anxiety that come our way, we shall emerge stronger because of the trials to be overcome. That has been the philosophy of the Rangers since the days of the gallant pioneers."

Triumph has emerged from adversity. Indeed, it was after another afternoon when the metaphorical dark clouds hung above Ibrox that the silver lining began to emerge. That day, Dave King – who would return as chairman as he, John Gilligan and Paul Murray won control of Rangers after a bitter and public fight that saw a reviled regime finally ousted from power – was perhaps the only man that knew it.

It was March 2018 and Rangers hosted Celtic in the third Old Firm fixture of the season. On the park and in the dugout, they would once again find themselves outclassed as Celtic – managed by Brendan Rodgers – earned the points that all-but secured a seventh consecutive Premiership title. The confirmation of that feat would come just weeks later for Celtic as a 4-0 victory at Hampden in the Scottish Cup was followed by a 5-0 win at Parkhead in another demolition derby.

It is difficult to pinpoint the moment where supporters felt at their lowest and most demoralised and when Rangers seemed as far away as ever from being able to compete with Celtic, never mind beat them. Those final ignominious and controversial days of Graeme Murty's second spell in charge were undoubtedly some of the most testing, though.

The 3-2 loss at Ibrox wasn't an embarrassment, like so many others of this period were for Rangers, but the issues in terms of leadership and quality were clear to those that contributed to the usual fevered and frenzied Old Firm atmosphere. In the Main Stand, Gerrard watched on. Within minutes of the final whistle, a chain of events started that would ultimately lead to Gerrard, then the Under-18s coach at Liverpool, becoming Rangers manager.

"Steven is a very interesting story in the sense that there is a certain sense of what I would call randomness about it," King said as he reflected on the process that saw Gerrard return to Glasgow just months later and agree a four-year contract with Rangers. "Not to be too philosophical, but that is something I believe in in life. Life is very random, and it is how you deal with events as they pass you by that makes a difference.

"Steven had come to a Rangers v Celtic game and he had brought up one of the Liverpool youth teams as well. It was the game when Celtic beat us with ten men when we thought we had a chance of winning the game.

"I had a meeting after the game which caused me to be delayed in terms of going into the boardroom where everyone met, and Steven was in the corner. So, I wandered over to him and asked how he was doing and I had met him a couple of times at Liverpool before with Kenny Dalglish. He made a comment to me and said that Rangers were technically very good but had no pace and power and we chatted about a few things.

"Towards the end of the conversation, I asked him if he had been missing playing and that side of things and he said yes and that he was really missing the buzz and the thrill of being there at three o'clock on a Saturday, European nights and just the buzz of the game.

"I asked if he was thinking of going into management and he said that is where he saw himself going next. Then I very casually said 'oh, that is interesting to know, we might give you a phone call one day' and it was a very casual, if you want to say flippant, comment from me."

By the time that call was made, Rangers were in disarray and King had reached a potentially defining moment in his chairmanship. If the appointment that summer had been the wrong one, Rangers would have been set back years. Progress wouldn't just have stalled, Rangers would have gone into reverse.

What has been labelled as 'The Ten' would have been gift-wrapped for Celtic and a fanbase that had been hugely supportive of King and his fellow investors and directors would have started to ask real questions over whether they were the right people to run the club and take it forward.

Rangers needed a manager, a leader, someone to inspire those around him and raise standards to the levels which a club with their history, tradition and aspirations should operate at. Those previously tasked with achieving just that had failed and, having only travelled some of the distance on the road to recovery, Rangers were in danger of taking a wrong turn once again.

Murty had firstly stepped in as caretaker following the departure of Mark Warburton and David Weir in February of the previous year. Rangers insisted that their management team had resigned, while Warburton and Weir claimed they were sacked. Within weeks, the pair were installed at Nottingham Forest, a proposition that Warburton had denied in his final days at Ibrox as relations with the board and sections of the press became increasingly strained.

By the time that Murty was relieved of his duties for the second time, Rangers had appointed Pedro Caixinha, sacked him and seen a move for Derek McInnes, the Aberdeen manager and a member of the Rangers nine-in-a-row winning squad, collapse at the last minute. The motives of the board and their affection for the club could not be questioned, but their decision making certainly could and Rangers lurched from calamity to crisis.

Warburton had at least ensured a second attempt at winning promotion from the Championship was a successful one, although the Scottish Cup final defeat to Hibernian would leave a scar on the squad and the support over the summer and into the new season.

On the day that Rangers returned to the Premiership, a 'Going for 55' card display filled the Sandy Jardine Stand. It was a message of hope as much as defiance, a rallying call from supporters to state where they believed Rangers were heading.

Warburton would not be the man to take them there and a 1-1 draw with Hamilton Academical was a sign of things to come. He had been serenaded by supporters who sang of chasing a 55th league title once promotion from the Championship had been achieved. The Englishman would deliver one part, but never looked like fulfilling the second ambition.

There was always a feeling that Warburton – a former City trader who had earned a sound reputation as a youth coach and then as a manager with Brentford – didn't 'get' Rangers and was unable to adapt to the nuances of life in Glasgow. It is a city where first is first and second is nowhere and Warburton seemed to struggle with the scrutiny and pressure that all Rangers and Celtic managers sign up for when they put pen to paper.

His insistence that 'Plan B was to do Plan A better' became a phrase used to mock him and his methods. He would suffer a 5-1 defeat at Parkhead and see the signing of Joey Barton backfire spectacularly as deals for the likes of Philippe Senderos and Niko Kranjcar proved to be costly mistakes that summed up a rapid decline in Warburton's fortunes.

He certainly left Rangers in a better place than they were when he arrived and, despite the failures, his tenure was an experiment that was certainly worthwhile embarking on at that time. But it would get worse, much worse, before there was even the chance of improvement and progress for Rangers and a stint under the caretaker guidance of their Under-20s coach was never going to be a turning point.

The first Murty reign was ended when Caixinha was appointed in March 2017. Come October, the Portuguese had departed as quickly as he had arrived. His tenure was short but far from sweet as Old Firm humiliations were inflicted by a Celtic side that contrasted starkly in every aspect – technically, physically and mentally – to a Rangers squad that contained many that were not fit to wear the shirt.

There have been several such sides in recent years, but the ridicule suffered on their stumbles in the lower leagues were nothing compared to Caixinha's evening of shame in Luxembourg. The defeat to Progres Niederkorn is only challenged by the famous Scottish Cup loss at Berwick Rangers in 1967 as the worst ever suffered by a Rangers side and the acrimony was as profound as the embarrassment in the early days of July 2017.

The pictures of Caixinha arguing with and gesticulating at supporters outside the Stade Josy Barthel will live with him forever and they encapsulated an era. Jordan Rossiter, the former Liverpool youngster, emerged from a dressing room containing far more experienced and culpable individuals to conduct the post-mortem with the press following the 2-0 defeat that saw Rangers eliminated from the Europa League by a side that had scored just one goal in their thirteen games in continental competition. It was a defeat that couldn't be believed even as the action unfolded in front of your eyes.

Caixinha – an unknown manager that had been plucked from the obscurity of Qatari outfit Al-Gharafa – wasn't fit to hold the position once held by Struth, Jock Wallace, Graeme Souness and Walter Smith and the time and money wasted during those ill-fated months set Rangers back considerably at all levels.

"The appointment of Pedro Caixinha was perplexing in itself," Andy Devlin, a sportswriter with *The Scottish Sun* and the man who would exclusively reveal the news of Gerrard's move to Rangers, said. "It was very left-field and people were almost scratching their head before he had a chance to get into the dugout. You could see very, very quickly that it was a massive gamble and it was never going to pay off with Caixinha.

"I remember sitting in one of the press conferences at Murray Park and he came out with the line about the dogs barking and the caravans keep moving. I remember sitting in the room and just putting my head in my hands and shaking my head as if to say, 'What is going on here? This is the manager of Rangers.'

"I looked across to the PR manager at the time and he had the same look on his face as I had. You could see that change was going to have to come.

"The writing was on the wall for Pedro from the moment that he found himself stood in a bush remonstrating with Rangers fans in Luxembourg. In hindsight, he really should have been relieved of his duties there and then."

Caixinha's tenure was defined by that night in Luxembourg but a defeat to Motherwell at Hampden was almost as unforgiveable. When Rangers were held by Kilmarnock at Ibrox, the Portuguese was sacked the next morning and his tenure was brought to an end after 229 costly and calamitous days.

It is remarkable, harrowing even, to reflect on those extraordinary months and time cannot forgive the appointment and financial backing of a boss that was clearly out of his depth from the first day that he took office. His media briefings were as erratic as his signing policy and team selections, which he once revealed at his pre-match press conference in an event that was more of an alarming insight into the workings of the man than merely a break with protocol. One early meeting with journalists, in which he attempted to explain his tactical philosophy by drawing obscure box diagrams on a piece of paper, left those there as bamboozled as his players and convinced he wouldn't last long at Ibrox, never mind be the man to deliver the next league title.

Caixinha would alienate the Scottish core of players in the squad but two of his acquisitions – Ryan Jack and Alfredo Morelos – would prove sound ones. Both emerged from the Caixinha era with their reputations intact and then survived the cull that Gerrard undertook to begin his Rangers revolution at the end of a barren campaign.

"We got to the situation with Pedro where he was obviously struggling on the park and off the park," King said. "And when I say off the park, I mean more in the sense that his manner of going about dealing with the media hadn't really worked and he came in for some criticism and abuse.

"I was very happy to defend him because my view was that Pedro couldn't be judged by what was happening on the media side of things but had to be judged by what was happening on the park.

"Unfortunately, every time I met with him I said 'Pedro, you have really got to turn this thing around. I am backing you, I know what you are trying to do, but you have got to get the team back on side.' I really gave him every opportunity, up until the Kilmarnock game and it just became too much for us. I said 'Pedro, I am sorry, I really love you, you are a great guy and I admire your passion,' but we just couldn't continue."

King had been the figure for supporters and investors to rally round in the months that culminated in regime change in 2015 and he would again come to the fore when it mattered most. He had delegated, to an extent, the recruitment of Warburton and

Caixinha to other members of the board but the knowledge that the third one had to be the right one saw him take a far more hands-on and firm approach to the process that would lead to Gerrard.

Rangers were a shadow of the club they used to be and should have been at that time, but the first two years of a new era had seen signs of progress. It didn't feel like it then, but Rangers were on their way back, although there were more blows to be absorbed before they could come out punching like the heavyweight force of yesteryear.

The fall-out and ramifications of the administration and liquidation process at Ibrox would continue long after Rangers returned to action in July 2012 with McCoist at the helm. It was the most bitter and tempestuous, even hateful, period that Scottish football has ever seen as Rangers and their fans were derided and kicked while they were down. Today, it is those same supporters that have the last laugh, and they who will celebrate the longest.

Rangers could easily have vanished that summer and become a footnote in Scottish football, but the club would survive thanks to the unwavering loyalty and commitment of their supporters. As they thrive once again, the list of those who have played their part and their achievements individually and collectively should be as fondly remembered and revered as the men who earned each result that gave Rangers a triumph that was ten years in the making.

Adulation that is normally reserved for players that win titles or trophies now bestows King, but the man himself is keen to acknowledge the team effort that was required to wrestle control away from the Charles Green and Mike Ashley power base, which saw the likes of the Easdale brothers, Sandy and James, David Somers and Derek Llambias cast as villains in a dark and complicated tale of many characters.

Had King, Gilligan and Murray, assisted by the Three Bears – Douglas Park, George Letham and George Taylor – not been successful in their moves to buy up large swathes of shares, Rangers would not be in the position they are now. Indeed, it does not bear thinking about for supporters just what state their club would have found itself in had those who cared about it not triumphed over those who only seemed to care about themselves.

"There are parts of that day that are very clear and parts of it that are just a blur and the sheer enormity of it didn't hit me until later on," Gilligan said of 6 March 2015, as power was transferred and Rangers were rescued. "The day that we won the EGM was monumental. Paul has said previously that the club was broken into bits. There were lots of pieces to it, but it was just so bad that it was hard to explain.

"What I would like to say is that the people that were working for the club were fantastic and all the people that were there when we arrived, they were all there because it was Rangers. They weren't there for the money, because it was miserable. But they worked for the love of Rangers."

Those that were returning to Ibrox had an idea of how wretched a condition the club was in, but it was only once they had the keys and could look inside for themselves that they could comprehend the scale of the task in hand. This was still Rangers, still their first love, and those feelings had only grown stronger through time and absence, even if their club was a shadow of its former glory at that time.

The day after regime change, Kenny McDowall's side were held to a goalless draw at Cowdenbeath. Central Park, with its stock car track surrounding the pitch and decaying, decrepit infrastructure, has a certain charm unique to Scottish football and it was perhaps an apt location for Rangers, the ultimate fallen giant, to begin the process of recovery. On that weekend six years later, Rangers would be crowned champions once again.

At a neglected Ibrox, the windows hadn't been cleaned, the wallpaper was peeling off and the carpets were threadbare. The offices hadn't been given a lick of paint for some time and the wood panelling had been allowed to fade as Rangers' iconic home summed up the state of a club that had lost its class through years of neglect by those who were supposed to be custodians of it.

"It was things like that that I remember," Gilligan said. "I remember thinking 'my goodness'. I had worked in Argyle House with McEwan's Lager and the dilapidation and the mess of the whole place was just so bad. You don't see it when there are 50,000 people there.

"We still had shareholders that we were trying to buy out or move on and come to arrangements with and they were still on the board even though we had won control of the board. It was challenging, very, very challenging and that was just off the pitch. On the pitch it was tough, really tough."

The work to bring Ibrox back up to standard and to give the stadium back its sense of occasion and grandeur was undertaken alongside the renovations to the team.

The first stage of that process saw McDowall, a man who took the side out of a duty to the club rather than a willingness and who cut a troubled figure for many weeks, relieved of his position. Stuart McCall would ultimately fail to win promotion from the Championship, but Rangers could at least build on sturdy foundations at board level as fans re-engaged with their club in huge numbers.

The call from Richard Gough to McCall was out of the blue as the former Motherwell manager was sounded out over a return to Ibrox. Gilligan pays a heartfelt thanks to McCall for stepping in during Rangers' hour of need but the nine-in-a-row hero was only too happy to help after being recommended for the role by Gough, John Brown and Walter Smith.

"I am just proud that I have played for and managed one of the most successful clubs in the world and a club that means a lot to me," McCall said. "From a performance point of view, we got so far and then lost in the play-off final and that was the end for me in the job at that point. But I would never have changed it for a second and never had any regrets.

"People said it wasn't the right time to go in there but I knew where the club was at and what they needed. I have got a lot of friends and family that support Rangers and they had lost a bit of connection with the club under the old board.

"When they went and Dave King, John Gilligan and Paul Murray came in, that all changed and there was a bit more positivity. The results picked up but we couldn't get over the line unfortunately. I would never have said no to it when the club asked me.

"At the time, I just thought 'what an honour to be asked to go in as Rangers manager'. The crowds at the start were 28,000 and the last games we played were both sell-outs so we managed to get a bit of belief back in the club. We obviously fell at the final hurdle unfortunately but, for that time, I was just so proud to be involved."

Given the paucity of the resources at his disposal, it was an achievement for McCall to take Rangers as far as he did before they eventually came up short, losing to former club Motherwell in the play-offs as Rangers were condemned to another season outside of the top flight. His affection for Rangers was always evident and he at least injected some pride and belief into a squad whose morale had plunged new depths as abject results and performances were produced amid the backdrop of supporter protests and the boardroom upheaval.

A new season promised to be a fresh start but, like so many before and after it, it was a false dawn. There was a renewed optimism upon Warburton's arrival but by the time the magic had vanished from his hat, Rangers found themselves at a crossroads once again. The route they went down in terms of Caixinha was very different and the mistake even costlier as another campaign was wasted and the chances of closing the gap across Glasgow seemed increasingly forlorn as Celtic enjoyed unrivalled and historic success under the guidance of Rodgers.

No Rangers manager should survive three seasons without silverware and the stakes were just as high for King and his board as the search for Caixinha's replacement intensified. Had they made the wrong call, then another power shift around the top table would surely have been required.

At that time, McInnes seemed destined to return to Ibrox after several steady, if unspectacular, years with Aberdeen. The pursuit was lengthy and ultimately unsuccessful as, despite being within hours of being named as Rangers manager, McInnes confirmed he was staying at Pittodrie. There would be no coronation for the man whom King had apprehensions about as he addressed the 'concomitant' risks of the move for McInnes.

"I made some calls and it became clear that there was a desire to go for Derek McInnes and I ran a story saying that Derek was the man Rangers wanted," Devlin said. "For his part, I think Derek McInnes at that point was keen to take the job, he wanted to move and he wanted it done quickly, if possible.

"Looking back, the one voice of concern on the board was Dave King and I don't think Dave King was convinced that Derek McInnes was the man. He had reservations and I think this is where Dave King is due a lot of credit and, as chairman, he stood his ground.

"There was a push for Derek to become Rangers manager and there were talks held and early on in that process Derek was keen on the Rangers job. The longer it went on, I was convinced that Derek wasn't going to get the job and however you want to look at it, whether he knocked it back or Rangers took the offer off the table, he didn't get it.

"Dave had reservations about Derek and while some on the board undoubtedly wanted him to become Rangers manager, it became clear that it wasn't going to happen."

When that news was confirmed late on a Thursday evening just a fortnight before Christmas, Rangers returned to a state of flux. Criticism was directed at the board from all angles of the media as King's detractors lined up to take shot after shot. If they had endeavoured to get to know the man rather than judge opinions on the caricature painted in some circles, they would have understood that the South Africa-based businessman was more than adept at repelling unfriendly fire.

The next appointment was going to be the most important of King's tenure and the most significant in a generation from Rangers' perspective. The move for Gerrard was an undoubted gamble, but the man that rolled the dice knew the prize that could be collected if it came off.

Of the names that were put to King, many were dismissed out of hand and the more high-profile ones – including four Premier League bosses and two former England managers – were deemed unsuitable because of track records that were blotched more than once. They were available and interested as a result of past failures, and that quite simply was not an option at Ibrox.

King had united a support that had become disillusioned and disheartened and brought them together for the good of Rangers in the build-up to his EGM win. It was success on the park that he required, though, if his legacy wasn't to be one of a job only half done and his mind would return to his early messages to fans as he considered his options going into 2018.

"I was looking very hard at that time and thinking that I had come in at regime change, I had promised supporters that there was a way forward there," King said. "But that wasn't just momentum forward to a better position, ultimately what I was saying to supporters was that I would deliver to them a Rangers team that would compete for the league.

"At that time, we were still in the Championship and just after we took over Stuart McCall came in and we had another year in the Championship. It was quite dire but I was mindful that, while there is nothing certain in football, that our goal that I was asking the supporters to buy in to was the re-emergence of Rangers as title contenders.

"I was very concerned looking at the applicants at that moment in time that, given whoever came in we would need to give more money to in terms of our budget, I just didn't feel there was a way forward that I felt comfortable with and confident that it might not get us back in the same situation in one or two years' time. I knew I didn't have another two or three years, I had to start making progress immediately."

As King deliberated, Rangers deteriorated. Murty had been appointed as interim manager just before Christmas but there was never any prospect of the youth coach becoming boss on a long-term basis. Given the fanfare that would later greet Gerrard at his unveiling, the way in which Murty was presented to the media was in keeping with the feelings of uncertainty as a sticking plaster was put on a gaping, self-inflicted wound.

A press release was distributed to journalists waiting at Auchenhowie for the pre-match media conference while Murty, director of football Mark Allen and Stewart Robertson, the managing director, quickly posed for photographs. Murty was friendly and engaging to deal with, but he was a coach in a manager's position and his reluctance to put himself forward as a candidate was indicative of the fact that he knew himself he wasn't the man for the job.

The obvious jibe that was directed towards Rangers when Gerrard was appointed was that they had exchanged one academy coach for another. Yet that overly simplistic view failed to take into account the characteristics and experiences of both men and there is an aura about the way in which Gerrard operates and carries himself that instantly impresses and captivates.

At a club where the cost of failure and the rewards of success are matched, it takes a certain kind of man to assume the role. Gerrard ticks all the boxes in that regard. He is polished and professional in front of the cameras and speaks with an authority and assertiveness to the media and his players.

There was a lure of Liverpool for King when it came to appointing the former Anfield captain, the man who had inspired the Miracle of Istanbul and who had represented his club, his community and his country with such distinction and loyalty until a premature end just months before Rodgers would leave Merseyside having failed to deliver the Premier League. King had adored Gerrard the player, now he wanted to give him a chance to be Gerrard the manager.

"I spoke to Mark Allen and said I had this chat with Steven Gerrard," King said. "And there was just something about it when I said to him about missing football and him wanting to be in management, and when I said 'I might give you a call someday' that stuck with me. It was almost like a 'you know, I wouldn't mind you chatting to me about that'.

"Mark and I had a chat and we discussed the obvious things like bringing in a guy who was a football legend, of which there are many. Diego Maradona was a football legend but he hadn't succeeded in management. Can you bring a football legend into Rangers and ask him to be manager at that time?

"This is where a little bit of a personal element comes into it for me. Being a huge Liverpool fan, I felt like I knew Steven in the sense that I had watched his debut under Gérard Houllier and I felt that I knew the man just from watching him play for Liverpool every week.

"I knew his character, I knew something about him that made me think that Steven would be the right person and that it would be a better risk, if you like, than going with one of the more experienced managers that hadn't achieved major success. Mark said to me it was an interesting possibility and that we should think about that."

While the wheels were coming off the season for Rangers, they were turning behind the scenes. A win over Hearts was sandwiched by those losses to Celtic and banners reading 'No fight, no pride, nowhere to hide. Incompetent on & off the pitch. We deserve better' and 'Mindless behind the scenes, heartless on the pitch. We deserve better' were unfurled before the match and at half-time by the Union Bears, the Ultras section located in the Broomloan Stand at Ibrox, as King's board faced their most serious and significant moments.

Murty wouldn't reach the end of the campaign as he was relieved of his duties following the Old Firm defeat at Parkhead, which came just a fortnight after a dressing room bust-up that saw Lee Wallace and Kenny Miller effectively forced out of the club as their proud Rangers careers came to an unsavoury end. It was symptomatic of a lack of leadership at Ibrox. Each party will have their view on whether a line was crossed as home truths were shared in the aftermath of a humiliating Scottish Cup semi-final defeat, but it was another example of Rangers being disjointed and another reason why Celtic seemed so out of sight as they lorded it over their Glasgow rivals.

Rangers would end the season with a third different boss as Jimmy Nicholl saw out the final fixtures. In a somewhat fitting manner, the campaign was brought to a close with a head-scratching, almost comical 5-5 draw with Hibernian at Easter Road.

The job that lay ahead was monumental for whoever was tasked with it. Allen had spent seven years with Manchester City before being appointed in 2017 and the then director of football was fully aware of the significance of Rangers' decision.

"It all started with firstly identifying what I thought Rangers needed in a manager," Allen said. "You can look at lots of different things, such as win ratios, but the challenge with that is that it is very difficult to compare leagues to leagues.

"How do you compare Eredivisie to La Liga to Bundesliga? How do you come up with a rationale when someone has a 40 per cent win ratio, someone has 70 per cent and someone has 50 per cent? Some leagues there are only two or three competing teams.

"So I said that we needed to take a step away from that and look at what we needed a manager at Rangers to be in terms of history, tradition, what we stand for and the supporters. That was someone who was a winner, a leader and someone who had the right character to cope with the adversity they were likely to encounter with the fans, media, etc, and that had the ability to work under high scrutiny.

"We were looking for someone to fit that criteria and Steven ticked all those boxes. He had those characteristics in abundance and the key then was to try and surround Steven with the team that would help support him on all the other areas – whether that be tactical, physical, mental, technical – and augment the skill set that he brought to the table."

The light bulb that had flashed in King's mind was now shining brightly in Allen's. Rangers had their target, but they didn't yet have their boss as supporters waited anxiously for news whilst deliberating their own preferences for the seventh man to take a seat in the dugout since regime change. It was Devlin who would give them the update that shook the support and his exclusive on Gerrard to Rangers would win him the Sports News Writer of the Year prize at the Scottish Press Awards.

There was no other suitable candidate in Scotland and Rangers couldn't take the risk with another foreign appointment given the unadulterated failures of Paul Le Guen and Caixinha. The next boss would cross the border and one observation would stick with Devlin throughout his pursuit of a story that would ultimately see the history books rewritten.

"At the beginning of the process, I always remember somebody telling me that when I found out who it was, I would sit back and think 'my goodness, what an appointment that is' and I always had that in my mind," Devlin said. "I started making calls, I had various guys I was talking to on the board, people outwith the board but that had strong connections to it and it really went quickly from there.

"Like every managerial appointment, there is an element of risk. I'll be honest, the first time that Steven Gerrard's name was put to me, it was in the context that he would be coming as an assistant to Neil Warnock. I had a number for Neil Warnock and people that represent Neil Warnock, so I had gone to them late afternoon.

"Neil had been at Ibrox a few times and been pictured there so it wasn't outwith the realms of possibility, but during the course of two conversations that afternoon I was able to rule Neil Warnock out of the running and out of proceedings. But Steven Gerrard's name had stuck in my head and through the course of the next 24 hours I hammered the phones, as you do, and was doing all I could to stand this up.

"It was such a leap of faith in a guy who was coaching Liverpool's Under-18s and you are acutely aware of the need for Rangers to get this appointment absolutely bang on. Again, at the back of my mind, I had the bells ringing of what someone told me at the outset that when I found out who it was I would think 'what an appointment'. I began to chase the Gerrard line and I took two calls, one around 8.00 p.m. and one again around 9.30 p.m. basically telling me that Gerrard was the man, he was the chosen one."

There was one final call that Devlin had to take. When he did, it was a case of hold the back page as *The Sun* got the story that everyone in Scottish sports journalism had been chasing.

The pursuit of the man to replace Caixinha had lasted seven months and the decision that Rangers were about to make would shape the club and Scottish football for years to come. Gerrard's name naturally carried significant weight, but his managerial experience amounted to nothing more than a stint back where it all began at Melwood, the Liverpool training centre, as he learned his trade whilst being tipped to eventually replace Jurgen Klopp at Anfield. The leap of faith from Rangers was sizeable, and *The Sun* had to take their own as well as they ran with what was the story of the season by some considerable distance.

"I spent the next hour-and-a-half frantically trying to stand this up and couldn't get anyone to answer their phones," Devlin said. "I had texted a couple of people and put the name out there and usually when you put a name to someone and it is a lot of rubbish you get a reply instantly to say forget it.

"This had gone on and on and it was maybe two days I had been pushing Gerrard because the Warnock thing was a non-starter. At 11.10 p.m. on the Wednesday night, I got a call from somebody saying 'go with Gerrard' and that was it. That was the extent of the conversation. It was just 'go with Gerrard'. We did.

"I was up against it in terms of deadlines. I phoned the desk and rattled out a couple of hundred words for the back page. When you go with a story as big as that, you don't get much sleep, so I had a restless night.

"I was 95 per cent certain that Steven Gerrard was the man, but I was aware that he had no real managerial experience and this was a huge task he was undertaking when you look at where Rangers had been and the state of the Rangers team that he inherited.

"There are always these nagging doubts but the following morning various news outlets had picked up on the story and obviously made calls themselves and, to my great relief, none of them were knocking it down. In fact, they were all endorsing it. When you come through that early morning, I knew it was right."

By that stage, the deal was almost done. Steven Gerrard would be the next Rangers manager. King had appointed his hero and supporters had a legend to rally round as the quest for 55 began all over again.

King had been the driving force behind the move for Gerrard, while Allen had been tasked with making it happen. There was only one other man, close friend Dalglish, involved as King asked The King for advice on the way forward for Rangers and whether Gerrard was the boss to lead the revolution that would draw comparisons with another Ibrox and Anfield great, Graeme Souness.

Once contact was made with Liverpool and permission granted to speak with their legendary former captain, King would travel to Merseyside and he was a guest of Dalglish's at the Champions League semi-final with Roma at Anfield. The following morning, King and Gerrard would meet once again at his house and Gerrard later appeared on BT Sport and confirmed he had held talks with Rangers. Within days, he was at Ibrox being paraded in front of 7,000 supporters and a new era dawned.

What had started with a chance conversation had become an opportunity that Rangers and Gerrard could not refuse. He had used his time in Major League Soccer with LA Galaxy to come to terms with leaving Liverpool, a place where he realised so many dreams and suffered the ultimate nightmare as he was denied the Premier League title that was so sought-after at Anfield. As he prepared to go down a different path, the lure of being a champion was the motivation once again.

"I organised it with Kenny that he would invite me to be his guest to Anfield and I would go there and spend the night with him and meet Steven the next day at his house," King said. "I went to the game and I met with Steven.

"We had a very frank discussion about what I was expecting from Rangers and where we needed to go from where we were. Steven made it very clear what his ambitions were and the support that he would need from me and the board to get there and we ended up having a meeting of minds that resulted in us progressing to the point, fairly quickly, that we were able to sign a contract with Steven."

The rest, as they say, is history. As King and Gerrard shook hands and the Liverpool legend put pen to paper, he embarked on the next stage of his career and assumed a responsibility and pressure he hadn't felt since he removed the Reds armband for the final time three years previously.

The rush of competition, the thrill of winning and the desire to improve were like drugs to Gerrard. Without those natural highs that only elite sport can induce, his life felt different and he needed an environment to test and challenge him. In that regard, he and Rangers were perfect for each other at that time and one can only look back and ponder what would have happened had a series of events in the previous three seasons unfolded differently.

One thing is for certain, Rangers were right to go with Gerrard.

TWO

LET'S GO. Two words were uttered but a thousand received by those inside the Blue Room. In the Ibrox stands, the people that Steven Gerrard was addressing waited to welcome him to Rangers.

The final answer of Gerrard's first press conference as manager was delivered with an assertive nod and a determined look. Asked what his message would be to supporters, Gerrard's reply of 'let's go' said it all. A marketing slogan was born in that instant, but Gerrard was there to win matches and to win trophies rather than sell jerseys and season tickets.

His previous statements had been eloquent and enlightening but that short, sharp response was evocative. It was time to get down to business and Gerrard, Dave King, Mark Allen, the Rangers director of football, and managing director, Stewart Robertson, would leave the press pack behind to return through the door to the Managers Office at Ibrox. A new era had begun and Scottish football had been changed forever.

The walls of the Blue Room celebrate and commemorate some of the finest names ever to pull on the famous Rangers jersey.

High up, a series of murals pay tribute to former chairmen, managers and players and all would look down on Gerrard on the day that so many looked up to him for hope and inspiration. He was surrounded by history and now had a chance to make his own at Ibrox.

Created by artist Senga Murray, the first illustrations were commissioned three decades ago by then chairman David Holmes and they are a unique addition to a room that has hosted the great and the good of Scottish, European and world football. To set foot inside it is a special feeling, and those there for Gerrard's unveiling knew that change was coming to Rangers. After years of abject failure, it felt like a turning point for the club.

Gerrard would have climbed the Marble Staircase and felt the tradition of Rangers. The bust of Bill Struth sits at the top of the first flight, while the Hall of Fame board comes into fuller view when you reach the landing and have the choice of entering the Managers Office, the Blue Room or the Trophy Room. The last time Gerrard was there, he was a youth coach at Liverpool. On that day, he was Rangers manager.

If the stomach was churning and the adrenaline was coursing through his veins, Gerrard didn't show it. He was sharp and composed, completely undaunted by the flashbulbs that lit up his face or any question that was directed his way from a media pack that hung on his every word. Gerrard looked, sounded and acted like a Rangers manager should and those standards set on the very first day have been matched throughout his tenure.

When he spoke about the size and history of Rangers, it was through an appreciation and understanding rather than for the sake of PR point scoring. Gerrard had missed the buzz and pressure of competition and Rangers would give him that back three years after he left Liverpool. He had arrived at an empty Ibrox and walked up the tunnel just hours earlier. When he headed back down it, thousands were waiting for him as a concoction of emotions surged through him. Gerrard was back in the kind of environment where he belonged.

"We got him up to sign a contract and that day was actually quite phenomenal because Steven arrived and signed and the crowds built and built," King said. "There was 50 people, 200 people, 1,000 people, 2,000 people and eventually Police Scotland got hold of our security guys and said we had to open the stadium and let people in. I think around 7,000 were there and we had the signing, did the media and then took Steven down and around.

"I tell you, that day, if Steven didn't really understand, which I think he did, what Rangers meant to the supporters, then that day told him everything he needed to know. The welcome he got that day was just unbelievable. When he came back in, he said to me 'Wow, what a buzz. Can I do that again?' He was genuinely blown away."

When he did do it again, there were more than 40,000 in attendance as a new era and Gerrard's reign began with a friendly victory over Bury. The 6-0 win that night is as irrelevant now as it was then, but it marked a moment of real change for Rangers and Scottish football. Steps back have been taken, of course, but the strides forward have been hugely impressive and Rangers have now earned the rewards for their efforts.

Gerrard officially didn't begin that work until a couple of weeks after his confirmation as manager and it was Jimmy Nicholl who took charge of the final fixtures as Rangers drew with Aberdeen and Hibernian. The task ahead of Gerrard was there in black and white as the Premiership standings confirmed a third place finish and a 12-point deficit to Celtic that could easily have been far more substantial given the shambolic nature of the campaign.

The appointment of Gerrard was never going to be an overnight fix. Many fans had concerns over his lack of managerial experience but found it impossible not to succumb to the attraction of his name and his status. King had been seduced by the prospect of having a Liverpool legend as Rangers manager and there was no denying that it was a bold, box-office move by the Ibrox board.

Whatever doubts supporters had over Gerrard's capabilities and credentials, nobody could deny it was an exciting time as all parties took a step into the unknown. As Gerrard strode purposefully down the touchline, it was love at first sight for many in scenes that brought back memories of the crowds that gathered to welcome Paul Gascoigne to Ibrox in 1995. Given Gerrard's stature and worldwide appeal, his arrival in Scottish football was the most high-profile since the day that a bleached-blond Gazza took the acclaim of an adoring support on Edmiston Drive following his arrival from Lazio.

"We were expecting a decent turnout of fans looking to catch a glimpse of Steven," David Martin, Rangers' head of security, said. "You let the police know, you have a chat with them, and we anticipated that there would be enough fans turning up at the front door to make it a problem for the police in terms of road safety. The flip side of that coin is to open up and let them into the stadium and make it a safe encounter.

"Our expectation was that we would get two or three thousand so we said we would open the Enclosures and accommodate them there. As you saw, we filled the Enclosures and we must have had about 7,000 in the stadium for him turning up.

"It was straightforward in terms of having police on site and also making announcements that if anyone comes over the wall looking for selfies and autographs then we would take him back up the tunnel.

"There were a lot of families that turned up. Steven did his piece upstairs with Dave King and we came down, out the tunnel and he did his walk and got the scarf and met the fans."

Events such as these are always carefully choreographed and controlled by clubs and many can become fairly mundane affairs.

Gerrard's unveiling was different, though, and there was an energy around the stadium that pointed to something more significant than just the naming of a new manager. Rangers had done that too often in the years since regime change in 2015 and the pressure was on Gerrard to deliver and prove King's gut instinct was right.

"It was a step into the unknown with a big name manager, but one who didn't have a track record," renowned sports photographer Willie Vass, who covered Gerrard's unveiling and has been with Rangers every step of the way throughout 'The Journey', said. "You look at where we were before with Mark Warburton, Pedro Caixinha and caretaker managers, so it was a gamble worth taking with Steven Gerrard.

"It wasn't going to be an overnight success but, on that day when Gerrard was unveiled, the feelgood factor was off the scale. All the fans came in off the street and that huge groundswell of emotion, you just hoped that would go to the next level and that Gerrard would be given the time to find his feet and learn his trade as a manager.

"To the credit of the club, they have stuck by him and he has learned on the job. He has learned what Rangers means. The first couple of seasons, he had to find out where he was, to get the map of Scottish football.

"He has done his homework, he is not a daft guy. Other clubs would have demanded instant success, especially with Celtic winning those Trebles, but Rangers gave him the time that he needed.

"After the Scottish Cup defeat to Hearts in the second season, I had my doubts and I thought he would walk away. The soundbites and the optics coming from Gerrard weren't good and he looked really down, but he reset himself and has never looked back from those times."

If Gerrard failed, the consequences would be dire individually and collectively at Ibrox.

In his years working for Rangers, Martin has seen all manner of managers, players, directors and staff come and go. Some succeeded and some failed, some will be remembered and some cannot be forgotten unfortunately. His previous career saw him rise to assistant chief constable with Strathclyde Police and he and security staff would accompany Gerrard on that first journey along the front of the Enclosures. Just yards before reaching the mouth of the tunnel and disappearing from view, a visceral roar and fist-pump showed the sense of excitement within Gerrard.

"It wasn't challenging in any way, shape or form," Martin said. "But you got the sense very quickly that we were entering a new era at the club, there was no doubt about that.

"It was a watershed moment and, I have to say, I can't compare him with anyone else that I have worked with at the club. I have been there since Walter and worked with Coisty and all the other guys that have been in charge of the team at different times.

"Steven Gerrard is a completely different animal. There is a presence about the guy, there is no doubt about it, and I have yet to come across or see anybody who is more accomplished with the press. He is top drawer when it comes to that."

As the crowds began to dissipate and pictures and videos were shared around social media, Gerrard found peace and quiet in the home dressing room. The wood panelled walls and portrait of The Queen give a sense of history and occasion for whoever walks through the door and Gerrard would attempt to stifle a broad smile as he looked around his new home from home.

As he did so, kitman Jimmy Bell prepared for the match with Kilmarnock the following day, which Rangers would win 1-0. It was very much a case of old meeting new.

"I had the impression before we got there that he wasn't nervous about it, but not over-confident about it," Martin said. "It was an environment he hadn't been in before, he had never seen it and he wasn't too sure where he was going.

"As soon as you took him under your wing, if you like, and started to take him into the dressing room and the boardroom and the Managers Office, you got the very strong sense that it was an environment that he was familiar with and would be comfortable with very quickly.

"He came round the Argyle House offices with Gary McAllister and the staff and they came through and met with everybody. He went through the whole office, shook everybody's hand and that went down really well with the staff. It is not an easy job, let's be honest. But early on you got a feeling about just what he was all about as a man and a manager."

In those initial days, that hunch was all that Gerrard's supporters had to go on. He had no track record as a boss and taking on a challenge like Rangers had the potential to end his managerial career before it had really got off and running. As he said himself, though, it just felt right when Rangers made the approach and he would say yes after declining several previous opportunities as a coach or manager.

"I have confidence in myself, in my ability," Gerrard said as he spoke with the authority of a man fit to hold such an office. "I have weighed the gamble up and the risk and I understand other people thinking it is because it is my first job in management, but I have confidence in myself that I can deliver for these supporters. That's the only thing that matters to me: do I think I can do a good job as the manager of Glasgow Rangers? In my mind, it's yes.

"I love a challenge. My parents brought me up in life to always front a challenge, if you feel like that challenge is the right one for you, go for it. Go and front it up and give it your best shot. That's exactly what I'm going to do here.

"Pressure's not a bad thing for me. I played under pressure, I have lived under pressure since I left school. In football, if you are working under pressure you are in a good place. Since I stopped playing football, I have missed that pressure of fighting for three points at the weekend. Being Rangers manager, I know there will be a lot of scrutiny and pressure but that's what I love about being involved in football.

"Bring it on. I don't mind being under intense pressure. I knew that before I decided to be Rangers manager and I'm up for the challenge. I will do my very best. The supporters were another big reason why I wanted to come here and be a leader for them. Their loyalty, how they stuck by this club, is certainly one of the values that I believe in. I can't wait to be out there leading this team in front of them."

The questions over him one day returning to Liverpool were predictable but that possibility would never be on the table unless he was a success at Ibrox. There have been real periods of angst in the years since and times when it looked as though the gamble wouldn't pay off for King or Gerrard, but the failures of the first two seasons are consigned to history, forever overshadowed by the glory of Premiership triumph.

Just days after breaking the story that the Liverpool legend would become the Rangers manager, Andy Devlin was at Ibrox to cover the most high-profile press conference in a generation for *The Scottish Sun*. Those that view life in hindsight always have 20-20 vision, but it is not being smart after the event to say that Gerrard seemed destined to deliver for Rangers.

"From day one, he has carried himself tremendously well and he has had to do it through some very difficult times," Devlin said. "I go back to what someone said to me right at the beginning of the process, that when I found out who it was that I would be taken aback.

"What really frustrated me at the outset was that I remember people saying that Ronny Deila was a bold appointment for Celtic and it was a fresh approach. Ian Cathro was thinking outside the box, what a terrific appointment, when he went to Hearts, we were told.

"I was really taken aback by the amount of people in my own profession who were so quick to judge Steven Gerrard and almost write him off before he had a chance to get his feet under the desk. One thing was for sure, this was a guy that was going to raise and drive the standards up at Rangers Football Club.

"He demanded nothing less as a player and you could see from day one and that press conference that he understood straight away the magnitude of the challenge, he got the expectation that had been thrust upon his shoulders.

"Look at the crowds that turned up at Ibrox to greet him that day. The club had been kicked from pillar to post, they had endured some horrific times and the supporters had been to hell and back. And you just sensed this wave of optimism sweeping over everyone that day and people realised that it was a new era, a fresh start and this was someone who could finally bring this fragmented club together."

The Rangers that King, John Gilligan and Paul Murray salvaged three years previously was battered and broken and the one which Gerrard inherited remained in a state of disrepair. The seasons before his arrival had fluctuated between shambolic and shameful and it cannot be underestimated just how extensive the rebuilding job was. The foundations were laid from the outset by Gerrard as Gary McAllister, Michael Beale, Tom Culshaw and Jordan Milsom followed him from Liverpool to Glasgow, while goalkeeper coach Colin Stewart was retained to complete the new-look backroom team.

The comparison to Graeme Souness was an obvious one to make at the outset. His appointment as player-manager in 1986 was a watershed moment for Scottish football and Souness would revolutionise Rangers in a whirlwind of headlines, big money deals and sustained success before returning to Anfield five years later. Souness – a winner of five league championships and three

European Cups – had seen it and done it all with Liverpool but that didn't prepare him for a colourful and controversial move into management.

It all started with a blaze of negativity and a flash of red as Souness was sent off on his debut in a defeat to Hibernian at Easter Road. Come May, a pitch invasion at Pittodrie was sparked by the final whistle that confirmed a first league title in nine years. The circumstances are not the same, but those fans who endured the barren years before the Souness Revolution will surely see similarities as they now celebrate after a decade without top flight silverware.

"I was off the board by the point that Steven was appointed," Gilligan, who stepped down from his position as a director in May 2017, said. "But I have always been in touch and I kept thinking of Graeme Souness, like a lot of people. When I saw Steven Gerrard standing out in front of the Enclosure in front of 7,000 Rangers fans, I had the feeling of Souness.

"Even with Gary McAllister coming in, like the Walter Smith situation, as the Rangers fan that played the game and that had come back to Rangers. I had a wonderful feeling, I thought this could be the one to get us back.

"I have only been in Steven's company a few times and I don't push myself. I was lucky enough to be on Walter's Testimonial Committee and I feel very close to Walter, and I was very close to Mark Warburton and Stuart McCall, who both deserve real credit for the jobs that they did for Rangers.

"What I will say is that when Steven walks into a room, he has got an aura and presence about him and he is very charismatic. He is a very nice guy, very pleasant and he has just got it."

When Souness was given a blank chequebook to overhaul the Rangers squad in the summer of 1986, he quickly put it to good use. England internationals Chris Woods and Terry Butcher were a remarkable sign of intent as Rangers brushed aside alternative offers from south of the border. Jimmy Nicholl would also re-join the club and Colin West was signed before Graham Roberts arrived from Tottenham Hotspur in December.

This is where there is the most marked difference between Souness and Gerrard. When it comes to the transfer market, Gerrard has had to operate in another realm. He has spent wisely and spent what he has earned, but he cannot be accused of buying success.

"I think he has attracted players and probably one of the biggest benefits that the club has had is that if Steven Gerrard is your manager and you go to sign a player, there is an attraction there," Gilligan said. "Players want to be involved with a former great player like that and work with someone of his name in the game.

"He has been fantastic and he is such a good speaker as well. I find him more like Walter than Graeme, I think he is probably more like Walter. With respect to Walter, as a player Steven and Graeme have more in common.

"But I think he has got more in common with Walter as a manager. He is very open but, and the press boys may tell me differently, he has got that stare as if to say 'I'm not answering that question' and he deals with that side of it so well. He has been a miracle for us, he really has."

Even miracle workers do not get results overnight. If Souness was a revolution, then Gerrard has been more evolution as a squad that was disparate and desperate has become one that will be forever revered amongst legendary sides of yesteryear.

There have been and there will be better Rangers teams to win the title and the arguments over where Gerrard's side rank in that regard can be bandied about on supporters' buses and in pubs for some time to come. None will hold such a unique place in the hearts and minds of fans, though.

The first transfer window in the summer of 2018 was the building block around which every other piece was laid. The strike rate wasn't perfect and mistakes were certainly made but Gerrard and Allen would assemble a group that at least restored some pride in the Premiership and surpassed all expectations in the Europa League.

The deals for Scott Arfield and Allan McGregor were completed in the days after the previous campaign had come to a close and Jamie Murphy's loan move from Brighton was converted into a permanent arrangement shortly afterwards.

It was then time for Gerrard to get down to business on the park and a training camp in Andalusia saw more new faces arrive. Rangers tried their best to keep the signings of Jon Flanagan and Ovie Ejaria under wraps and away from the travelling press contingent, but it was the presence of Connor Goldson and Nikola Katic that was more significant in the long run for Gerrard.

Flanagan had been quietly marshalled in whilst interviews were taking place away from the hotel reception, while Ejaria was greeted at Malaga airport by photographers. A scarf was put around his neck and shots quickly taken as the lift button was continually pressed to stop the midfielder, who had agreed a loan move from Liverpool, leaving the scene before the snappers had what they had waited several hours for.

Those days provided an opportunity to see Gerrard at closer quarters and there was an intensity about the way in which Rangers worked. His media dealings were prompt and professional and a low-slung thumbs-up accompanied an 'orite, lads?' whenever he passed the assorted writers and broadcasters at the team hotel. He kept transfer business close to his chest but was eloquent and engaging on other topics and those early weeks offered insights for both parties into how the other operated.

Those that were in Croatia to see Gerrard's side beat Osijek in the second Europa League qualifier couldn't help but be impressed with Borna Barisic and he would sign just days later.

Ryan Kent made his debut that night after moving on loan from Liverpool and a style of play and management and identikit of player was beginning to emerge as Gerrard settled in at Ibrox.

"You are looking for that mix-and-match and some players will be better suited to some rather than the other," Allen said of the task of building a group that could compete in both the Premiership and the Europa League in Gerrard's first season. "The overall goal was to have a group of players that was capable of achieving both and we knew that would take a few windows to do, but we were quite active and aggressive in the field in those first few windows.

"You have to be realistic in that first window and there were two things, really. The first was to try and be in early because that would give us a competitive advantage, so that is players that had been released or who had been made available early in the window. Of course, they had to be of the relevant quality.

"And the second reason was to put that squad together as quickly and practicably as possible so that Steven could hit the ground running when we reported back for pre-season. We were in very quickly and I think that helped enormously for the preparations for Europe that season."

It was a European campaign that would take Rangers much further than expected. The humiliation of Progres was still raw and vivid but Gerrard would restore Rangers' reputation on the continent with a run that saw his side overcome the odds and their seeding.

A first round victory over Macedonian minnows FK Shkupi was followed by that away win and a home draw against Osijek and the third tie offered a glimpse into just what Gerrard was building. Maribor were beaten 3-1 at Ibrox and the return leg the following week would end goalless as Gerrard's side showed a strength of character and tactical awareness that Rangers hadn't possessed for some time.

The man of the match that night was McGregor as he rolled back the years and put in a display to match anything he had produced during his first spell at Ibrox. It was a sign of things to come from the former Scotland keeper and there has arguably not been a more influential or important signing in the three seasons that Gerrard has been boss.

"It is doing your homework and your due diligence and you know who is available," Allen said. "As soon as I knew Greegs was available, I was on to his representatives to say that we wanted to be at the front of that queue to bring him back in.

"I knew he was of the requisite quality, I knew he had the experience of playing with Rangers, I knew he could cope with the intensity and scrutiny that goes on the players and it was an easy decision.

"It was easy to convince Steven as well because he was in transition at the time. I still wouldn't have rubber-stamped it had the manager not been happy, but I knew it was a no-brainer."

The Europa League would provide Gerrard with moments that would stress him out and send him wild during his first season. The range of emotions and opportunities were only available at a club of Rangers' stature and it became clear that he wouldn't be a boss that would take his chances on the managerial merry-go-round and bounce from job to job for decades to come. He is an elite operator, and he needed an elite environment.

From the nerve-shredding night in Ufa as his nine-man side held on to qualify for the group stages to the win over Braga that clinched a place in the last 16 during his second term at Ibrox, Gerrard would go through the wringer and experience the full scale of highs and lows.

It was a rollercoaster that supporters simply had to enjoy and one which was a privilege to be part of. Rangers would fail to qualify from a section that included Villarreal, Spartak Moscow and Rapid Vienna first time out, but only Porto finished above them in their second group stage appearance as Feyenoord and Young Boys were overcome.

Rangers were not surviving at that level, they were competing at it and there were signs of development individually and collectively. The squad became stronger ahead of the second season and Gerrard's side moved through the gears efficiently. As they became a force in Europe, the farce of Progres was laid to rest as a goalless draw in Luxembourg was enough to continue on their way to the group stages for a second consecutive season.

When looking at Gerrard's first two campaigns on their own merits and as a whole, the Europa League stands out as the area where the most significant signs of development were evident. There were difficult and demoralising times domestically, but the way in which Rangers operated against a higher calibre of opposition undoubtedly bought Gerrard time and put further credit, and money, in the bank ahead of his third season.

His mission, of course, was to win silverware but Gerrard's impact cannot solely be judged on his successes or failures on the park. His influence stretches into every area of the club as Rangers have been modernised from the inside during the last three years.

The Auchenhowie training base on the outskirts of Milngavie celebrated two decades in operation in July 2021 and that was the first area that Gerrard put his stamp on. After a career spent in the highest echelons of the game, Gerrard knew the importance of creating an elite environment for his players to work and rest in and then to play in at Ibrox.

"To be fair to him and his staff, over the three seasons that they have been here at Rangers, they have absolutely transformed the place, I don't think you could describe it in any other way," Martin said. "There has been a lot of money spent at the training ground to upgrade it and modernise it in terms of the eating facilities, the training facilities, the changing facilities.

"There has been a small fortune spent up there and it is top drawer. And obviously they have spent money at Ibrox as well. When you go through the corridors now, a lot of it is a lift from Liverpool and the signs on the walls have so many league titles, so many cups and so forth.

"A lot of that comes from Liverpool but there is no doubt that it has gone down very well. He is the kind of guy that would just not entertain second best, I think that is how I would describe him. He is a winner, there is no doubt about it."

The changes implemented by Gerrard and his staff are not merely cosmetic. A refurbished media and analysis room and new reception are the last areas seen by many visitors, while the corridors that link the Academy and the first team department are beyond doors that few outsiders enter through. Another visible upgrade is the blue sheeting around the first team training pitch as, after stories and team selections were leaked, Gerrard sought to ensure privacy whilst Rangers were working. In every aspect – from the gym equipment to the food on offer in the canteen – Rangers now operate at a higher level and those refinements undoubtedly played their part in taking them to the point where they were able to mount a sustained and ultimately successful title bid.

At Ibrox, a lounge for players to use before and after matches has been built after Gerrard took issue with his squad having to utilise various rooms in the stadium for meals and to spend time with friends and family. The gains are marginal, but they all add up and each one percentage point can earn three on the park.

"I think it is an important part and environment plays a huge part in success," Allen said. "If you are looking to attract, retain and develop the best talent, the environment offers two things.

"Firstly, it offers a sense of where the club is and shows that you are a top club, that you do things the right way and we invest in the right areas, such as hybrid pitches, cryotherapy chambers, gym equipment.

"And secondly, it creates a no-excuse culture. We give the players the best that we possibly can and you take away as much of the noise, for want of a better description, and it is a case of 'go on, you have no excuse but to go out and perform'.

"The canteen is a hub for where a lot of activity takes place in terms of communication and the more you can persuade the players to be in and around that area, the better that is for everyone. I have got several board presentations that talk about that and the need for a high-performance arena to attract high-performance players and it is an integral part of any successful side.

"People think it is all about the recruitment, and of course you need the right quality of player, but you need to know that once you have the right player in that they have the adequate environment in which to perform."

If the Gerrard gamble had failed and Rangers hadn't won that sought-after 55th title under his guidance, it would have started another period of soul-searching and change at Ibrox. As a club and a football operation, Rangers would still have been in a far healthier position than they were when he arrived, though.

There is a natural energy and feelgood factor when results are going the right way on the park but the progression of Rangers at all levels is enough to raise morale. This has never just been about constructing a team, but more about the rebuilding of a club whose wounds had been inflicted by those who enjoyed the privileges of their positions whilst failing to fulfil their responsibilities associated with them.

In his role as a club ambassador, Mark Hateley had seen all the characters in the tale come and go. He would give fans some heady days during the run to nine-in-a-row under Walter Smith and the arrival of Gerrard would remind the former striker of the standards that used to be the norm around a club that was associated with class and dignity.

"One of the first days he is in at the club, I was in the Main

Stand looking at an area that we were looking to develop down by the dressing room," Hateley said. "I saw Gary Mac and I know him well from long summers golfing in Portugal together and through our playing careers. He came over and gave me a handshake and a hug and then he shouted on Steven.

"He was in where the old gym was with his staff and Steven came through and gave me a big hug. He was really nice and said that guys like myself were ones he needed at the club because it made his job easier.

"People with the experience and wisdom of being there for so long does help a manager and that was the first time I had heard it from a guy in his position. He was so positive and then he went round the whole building and introduced himself.

"That had not been done for a very, very long time. That is the old days of Graeme and Walter and Steven introduced himself to everyone in the building. That, for me, was a sign of good things and from that good things can come.

"You get that sort of response from a manager to normal, hardworking people that are trying to do the club justice and trying to get it back on a right footing. He has brought a presence and a professionalism and I think he has handled it very well. He has learned some lessons along the way."

That curve has certainly been a steep one for Gerrard at times, but he is unquestionably a better coach and manager for having had those experiences. The demands that he places on his players are as high as those that he puts on himself and while he is the figurehead and the one who carries the ultimate responsibility, he expects those around him to commit and sacrifice as much as he does. Another two word phrase – 'all in' – encapsulates his mantra and mindset.

Players that do not buy into his methods or who do not aspire to reach his levels will not last long at Ibrox and there is a camaraderie within the squad that reinforces the all-for-one and one-for-all attitude that has been fostered over the last three seasons. That process cannot be forced and naturally takes time, but Gerrard has reconnected Rangers past and present, on the park and off it.

"A big shout has to go to Mark Allen and between him and Steven's team, they really did put an edge back at the training ground and then onto the pitch and into performances," Hateley said. "It was the way that we should be conducting ourselves.

"I got on really well with Mark, he asked me for things and I went back to him and we delivered both ways. All that started with Steven and him putting things in place and making it how it should be at Rangers.

"It was refreshingly good and within three or four months of being there I suggested that we get all the older players that work for the club or are there on a match day, guys who had seen it all and done it all, to come up and see what was happening there.

"Mark was bang on it, Steven was bang on it and we had them all up, we had a bit of lunch and watched a training session and had a chat. It was making everybody feel part of this epic club that we are.

"You put all of these things together, you have marginal gains and the standards become higher, the professionalism is more acute. You have got a manager that leads the way and you just have to get better in that setup.

"A lot of that comes down to results, of course it does, but they get those results because of the process and I still can't believe how quicky we have clawed the gap back."

Those initial efforts were undoubtedly important to the success that Rangers now savour. As they do so, Allen watches on from afar. He would leave Ibrox in September 2019 after overseeing a transfer window that culminated in the permanent signing of Kent for £7million. Joe Aribo and Filip Helander were the other success stories from that summer as more remnants of the Mark Warburton and Pedro Caixinha eras were finally moved on.

The Welshman would take up a new position as the academy director at Swansea City in January 2021 but his interest in Rangers remains strong. Like so much of the Rangers story, there are those who gave more and did more, but many who played significant parts in restoring the club bit by bit and who can take satisfaction from their efforts that would culminate in league flag number 55.

"I am someone who likes others to do my bidding, if you like, in many respects and say 'he did a good job' or whatever," Allen said. "But look, we have to be honest and I think I can fairly say that Rangers were in a significantly better place after I left than when I went in.

"That is in terms of player levels and quality, systems, processes, procedures, facilities, and all of those things I would like to think I played a part in, without trying to blow my own trumpet.

"My task, as I laid it out to the board, was threefold. One was to close gaps, two was to win the title and three was get back to that position where Rangers were the number one team.

"They were my short-, medium- and long-term plans and we have seen the fruition of the first two certainly. We have closed the gap, without any shadow of a doubt, we have won the title and I think if you look at the foundations that have been put in place then there is a very solid platform to build for the future and be number one for years to come. That is what I hope.

"I can't wait for the fans to be back at Ibrox and start singing about 55 titles and that will mean such a lot to me when I hear that. I can honestly say that Rangers has become part of me, I have followed every single result since I left, I have watched every game that I could and it is the first result that I look for whenever they play.

"I consider myself that there will only ever be one team in Scotland that I follow and support and that will be Rangers. It is a very, very special club."

It is now, finally, a club that is back on top of Scottish football but the process that led to the achievement was far from straightforward. There was a fear of the unknown in 2012 when Craig Whyte had Rangers peering over the precipice and dismay of a bleak future before regime change in 2015. Two more three-year milestones – the appointment of Gerrard and the title win – complete the story and ensure there is a happy ending.

The wait has been too long for Rangers, but it has ultimately been worth it in the end. Supporters would surely change various scenarios that unfolded over the years, but each has enhanced the feelings of jubilation that have been felt in recent months as Gerrard has delivered the Premiership crown.

In truth, it could have been done before now. It was not a case of third time lucky for Gerrard, but it could have been three strikes and out if he had not succeeded. For all the positives and all the progress during his first two campaigns, he would have been well aware of the cost of failure this time around.

When Gerrard's side beat Celtic in December 2018, Rangers were level with their Old Firm rivals at the top of the table as Brendan Rodgers suffered his first defeat in 13 derbies. After a period of unchallenged dominance, there was the potential for the pendulum to swing from blue to green but Ryan Jack's strike that clinched victory would prove futile in terms of the title race.

The same can be said for the corresponding fixture 12 months later. Katic was the Old Firm hero on that occasion but Rangers couldn't capitalise on their triumph and the drop-off in the following weeks was even harder to take and explain. They had the look of challengers, but not the mark of champions as they collapsed for the second successive season.

A fortnight earlier, Gerrard had signed a new contract at Ibrox until the summer of 2024 and spoke of how Rangers were 'building something special'. At the same time, Jurgen Klopp put pen to paper on an extension to his Anfield deal and there were dots being joined in Glasgow and Liverpool but Gerrard's name and standing alone wouldn't be enough to take him home and to his dream job. He needed to win.

He would come close, but not close enough in his first two seasons as those wins against Celtic were remembered for celebrations that were raw yet premature. The victory at Ibrox was Rangers' first on league duty over Celtic since the day in 2012 that they denied them the title, while it had been two years previously that they had last won at Parkhead and each achievement felt like another box being ticked in terms of their recovery.

The footage of Gerrard hugging and high-fiving his players and famously roaring into the camera stirred the senses of supporters. Rangers were right to savour the moments, but they were not good enough when it mattered most in the Premiership or the cup competitions.

Defeat to Celtic in the Betfred Cup final was a demoralising blow for Rangers and hurt even more so than the early exits to Aberdeen in Gerrard's first term. When Rangers lost to Hearts in the Scottish Cup in February 2020, Gerrard was heading for zero from six in terms of silverware and seemingly as close to leaving Rangers as he has ever been.

His demeanour in the post-match press conference was of a man who feared he had come to the end of the road. He stressed his desire to win with Rangers but admitted to needing a period of the next 48 hours 'to do some real, serious thinking'. He would remain in post, but a defeat to Hamilton the following Wednesday was the lowest point of his tenure.

Supporters didn't know it at the time, but that would be the penultimate occasion that they would be at Ibrox before Coronavirus changed the game and the world. The league title was gone and there was a feeling that Gerrard might have been too if the situation had deteriorated further.

It is a theory that seems unthinkable now, but one which David

Edgar, a former board member with the Rangers Supporters Trust and now host of the Heart and Hand podcast, can buy into. A 1-0 win at Ross County was the final Premiership fixture before Scottish football was closed down and a summer of acrimony and accusation followed. It would give Gerrard time to reflect and recover.

"He might have made the decision himself," Edgar said when asked if Gerrard could have left Rangers at the end of his second season. "I had invested a lot in Steven Gerrard emotionally, right from the start I was accused of being a Gerrard fanboy and all the rest of it.

"I can be very smug right now! But that night after the Hearts defeat, it looked like a man, to me, who was ready to fold in his cards and the Hamilton defeat was really bad.

"Then we had Celtic to play twice. Sure, we could have beaten them twice, but if we had lost twice then the pressure would have been huge.

"What I think history will show is that we weren't far away and sometimes you are too close to something to see it and you need to step back to get perspective. We were forced to do that. It is very difficult at Rangers because of the pressure that everyone is under and this is everybody's life.

"At that point, he was forced by Covid to take a step back. He looked at it, knew what went wrong last season and knew that he was only a couple of players short. It is fine margins and it is scary to think that if the season had continued then Steven Gerrard might well have left Rangers. Then someone else would have come in, ripped it up and started again. But it didn't need starting from scratch, as we have discovered this season."

In sport, as in life, there is no reset button and one cannot go back in time to take a different path in search of a different outcome. Those final weeks of the campaign may have allowed Gerrard a chance to cure the ills that had seeped into his side, but given the form and the feeling, that seemed unlikely and the Covid-enforced break undoubtedly came at a good time for Rangers, even if Celtic were awarded a ninth straight league title in farcical circumstances that shamed Scottish football.

If the supporters that packed Ibrox for the Europa League tie with Bayer Leverkusen had known then what would unfold in the months to follow, they would surely have taken one final glance around the stadium or said longer farewells to those seated next to them before heading for the exits. The 3-1 defeat in the last 16 was followed by a loss in Germany months later as the European run came to an end but the focus by that stage was on the new campaign rather than the old one.

The months in isolation were put to good use by Gerrard and his staff. Regular meetings were held online and the camaraderie that had been forged, and which is such an invaluable component of any successful side, was maintained despite the distances between them as some stayed in Glasgow and others returned to family homes around the world.

There was much to consider in those times as Rangers were forced to answer the same questions for a second consecutive season. Losses to Hearts and Kilmarnock and draws with Aberdeen and St Johnstone had wrecked their title aspirations and, despite their continued protestations to restart the campaign, there was little chance of Rangers overhauling Celtic.

The first two seasons showed that Rangers could beat Celtic over 90 minutes. It is only in Gerrard's third that he has proven his side can emerge victorious over the course of the campaign. Finally, Rangers have the ultimate reason to be cheerful.

"You look at the exuberance of the celebrations at Parkhead in December 2019," Devlin said. "Completely understandable because Rangers hadn't won at Parkhead in ten years and at that point they were motoring. You felt this could be the season, everyone got carried away and history tells us that they collapsed after coming back from Dubai, as they had done the previous season after the trip to Tenerife.

"This year, the mantra has been one game at a time since the get go and that is down to experience, down to Steven Gerrard learning on his feet and on the job and learning the demands of managing Rangers.

"For him to do all of this in the space of two years is incredible and all credit must go to him, his coaching staff and his players for sorting out the mentality, which was a huge problem amongst the Rangers players. Steven spoke about the players that had suffered against Celtic and they weren't able to mentally get themselves into a position to challenge them over 90 minutes.

"Gerrard has realised that it is all well and good beating Celtic in one-off games, but you need to go to St Johnstone, Motherwell, Hibernian and get results and he has done that. For a guy who was written off by so many people at the start, it is absolutely remarkable the job that he has done."

The mission that Gerrard accepted in May 2018 was almost never completed but the work that was put in was never going to go to waste. Rangers had been modernised on and off the park and were suitably equipped to challenge for domestic honours and further enhance their standing on the continent. All the pieces were finally there, but they still had to be put together.

It is silverware that Gerrard had to deliver, and he appreciated that as well as anyone. He started his second term with a defiant 'let's go again' and time would tell what his message would be to supporters at the end of year three.

The 2020/21 campaign was destined to be historic as Rangers chased 55 and Celtic sought 'The Ten'. There could only be one winner and legends would be made at Ibrox.

THREE

SCOTTISH FOOTBALL: a rubbish watch, but a great read. It is unlikely that the SPFL will adopt the line as the new motto for our game, but what began as a joke amongst the sports media here was no laughing matter during the summer of 2020.

In fact, our game became more of a laughing stock. In a time of great uncertainty and of widespread fear, both of the unknown and of the virus that was sweeping the nation, leadership was required at Hampden and Holyrood.

The decisions made by Nicola Sturgeon, the First Minister, and her Government will be debated for some time and it is at the ballot box where the people of Scotland will always cast their judgement. Thankfully, the democratic processes that leads to our political powers being elected are not as contentious as the one which Neil Doncaster, the SPFL chief executive, and his board oversaw in April 2020.

The summer of 2012 had been the most vitriolic close season that Scottish football had ever endured as our game came to terms with Rangers' financial implosion. It was a time of accusation and recrimination, but the anger was mainly from Ibrox as the club and its supporters became entrenched, fighting for their survival and battling against those who sought to inflict further damage on an institution who had suffered self-harm at the hands of its supposed custodians.

Eight years on, tensions would run even higher. Rangers were at the centre of it once again but this time they were not alone and the wounds opened through several headline-grabbing weeks will take years to heal after Hearts, Partick Thistle and Stranraer found themselves unfairly punished by their contemporaries as any semblance of sporting integrity was lost. Others would later join their cause in demand of answers as the governance and competence of those running our game was cast into doubt and called into question by some of their most established clubs.

It was on Friday 13 March 2020 that Scottish football was placed into cold storage amid the Coronavirus outbreak. The decision was inevitable but those that took it would have barely believed what would unfold as a result. This wasn't just a season being brought to a premature close, it was a seismic shift in the landscape of our game, both politically and financially, at a time when Scotland was searching for answers and assurances.

The previous night, Rangers had hosted Bayer Leverkusen in the Europa League and more than 47,000 supporters packed Ibrox. Steven Gerrard's side wouldn't step on to the park again until August, but there would be no fans to take their seats when they did so. The second leg, a 1-0 defeat in Germany, was one of seven fixtures that Rangers would play in August as clubs and those that follow them had to adjust to the new normal of behind-closed-doors fixtures. The sight of an empty Ibrox – one which looked like home but didn't feel like it – would be difficult to stomach for many months to come.

Within weeks of that first fixture in the last 16, the season was officially declared finished. Celtic had their ninth successive league title, while Dundee United, Raith Rovers and Cove Rangers were announced as champions of their respective divisions on a points-per-game basis. Those that had been denied the chance to challenge for titles were rightly furious, but their ire was nothing compared to the clubs who found themselves relegated with several games still to be played in each of the leagues. Social distancing may have kept supporters apart, but many were united in their condemnation of those running our game.

"I always felt that it was a mistake to cancel the season and I felt they could have postponed it at that time with a view to restarting it, as many other nations did," Gordon Smith, the former chief executive of the Scottish Football Association, said. "The big argument was that this was so money could be handed out and teams could get their funds from the SPFL based on position.

"They could have handed out a proportion of that to clubs then completed the season and if there were any changes to the positions, the clubs could either owe or be owed money at that time. I didn't think that was a reason to stop the season and it shouldn't have been done to give out the payments.

"Look at who else suffered in that scenario: Hearts were relegated when they might have stayed up, Partick Thistle were relegated when they might have stayed up and Stranraer were relegated when they might have stayed up. That doesn't make sense. Rangers suffered in the summer and it would have been even harsher if the league had been tighter."

Given how alarmingly Rangers had fallen away after the winter break, there was little realistic chance of Gerrard's side catching Celtic but the only predictable aspect of sport is its unpredictability. Even if their game in hand had been won, a deficit of ten points over the final eight games looked insurmountable – but that wasn't the point. As leagues across the continent, including in England, were played to the finish, the ball was picked up and put away in Scotland.

Hearts were relegated despite a deficit of just four points to eleventh-placed Hamilton, while Partick Thistle, who had played a game fewer than Queen of the South, were just two points adrift at the foot of the Championship. Raith were crowned League One champions courtesy of a 1.89 points-per-game ratio compared to Falkirk's 1.86 and in League Two there was no relegation as Brechin City, whose chairman Ken Ferguson was a member of the SPFL board, did not have to play for their League status as the pyramid play-offs were scrapped.

The process that led to those decisions attracted comment and criticism from many quarters. Rangers were at the forefront of the calls for change, but it was Dundee who were at the centre of the storm following the ballot to call the season, which had been repeatedly championed by Doncaster during what felt like an election campaign.

At 5.10 p.m. on Friday 10 April, a total of 39 of the 42 clubs had submitted a return on whether they wished to call the leagues and end the season. The minutes that followed were later the subject of an internal investigation by Deloitte as the timeline of who said what to whom and when became key. Doncaster and John Nelms, the Dundee managing director, would speak at 5.39 p.m., while SPFL company secretary Ian Blair and Dundee secretary Eric Drysdale spoke at 5.50 p.m. Ten minutes later, a text from Drysdale to Blair intimated that the Dundee vote should not be considered as cast.

It was only at 8.30 p.m. that the SPFL email quarantine system was checked and 25 minutes later an unread email from Dundee, sent at 4.48 p.m., was released. The 'no' vote, which would have prevented the season being declared finished, was effectively withdrawn and it was five days later before the Dens Park board would eventually submit a 'yes' ballot as the Championship,

League One and League Two were called. The Premiership would subsequently and inevitably follow on 18 May.

"I think from the supporters' point of view, and certainly from my own, there was a real sense of frustration and a sense that it was totally unfair," Steven Clifford, founder of the Four Lads Had A Dream blog and a prominent Rangers podcaster, said. "If Rangers are to lose a league, we had to lose it on our own terms. So for it to be taken out of our hands and for it to be awarded, despite it not being mathematically impossible for us to win it, to our biggest rivals was the worst possible outcome.

"It was grossly unfair. As it turned out, other countries were able to finish their leagues and that certainly galvanised the support and the feeling that there are unfavourable individuals within the governing bodies.

"I think the club's reaction was correct and there was a bit of a shock factor in terms of what they did because they were trying to galvanise the support. But the clubs were basically blackmailed and told if the season wasn't voted to a finish then they wouldn't get their money.

"We know the Scottish game is in such a precarious situation and everyone was desperate for that money. So when you are given the choice between taking that money and surviving as a club or listening to concerns from other clubs, there is only one outcome. Unfortunately, Rangers were in a situation where they were never going to win that fight."

Celtic were handed the Premiership title on 18 May but the fact was largely irrelevant to anyone other than their own supporters. Weeks before, Rangers had called for the suspension of Doncaster, the removal of legal advisor Rod McKenzie and an independent investigation to be held into the voting process and the conduct of the SPFL.

Rangers claimed the voting debacle and whistle-blower evidence they had received raised 'serious questions concerning the corporate governance of the SPFL' as allegations of coercion and bullying were made from Ibrox and rejected at Hampden. Those who suggested that Rangers had to produce a smoking gun missed the point and the body of evidence they put forward ultimately wasn't enough to convince clubs to vote in their favour. Doncaster and McKenzie would survive.

"It was quite a step for Rangers to take that action and the way that they put it across was that they had a good case and they could prove that things had not been handled correctly," Smith, who served for almost three years as chief executive of the Scottish FA before leaving his post in April 2010, said. "In the end, it was all dropped and it wasn't pursued once the vote went against them. Rangers had their case against Neil Doncaster and the SPFL, but the investigation never happened.

"You have to wonder why clubs didn't at least want to have the investigation. The SPFL were saying that they had done nothing wrong, so surely it would have been better from their point of view if the investigation had gone ahead?

"If they were quite comfortable with how they acted and that everything was totally above board, they should have been welcoming the investigation and that, as far as they were concerned, any issues and accusations wouldn't have been proven. If a club says they have evidence against you, why not prove that evidence wrong when you have the chance rather than dismiss the possibility of an investigation?

"That anger and those questions will still be there for some people and some clubs, but Neil will probably say he had the backing of so many clubs and will be comfortable with that. The SPFL were adamant they hadn't done anything wrong and Neil had a certain level of support. Rather than investigating the evidence that had been raised, a number of clubs didn't want it looked in to.

"That was a sign that Neil was in a strong position, even though he had been accused strongly by Rangers of wrongdoing and they felt an investigation was required. It is incredible that it was just dismissed by the members."

The ramifications in terms of relationships will be long lasting in Scottish football but the fall-out from last season threatened to impact on the new one. Talk of league reconstruction was a red herring and always doomed to failure but court action from Hearts and Partick Thistle could have had serious consequences for the game.

A hearing at the Court of Session ruled that their claims for compensation should be heard by an arbitration panel overseen by the Scottish FA and Lord Clark would pass the case back to Hampden. Just days before the new Premiership campaign began, Hearts and Thistle would lose their arbitration proceedings as their relegations were confirmed and attempts to receive £10million in compensation were dismissed. Finally, the damaging saga was brought to a conclusion, albeit an unsatisfactory one for many, and the focus was on football once again.

In the end, Rangers just didn't have enough support to put the necessary pressure on Doncaster, never mind topple him. Their resolution was supported by 13 clubs, while 27 voted against and three abstained. Whatever side of the debate you were on, it was time to look to the future.

"It was a good meeting, there was some good exchanges of views, but ultimately the clubs have spoken," Doncaster said. "They have given a very clear indication that they do not want to see this independent review that was being sought by three clubs.

"My view is very clear that the board should devote all of our time and our attention to the crucial work of getting the game back up and running in Scotland as soon as we can and as safe as we can.

"I am very pleased with the result and the work starts now. It was a very respectful exchange of views and you would expect that.

"I think statements can often be misconstrued, but there was a good exchange, we had all 42 clubs represented in the meeting and ultimately the clubs have given a very clear indication that they see the way forward with being engaging with the Scottish Government, getting games up and running as soon as it is safely possible and that is what we will be doing immediately."

The summer had been a classic Scottish football soap opera. It became a case of he said, she said as statements were dispatched from Ibrox and Hampden, and all around the country in fact, with regularity.

Rangers' final say on the matter wasn't exactly an olive branch but the return of competitive football soon saw the agenda move away from the politics of the game. Time would pass but it wouldn't see positions soften.

"Member clubs, recognising the need for Scottish football to improve its governance and professionalism, have moved beyond sporting rivalries and it would be unwise to regard this result as any kind of endorsement of the SPFL executive," Rangers said in a statement. "A light has been shone on the SPFL's governance and regardless of the attempts to debunk our report, there is widespread acknowledgement that it highlighted serious issues and failings which remain to be addressed.

"A management culture which not only fears accountability and scrutiny, but which actively campaigns against it, is unhealthy and breeds continued mistrust. This culture, so deeply embedded, must be addressed if Scottish football is to flourish.

"It is clear that many members have lost confidence in the SPFL leadership and the need for change will not diminish. The status quo cannot hold."

Rangers had found themselves on an almost constant war footing with the Hampden authorities for some time and

Stewart Robertson, the managing director, was a frustrated voice around the SPFL table. Given the myriad issues that Rangers had to contend with following regime change in 2015, it was no surprise that their influence at Hampden had significantly waned, but their status as champions, coupled with the departure of Celtic chief executive Peter Lawwell, could change the dynamic in Scottish football.

If the story of how this season would unfold was told at this stage of the campaign, few would have believed it. Rangers had spent so long trying to attain Old Firm equilibrium, yet their success on the park and stability off it has swung the balance of power completely in their favour. The only regret at Ibrox is that it has taken as long for Rangers to become the pre-eminent club in Scotland once again.

"I'll tell you this, and I firmly believe it," Jim Traynor, the respected journalist, broadcaster and former public relations advisor to Rangers, said. "I have huge respect for Peter Lawwell and what he has achieved, but had Dave King been based in Scotland, Rangers would have been a hundred miles further down the road in terms of challenging Celtic on and off the pitch. Also, the governance of the Scottish FA and the SPFL in particular would have been scrutinised much more robustly and some of the things these bodies, particularly the SPFL, got away with wouldn't have happened if Dave King had spent those five years in Glasgow.

"When it comes to getting things done and finding ways of forcing change he is in a different league. He is never flustered and he never wavers when he feels he is in the right. He is unsurpassed, although David Murray was like that as well.

"It would be churlish not to have respect for Peter Lawwell, especially when you look at Celtic's trophy haul. However, it should also be necessary to step back and factor in the strength of their opposition. Of course the game's old mantra that you can only beat what is in front of you holds, but if what stands before you is weak and wounded then your chances of continued success are just about guaranteed. It would be equally churlish not to acknowledge that."

When Rangers were under the control of those supposed custodians before regime change in 2015, the club were as weak in the boardroom as they were toothless in the dressing room. Rangers still had their history and their support, but their stature and influence had diminished and it would be some time before they were able to look Celtic in the eye again. Now, they have a chance to glance at them over their shoulders.

This isn't just about reconstructing a football team, it is the rebuilding of a club and an institution and that is what makes Rangers' trials and tribulations as compelling a tale. The story can now take a different turn as Rangers seek to become Scotland's dominant voice once again.

"Peter was there when David Murray was still at Ibrox and Rangers were winning and getting to the UEFA Cup final," Traynor said. "Where was Peter Lawwell then? Rangers were ailing, apparently, and apparently crippled with debt, which was a myth.

"Peter wasn't dominant in that scenario. David Murray had the measure of Peter Lawwell and so did Dave King. And so, too, would Douglas Park had Peter decided to stay on.

"Without wishing to demean other clubs, the fact is Peter and his club have had free rein while Rangers were striving just to get back on their feet. Dave stood tall and dragged that club up.

"Dave and Douglas, I thought, formed a great partnership, a powerful one, and although there might have been signs of fracturing at the end, there is a mutual respect there. Dave was probably the driving force, but he couldn't have done it without the likes of Douglas, John Bennett, George Letham, John Gilligan and Paul Murray behind him, he couldn't have."

Later in the campaign, Robertson would express his

frustrations at the way the SFA and SPFL had handled a proposal regarding the introduction of colt teams into the League structure. He was rebuked on that occasion by Rod Petrie, the SFA chairman and accused of 'inaccuracies' in his version of events relating to the process as the Old Firm pushed their case over a controversial blueprint.

In public and behind closed doors, Rangers have still to really show a strength in terms of exerting their influence on the Scottish game. Time will tell if they are able to shift the balance of power in their favour, but they are at least now operating with the clout of champions.

"I think the most important thing for Rangers, first and foremost, is that they won the title and 55 was paramount for the club," Clifford, a season ticket holder and member of the Rangers 'fan media' rise, said. "Now that has been done the club can go back to trying to influence and work with other clubs and pointing out the unfairness and the issues with the governance of the game.

"Rangers may be able to garner further support from those in the lower leagues that weren't convinced. Rangers pointed out a lot of high-profile issues but it was painted as this smoking gun full of revelations and accusations of cheating. But that was never what Rangers were trying to say and what they were trying to achieve.

"This was about the governance of our game and those running our game. Now that Rangers have achieved their objective on the park, they are approaching this as the champions of Scotland and they can go back to those clubs. They can say 'Look, this is what happened last year and this is what happened since and it is not a strong place for our game to be in.'

"When Rangers talk about refereeing and the governing of the game, we just want a stronger and more balanced outlook in terms of how everyone gets treated. This isn't for Rangers' self-gain, it is for the game as a whole. If you have someone like Steven Gerrard in the game, you should be listening to him and using him any way you can to grow and move our game forward as best we can."

The Gerrard factor hadn't been fully capitalised on by Scottish football in terms of sponsorship and exposure, but Rangers were ready to really reap the rewards of the presence of the most high-profile figure in our game. Gerrard, of course, was at Ibrox to win trophies rather than sell season tickets and August began his third attempt at that very ambition.

A summer of hostility mercifully gave way to the new campaign and Rangers would begin their title bid with a 1-0 win at Aberdeen as Ryan Kent scored the only goal of the game. A trip to Pittodrie is so often an occasion to savour given the animosity between the respective supports but this fixture, and the rest of the Premiership card that weekend, only opened fans' eyes as to what the campaign would look like as matches were played in front of empty stands and watched on television.

Like so many aspects of the Rangers story, even when the focus is on looking forward, it is impossible to avoid glancing back. On the day that Gerrard's side saw the previous season's Europa League run come to an end as they lost 1-0 in Leverkusen, Rangers brought a close to the final legacy issue that King, Murray and Gilligan had inherited in March 2015. Rangers had announced a new long-term retail agreement with Castore several weeks previously, but it was the opening of the refurbished club shop at Ibrox that really marked a new era. All the time, all the money and all the effort was worth it in the end.

"It is where you place the money that was available at that time, it was best use of the money," Traynor said. "When Dave believes he is right on something, he is the immovable object. He will not bend and he won't stop, even if you think it is a lost cause.

"He always had a way of getting round problems you thought were insurmountable. He knew a way. A lot of times, it was something that nobody had thought of and the Sports Direct saga is the perfect example. He believed he was right, and it was fortunate he was so utterly resolute in his stance because that was a ridiculous situation which had to be resolved in Rangers' favour.

"There were people in his ear saying 'give that one up' and I know there were people, quite wealthy Rangers supporters, urging him to do a deal with Ashley, but he just wouldn't because he knew he was right. He got there in the end.

"He had all sorts of people conveying messages, some of those messages hidden beneath superficial chit chat and there were always people seeking an audience with him to pass on information 'which could help Rangers' but he never wavered because he knew he was right in that Sports Direct one.

"If he knew he was right, he was immovable. That was one of his strengths, I always felt. When he felt he was right he just stuck with it."

The cost of litigation, both in terms of time and money, towards fighting Sports Direct was immense and it had taken a toll on King as well. This wasn't just a business deal to be thrashed out, it was personal as King attempted to remove every last trace of Mike Ashley's influence over Rangers.

There had been times when King believed he had won, others where supporters feared they would forever lose. Victories on the park will always be the most important ones for Rangers, but the moment that pen was put to paper with Castore was as significant as any final whistle this season and the ramifications for the club and the support cannot be underestimated.

"Mike Ashley tried to put me in jail one Christmas and take me away from my family," King said. "People ask me why I put up with that? I did it because of two things.

"I made a commitment to the supporters and my view on life has always been that if there is a problem like Mike Ashley you run towards it, you don't run away from it. That is just my philosophy.

"And secondly, the energy that I could draw from supporters, I knew that whatever I was doing I was doing it for the supporters who were alienated from their club. I say this with the absolute most sincerity. When I was making calls for supporters to boycott their club, I didn't do that lightly and I knew emotionally what that meant to say to people 'abandon your club'.

"I still felt at that point in time that it was only by abandoning their club in the short term that we could guarantee its future in the long term. The fact that so many supporters backed me, that gave me a hell of a responsibility to deliver on that. It was very important to me."

The issues with Sports Direct had dominated the agenda since regime change. It was natural that supporters focused more on matters in a football sense, but the financial implications of a retail operation that couldn't fully function were debilitating for Rangers and the club would not be able to look forward to future seasons had the Sports Direct affair not been resolved.

Matters became increasingly convoluted and complicated as the wheels of the court system turned slowly. Many fans may not have been able to follow the minutiae details, but they remained mindful of where they spent their money.

For so many years, the Megastore at Ibrox was the focal point for protests against Sports Direct as banners were unfurled and rallies held. On the day that James Bisgrove, Rangers' director of commercial and marketing, joined Castore founders Phil and Tom Beahon, the crowds that gathered were there for a very different reason as chairman Douglas Park cut the ribbons on the new-look retail outlet.

The spectre of Ashley had haunted Rangers for too long and fans were right to be inquisitive about any new deal that was signed.

"The powerful thing about today is that we are able to look forward," Bisgrove said on day one of the new partnership. "We have said before the legacy of the club and the previous relationships we have had from a kit and retail perspective are now behind us.

"I think, again, it goes back to the conversations that Tom and Phil and I have had from March onwards. The ambition, the professionalism, the passion that Castore showed in terms of selecting Rangers to be their flagship club within football, from the start of that conversation we were quickly able to see what the potential of this partnership is. To be candid, it was a challenge to get to that point so that is why today is even more satisfying.

"I think Tom and Phil have been very clear on that [Sports Direct] before. Rangers and Castore's ambition is to have Rangers strips far and wide so there is a global distribution plan that will get us there. Indeed, it is not uncommon that a number of high street retailers and third-party wholesale relationships will be put in place. That is certainly not uncommon in football retail.

"Today, the focus is on this store. We have got a new online store that is up and running as well from a Rangers perspective. In order for this partnership to get to where we and Tom and Phil get it to be at, there are going to be a number of periphery partners that will help us get there."

There were issues over supplies and the quality of some items early on and supporters voiced their concerns and unhappiness online as a level of understanding at the timeframe and turnaround bought Castore and the club some leeway.

The queues around Ibrox spoke for themselves as supporters re-engaged with Rangers and Castore cashed in at the start of what would become a historic campaign. After waiting so long to be able to feel able to spend their money on their club, these were reassuring times for supporters, but their loyalty and their backing should not be taken for granted and their demands off the park are as vehement as those on it.

It was the end of an era and a point at which Rangers could move on from. Time will tell just how successful the partnership really is as Castore look to live up to their 'better never stops' mantra and seek to further expand a client list that also now includes the likes of Patrick Reed, the 2018 Masters champion, and sports car manufacturer and Formula One team McLaren.

Their deal with Rangers was a step into the unknown at a time when there was little certainty in society and business. The following months would see Scottish football's greatest and most remarkable story written, but Rangers wouldn't have been able to fully capitalise on their sporting achievement if their retail operation was effectively handcuffed.

"It wasn't just financially because that was OK," King said as he considered his emotional and monetary input following his return to Rangers. "I had lost money before and I could lose money again. There was no point in me fronting this thing unless I had the character and mentality to face up to the likes of Mike Ashley.

"It wasn't about money, you can put money in. It wasn't about a cheque. We had to unlock so many things away from the football team to make the club successful and the vice-like grip of Mike Ashley and the Easdales (brothers James and Sandy) was critical to that.

"If I look at my investment and involvement in Rangers, I don't see it being the money. The money was important and for every pound I put in other people put in a pound. I couldn't throw money at the problem, it was the time and effort that I put in more than the money. It was standing up and being the businessman with the character and the temperament to take these people on.

"If I look back at my legacy, I think it is more my mental effort that I am more grateful of than the money. I can write out a cheque, but the time and effort I personally put in and the challenge I took on when Mike Ashley is threatening to sue me, liquidate me, jail me, I think that was more my contribution to the club."

When it comes to input, to doing your bit for the cause, then there are few who have done more than Craig Houston over the last decade. As the founder and public face of the Sons of Struth group, he became a figure for supporters to rally round, a voice for them to listen to through the darkest days of the escalating tensions between supporters and directors before King, Murray and Gilligan regained control of Rangers.

Houston was an ordinary man, an ordinary fan, that assumed an extraordinary role and his story is a remarkable one. What began as a Facebook page set up before he headed to Ibrox for a game became a source of information for his fellow supporters, a voice of the people that became increasingly influential over the next two years.

It would take its own toll, though. Houston's love of Rangers and his dedication to the cause saw the break-up of his long-term relationship and he would temporarily become estranged from his two young children.

A battle with depression was fought with the help of friend Sandy Chugg, a once notorious member of the feared Inter City Firm. His business would collapse and he faced bankruptcy after Sandy Easdale launched a £200,000 claim for defamation of character at the Court of Session.

The case was later resolved out of court, but it was just one of many run-ins that Houston had with Easdale and his brother, James, in a battle that would take him from the stands to the streets and ultimately to the Blue Room. Houston and his father were guests at the match with Queen of the South in March 2015, the first at Ibrox following regime change, as legends from yesteryear thanked him for his efforts in ensuring Rangers had a future.

A football academy for Glasgow kids is now run under the name of Rangers' most successful manager and the funds raised for good causes throughout his time on the frontline were gratefully received and warmly welcomed. The Rangers Youth Development Company and Rangers Charity Foundations are two such benefactors as SoS, like Rangers, has moved onwards and upwards following the overthrowing of the board in 2015.

One such charitable gesture attracted the interest of Ashley, though, and a call from King regarding the sale of Rangers merchandise prompted head-scratching. Houston had made a donation to the Rangers Former Players Benevolent Fund to purchase their unused merchandise items and would then sell the crested pin badges and put the money back into the Fund which helps those that represented the club who have fallen on hard times. A gesture of goodwill from Houston had attracted the ire of Sports Direct but the arrival of legal letters or spectre of litigation did not dissuade him in his fight.

The efforts of Houston had been crucial in alerting supporters to the deals that saw Rangers receive just a few pence-in-the-pound on every sale of replica merchandise. The £25million agreement with Castore, then, was transformative and one that Bisgrove believed had 'the potential to be the most valuable partnership in Scottish sport' as a £250,000 revamp of the Ibrox store was undertaken ahead of the August launch.

"All we ever wanted was two things," Houston said as he reflected on the end of the Sports Direct era and his role throughout the controversial period. "One was for the club to get a fair market deal and a deal that was fair for both parties. And we wanted Rangers fans to be able to go into the shop and spend their money and have their kids going about with strips and hats and merchandise like any supporter of any other club.

"That has come to pass. It took a long time to get there but those were the reasons for the actions that we took. It was good to see the numbers at the shop over the summer and the queues long before the store opened. I think a lot more orders came in than even Rangers could expect and you could see that they were bursting at the seams at times to cope with the demand.

"That was really warming. The fact that Rangers fans could go and buy a jersey and know that the club were getting pounds for every tenner that was spent rather than pennies for every tenner that was spent was great."

Houston had risen to prominence amongst the Rangers support long before the EGM victory that saw power transferred and hope restored. When it came to raising awareness or voicing concerns, he was front and centre, whether it be through Press interviews or stunts such as hiring mobile advertising lorries or leading protests at Ibrox or further afield.

His ire was often directed at the Easdales but the list of characters that he called out is comprehensive. Given Ashley's wealth and his business standing, taking on the Newcastle United owner was Houston's own David versus Goliath moment. He would never speak to the man himself, but legal correspondence accompanied regular conversations with police services in Glasgow and Northumberland.

"We knew that when we had a call for action to the Rangers fans for other things that we were doing at the time that they had responded well and were supportive of what we were doing," Houston said. "So that gave us a bit of confidence, but when you are taking on multi-millionaires and trying to get them to see sense, there is always a bit of doubt in your mind. We couldn't have done it without the Rangers fans.

"We never told anybody not to shop. We just said that we wouldn't be giving them any money and why and the support came with us. It wasn't Sons of Struth telling them what to do, it was people making their own decisions and that was massive in getting him to the table and getting to where we are and Sports Direct no longer being our retail partner."

Enquiries about whether Houston was sending a busload of supporters for a demonstration at a store in Newcastle were frequent. He never would, but the fact that Ashley had to be prepared for the eventuality was enough to cause him an issue and ensure a cost in terms of security staff. An idea of blockading his Shirebrook base in conjunction with Newcastle supporters was dismissed over fears of the impact on lorry drivers but Houston would take to the streets and internet in an attempt to play his part in forcing Ashley's hand.

The influence of Houston must surely have been a source of irritation to Ashley and Rangers just couldn't have been worth the time and the effort for so long given the stance of supporters. Once the doors opened at the Ibrox Store, so did the floodgates as Castore were given an early insight into just what they had signed up for with Rangers.

Like at so many times this season, those days offered a chance for reflection. Whether it regards merchandise or managers, supporters are right to remember just where Rangers have been at various stages throughout their recent history and to be thankful for the progress that has been made on and off the park.

"What we wanted to do was stop his tills working and you have got to be mindful of legal and moral obligations there," Houston said. "The staff that are in these shops might not like him but they had nothing to do with it and you had to be aware of the legalities. We had loads of ideas, some were a bit crackpot right enough! We just considered each one.

"Going into a shop on a Saturday with 100 Rangers fans, filling up their baskets and getting to the cash desk and offering £1 for whatever you wanted to buy seemed a logical thing. It disrupted his trading. The staff weren't getting abused, some of them were laughing and smiling with us and anybody that was outside the shop saw the crowd and thought 'look at the queues, I'm not going in there'.

"It was all for the same thing, to stop his tills from working for a while on a busy day. We had some success. I don't know how much it impacted on the bottom line of Sports Direct, but he was certainly aware of it because it was costing him tens of thousands of pounds in security staff each time we took action."

As Park officially opened the new Rangers Store and supporters walked out with their money spent and their bags packed, there would have been a feeling of job done for both King and Houston. Others, of course, had played their part in getting Rangers to that position and the Castore deal will go down as the most significant one that Bisgrove has struck. The list of commercial partners is now extensive at Ibrox and there is further scope for expansion as Rangers build on their status as champions and stability in a business and sporting sense.

The impact of Gerrard in that regard cannot be underestimated and the benefits that Rangers will garner for seasons to come are in large part due to the manager. Even right at the start of the campaign, Gerrard had a feeling that this year could be the year.

King may no longer have been calling the shots at Ibrox but he remained an important ally of Gerrard and was still in regular dialogue with the man that he brought from Liverpool two seasons previously. He had done so with the belief that Gerrard was the man to deliver title 55 and there was an optimism about Gerrard's manner that gave King hope. The summer had been contentious at boardroom level as Rangers took the fight to the Hampden authorities, but the football department had benefitted from the chance to take stock and transfer business was done promptly as Rangers prepared for their third attempt to win the Premiership on Gerrard's watch.

"If you come to the beginning of this season, there was a level of apprehension," King said. "Steven had made progress, he had learned more about playing football in Scotland and going away to difficult games like St Johnstone, Livingston, Kilmarnock and playing on difficult pitches.

"I felt that Steven had gained a lot, his management team had gained a lot and the players had gained a lot and I think Steven had learned about the type of football that is likely to be successful in Scotland, which is not necessarily what would work in other leagues.

"He adapted to what he thought could win in Scotland and with the transfer business that we did in the summer, Steven went into it and his comment to me was 'I think I can compete this year'. Obviously there were no guarantees but he really thought he could compete this year, which was quite a big attitude given that we had had a meltdown the previous season."

The passing of time between that abject defeat to Hamilton in March and the win over Aberdeen in August had been significant for Gerrard. Scotland remained under the grip of Coronavirus, but Rangers were ready to grasp their opportunity in the Premiership.

The goalless draw with Livingston was an off-day for Rangers, yet it was one that proved to be a rare occurrence. The other four Premiership fixtures, against St Mirren and St Johnstone before it and Kilmarnock and Hamilton after it, were won comfortably, although Gerrard would rue the wastefulness in the final third after the victory in Lanarkshire that should have been by a far greater margin.

"If you look at our results this season there has been three or four times that I'm going away thinking we should have got more goals today," Gerrard said after Ianis Hagi and James Tavernier were somehow the only scorers on a day where Rangers were profligate in front of goal. "At some point that might come back to bite us.

"That tells me we still need to get better. We still need to improve, keep working on the training pitch and if we can add that one or two bits of quality through the squad."

Those enhancements would come from within rather than fresh faces and the group that Gerrard had assembled early would evolve individually and collectively over time. It may only have been weeks into the season, but Rangers had clearly improved once again and had the look of genuine title contenders about them.

The issue at that stage for Gerrard surrounded keeping his key players rather than adding to his squad. Interest in Ryan Kent from Leeds United was serious but thankfully fleeting for Rangers and the winger would go on to be an integral part of a successful side.

"The relationship with the manager is key, as it is for any footballer," Kent, who added to his goal against Aberdeen with strikes in the wins over St Johnstone and Kilmarnock, said following the victory at Hamilton. "Especially for a forward player, you need to feel comfortable and enjoy your football. I certainly do here. The coaching staff have put a lot of faith in me and a lot of work into me to get numbers into my game.

"That's showing this season, I'm getting into the right areas now and putting away finishes that I wasn't last season. I want to repay the manager for that backing, this is the season to do that.

"Steven Gerrard, the coaching staff, my team-mates, the fans, I'll continue to do my best for them. I have high expectations of myself on the pitch so everyone can be reassured that I'll continue to do my best for Rangers."

The stumble against Livingston aside, Gerrard couldn't have asked for more from the opening month of the campaign. As Rangers started with authority, Celtic began to unravel almost from the off and, like so many of their problems, the damage was self-inflicted.

A 1-1 draw with Kilmarnock was costly for Celtic but the revelation that defender Boli Bolingoli had travelled to Spain and didn't isolate on his return before taking to the field at Rugby Park would put our game in the dock for the first time this season. His actions incurred the wrath of First Minister Sturgeon and Celtic's fixtures with St Mirren and Aberdeen – who had their own Covid issues as eight players broke guidelines by gathering in a city centre restaurant following the defeat to Rangers – were postponed as Sturgeon issued a cliché and political points scoring 'yellow card' to our game.

Celtic were already playing catch-up in the title race and it soon became apparent that they would be unable to close the gap. Rangers' squad had the strength and the depth to go the distance and the crucial box of mindset was one that Gerrard had expressed confidence that he had ticked.

"What was there to justify the difference between the previous season and this season, other than the transfer business that we had done? Steven had his reasons," King said. "He felt the business was good and that the mentality of the team had improved.

"From Steven's point of view, a big aspect of what he was doing was improving the mentality of the team, creating more winners and resilience and really having a good go at winning the league. We started the league and Steven felt he had a chance of having a really good go.

"Everyone knew this was the season so the emphasis all around the club was the title. It was actually quite nice, in retrospect, to go in as underdogs because the view of the media was the same as when Rangers won nine-in-a-row and that was that we couldn't lose the next one. The view was that Rangers were still so far behind."

That opinion wouldn't stand up to scrutiny for long. Rangers had been edging closer and closer to Celtic in every area since the day that Gerrard was appointed but the way that the balance of power shifted so quickly still came as a surprise to even the most experienced Old Firm observers.

Celtic's defeat to Ferencvaros in the Champions League will go down as one of the defining moments in the campaign. The money from that competition had become so critical to the Parkhead model but the usual response of selling a key player didn't unfold this time as Celtic chased 'The Ten'. The comments from manager Neil Lennon offered an insight into the mentality of the Celtic squad as he insisted that those who didn't want to be there were free to go. No big names departed but Celtic were in the ultimate catch-22 situation as those that remained showed that they either weren't up for the fight or weren't good enough to win it.

Even at that stage, it was clear there was an opportunity for Rangers to really apply the kind of pressure they had failed to do in previous seasons and test Celtic's mettle. Rangers wouldn't make the same mistake thrice.

"I have to say, I have reflected on that and I had a conversation with my boys and said to them that football was a funny thing," King said. "I get that they had the gap financially, but we had narrowed that gap because they hadn't done well in the Champions League and I had the pack of cards comment saying that we just had to take Celtic's revenue away from them.

"Even though we didn't win the league, we did better in Europe than they did and I just felt it was a potential turning point. I said to my boys 'you know, I have been around this game a long time and the football gods have got a certain way of working'.

"The unbeatable Celtic side that did nine-in-a-row didn't do the ten, the unbeatable Rangers team didn't do the ten. I just had a feeling that this might be the season and everyone was focused on it."

The belief from Gerrard and the hunch from King would prove to be astute. It would take until the Old Firm win at Parkhead the following month for Rangers to inflict another blow on Celtic, but this season was about what Gerrard's side did rather than their title rivals.

Recent history had scarred many supporters and they were right not to get ahead of themselves just weeks into the campaign. They had suffered through a series of false dawns, yet this season felt different somehow. And so it was to prove.

Those that believed Rangers would win the title were ultimately correct in their assertion, but few would have predicted the emphatic nature of it. Rangers had emerged stronger from their hardships and were now on their way to title 55.

"The logical side of my brain was saying that Celtic won the league by a mile last season and we collapsed after the break," King said. "I was really feeding off the enthusiasm that Steven had and him saying 'listen, forget that, we have figured this out'.

"This year, he said we could start as equals and really give it a go. It was basically my trust of Steven. He wasn't a manager who had come in from the cold for me, I felt that I knew him as a person, I had followed him as a player and had a good recommendation from Kenny Dalglish. I really thought we could have a good go this year.

"But, having said that, if we were in it with three games to go and one point ahead or behind, that was a challenge. I never in my wildest dreams believed that we would be in the situation where we would comfortably win the league like we did."

Over the last decade, there have been so many things that Rangers fans could only dream of at times. This season would be the season where they would become a reality.

The title win is, of course, the most important of all but off-field events were significant and fed into the feeling of progression at Ibrox. The difficult times that King and Houston were so involved in would be left in the past and by the end of the season there became no need to constantly remember where Rangers had been as those with an attachment to the club considered where they were heading ahead of their 150th year.

There will hopefully never be another one like it in a societal sense. The sporting recriminations of the summer may have been insignificant compared to the public health crisis in Scotland but they were highly-charged days of high-stakes decisions.

This season would be all about Rangers. They were a great watch, a great read and they were champions in waiting.

FOUR

READY. The word on the Rangers badge and the motto of the club was fitting for Steven Gerrard and his players. Could the same be said for the supporters?

The campaign may only have been weeks old, but Rangers had the look of genuine title contenders about them. So much had been said and written about the mentality of the Ibrox squad, but there were questions for the fans to answer individually and collectively.

After nine years of crushing disappointments and false dawns, it would take a shift in the mindset from the support if they were to play their part in the bid for 55. They too had to prove their mettle in the title race and show that they could live up to the club's mantra.

The famous circular crest was updated in July 2020 as Rangers unveiled a new look as part of its brand evolution and digital transformation strategy. An official club typography was commissioned and the badge was tweaked, with the lion rampant sharpened and the word 'Ready' moved inside the old-style leather football as the club name was realigned. The changes weren't radical, but they were another sign of the modernisation programme that was being undertaken at Ibrox as Rangers prepared to celebrate their 150th anniversary.

The ultimate ambition, of course, was to do so as champions. Come the end of September, they were still unbeaten in the Premiership, yet two results had seen supporters keep their expectations in check. The goalless draw with Livingston the previous month was the first stumble of the season and when Hibernian came from behind to earn a point at Easter Road just weeks later, there were fears that lessons hadn't been learned.

As it transpired, that 2-2 draw was the last time that points would be dropped until the match with Motherwell in January. The opener from Drey Wright was the first goal that Rangers had conceded all season as the run of seven consecutive league shut-outs, which surpassed a 114-year-old club record, came to an end. But it was the second goal, scored by Christian Doidge, that really hurt Rangers as efforts from Alfredo Morelos and Scott Arfield ultimately didn't prove enough to earn another Premiership victory.

It was seen as the kind of result that can, and had previously, cost Rangers a shot at the title. History shows that supporters need not have worried, however. It may have been a familiar kind of mistake, but it would prove to be a rare one and the reaction this time spoke volumes about where Gerrard's side were.

Given how high the stakes were this season, it was understandable that supporters would spend it on edge and there was a nervousness permeating the fanbase at that stage. If they knew then how comfortable the campaign would turn out to be, there would not have been the outpouring of concern and criticism when four points were dropped in the opening weeks of the season.

When Rangers started September with a 4-0 win at home to Dundee United, Gerrard's assessment offered an insight into his standards and the levels he believed his side could reach. The performance and result that day were the kind that championship challenging sides produce as an inferior opponent was beaten comfortably.

Gerrard, though, was right to demand better from his players and the fans should have bought into his messages. In the end, there would be many more such afternoons as Rangers took care of business in an efficient and ultimately unstoppable manner.

"We are not relentless yet, we haven't been relentless yet," Gerrard said after the 4-0 win as Ryan Kent, James Tavernier, Kemar Roofe and Arfield netted. "If there is one criticism or area where we can improve, it is to be more ruthless over the course of the games we have played so far.

"Today, we showed signs we could have gone on to get five or six. But if you look at the games collectively, once we get [Cedric] Itten 100 per cent, Roofe 100 per cent, Alfredo 100 per cent, then I think it could be interesting."

Those weren't the only comments that stood out that afternoon and Gerrard would find himself charged by the Scottish FA after discussing an incident that saw Morelos on the end of a crude challenge from Ryan Edwards. The Colombian was left with a nasty gash on his leg, but referee Kevin Clancy didn't deem the tackle worthy of a red card and Gerrard's observations saw him issued with a Notice of Complaint.

"I don't want to make headlines and say a kid should have got this or that," Gerrard said of Edwards' challenge. "I don't want to be that type of manager. What I would say is that I'd be very interested to see what the decision would have been from the officials had the shoe been on the other foot and it was Alfredo who had made that tackle."

Rangers would express their bemusement when Gerrard was charged and then reaffirm that feeling when he was subsequently cleared at a delayed hearing. It was the first of several issues

Rangers would have with the disciplinary system throughout the season, but it perhaps played into the siege mentality amongst the support and there was a unity between club and fan despite the Government-enforced distance that sadly separated them.

Given how unaccustomed Rangers fans were to success and how desperate they were for it, the feelings of anxiety were only natural. The fact that they had to watch on from home and in isolation served to exacerbate the issue and the only comfort many could find was virtually as they helped each other through the campaign. Rangers had proven that they were capable of challenging for the title and the support had to show they were able to keep calm and carry on while they did so at the third time of asking.

As the main host of the Heart and Hand podcast, David Edgar was given access to Ibrox this season as a 'fan media' representative. It was a change of direction from the club and one overseen by David Graham, who was appointed as head of communications and media relations in March 2020. It allowed Edgar to see the action and the fall-out at close quarters throughout the season.

"I remember after the Livingston game that the social media reaction was huge and there was a bit of a meltdown," Edgar said. "I commented on it on our shows and said that we have got to get better at being able to go up and down over a season. There will be times where the team doesn't play particularly well and we can't have this reaction, this early in the season, to one draw.

"It is explainable in the sense that it was the scars of the last ten years. It is difficult to imagine this now, but in September football had just started back up again and there had been a long time for the end of last season to fester. There was the way that it ended – the summer was very vitriolic with the situation with the SPFL – and people were unsettled, especially when you take into account the wider world.

"People were jumpy, if you like, and that reaction to Livingston summed it up. After Hibernian it was slightly better and I think that is down to perception. Livingston this season were one of the better sides, that is a very difficult place to go for Rangers and Celtic, but there is a more traditional respect for Hibs and it's almost not as bad dropping points there. Maybe that had something to do with it but people were still unhappy at the result. That was the kind of thing that can happen over a season though and we had to remember that."

When Rangers had encountered adversity in Gerrard's first two terms, they had a tendency to compound the problems rather than solve them. If the third season was going to have a different outcome, that was one area where Rangers certainly had to improve.

Drawing with Spartak Moscow, for example, was followed by a defeat to Aberdeen and stalemate with Kilmarnock before a 4-3 defeat in Russia that would hinder their prospects of progression in the Europa League. Later in the campaign, a loss to Rapid Vienna ended those chances and came after another defeat to Aberdeen and a draw with Dundee. In March, a run of five without a win ended their Scottish Cup ambitions and chance of winning the title.

The stumbles were more sporadic but just as costly in the second season under Gerrard's guidance. A draw with Aberdeen and defeat to Celtic in the League Cup final in December didn't derail Rangers but Hearts and Kilmarnock would beat them and the Dons would take another point before the losses to Killie, Hearts and Hamilton that saw the campaign spiral out of control in the days that were the precursor to Covid closing down the game and the nation.

Gerrard had used the long months since in search of answers. He would have preferred, of course, not to draw with Livingston or Hibernian early on but those results wouldn't prove costly for Rangers. In fact, they were beneficial as they provided an opportunity for Gerrard's side to prove their character to a support that needed all the reassuring it could get.

"Noticeably, Gerrard as a manager and the players collectively and individually, there was a maturity about them this season," Edgar said. "There were times in his first couple of seasons where he was too emotional after matches and that went both ways, it wasn't just that he was too critical of the players.

"I think he over-praised them at times and there were times where you felt he hadn't quite made the transition from being the captain of a side that literally kicked every ball and lived every moment and hadn't quite achieved that distance.

"Look at Walter Smith, there was a gap between Walter and the playing squad and he made sure of that. Having that opportunity, or forced opportunity, to take a step back and have very little to do except review videos and discuss with your staff where it had gone wrong worked in Steven's favour."

The aura that Gerrard had exuded when he took those first steps along the Ibrox touchline hadn't diminished through a sense of familiarity. He still spoke with authority to his players and the press and he had the respect of those that he worked with and for.

His two seasons had provided him with significant highs and real lows, yet it is not in his nature to let failures define or impede him. The first few weeks of his third campaign saw that steely determination come to the fore once again and there was a quiet belief that this time could be his time.

As Dave King and Mark Allen conceded, there were boxes that Gerrard did not tick in terms of managerial experience before they appointed him. When it came to being a leader, a man of the people, they could not have picked a more suitable candidate, however, and it was those inspirational qualities that would ultimately allow Gerrard to rally those around him and form a bond that even adversity could not break.

"Someone who is a seasoned pro, that has played a lot of football and been in a lot of changing rooms, will have seen players coming into teams that he was playing in," Dr Robbie Anderson, an experienced and respected sports psychologist and managing director with Chimp Management, said. "He will recognise the value of going round and putting his arm around a player and saying 'great job'.

"The emotional intelligence of someone who has been successful tends to be high and research shows us that one of the success factors of successful people is emotional intelligence. The people who understand their own emotions and can manage them and can understand the emotions in other people and manage it and communicate well tend to do well in any setting. If Steven has been able to transfer the emotional intelligence he had as a player into being a manager then that will only stand him in good stead and only help the people around him."

The theory by which Dr Anderson operates is defined as the Chimp Model. In essence, it splits the brain into three segments: the 'inner Chimp' that thinks and acts without our permission, the compassionate and rational 'Human' and the 'Computer', which represents the memory banks within our minds. The model is not pure scientific fact, but instead an aid to further understand the science and the concept is used by Professor Steve Peters, who helped Gerrard overcome a career-threatening groin injury and would later accompany the England squad to the 2014 World Cup finals in Brazil.

At a club like Rangers, a natural talent will only get you so far. The history of the club is littered with players who were supremely gifted but who couldn't adjust to the incessant demands at Ibrox. Conversely, those who had the right mental fortitude could out-perform their physical gifts and become integral members of successful teams.

When it comes to a title race, it can often be a case of mind over matter. For David Warner, there can be a more scientific approach to the issues presented by expectation and demands on players.

"If we take a step back and say fundamentally what is pressure?" Warner, a psychological skills mentor and quality control officer with Chimp Management, said. "Pressure comes from a fear of not being able to live with the consequences of what might happen. If you are very outcome and results focused, and let's be fair and say that football is a results business, but if you focus purely on the outcome and you are consumed with what the outcome is going to be and what that might mean, that is more likely to create pressure than if you focus on things that are within your control.

"The outcome is outside of your control. Once you both address consequences and focus on the processes that get you the best chance of the outcome that you want, then you are focusing on what is within your control. There will be stuff that has gone on before and some of that will reside in the Computer.

"We have experiences that are unpleasant and we remember those because we want to avoid them again and some of that will be around. The job of any leader is to reassure the team that they will be able to deal with any consequences and to focus on what processes will give the best results and start measuring results by how well they deliver those processes. Then the results come as a by-product of that."

Rangers had already proven themselves adept at earning individual wins during Gerrard's first two seasons, but the goal was to turn a title challenge into a title triumph. They had been able to go so far, yet for multiple reasons they had stumbled with the finishing line in sight.

A 5-1 win away to Motherwell was the only other Premiership fixture that Gerrard's side played in September. It was as comfortable as the scoreline suggested as Tavernier and Itten netted twice, either side of a strike from Jordan Jones, and Motherwell's consolation came via the unfortunate George Edmundson with three minutes remaining.

A 5-0 victory over Lincoln Red Imps was followed by a 4-0 win away to Willem II as Rangers moved to within 90 minutes of the Europa League group stages once again. It was still early in the season, but there was an encouraging momentum behind Gerrard's side and a confidence that they could overcome the challenges that were quickly coming into view.

By the time attentions had turned to the meeting with Galatasaray on 1 October, Gerrard had already completed almost all of his transfer business during his fifth window. This was now his squad and his team and there was a need to deliver results and silverware over the months that would follow.

The signing of Bongani Zungu would come on deadline day but ultimately matter little. Rangers had pursued the South African earlier in the summer, yet it took until the final hours of business for the deal to be done. His handful of appearances did little to convince that the effort was worth it and he was fortunate to play again following his Covid rules breach later in the season.

The majority of the work that Gerrard and Ross Wilson, the sporting director, completed proved successful, though. Wilson had been appointed as Allen's successor in October 2019 and this window was his first real opportunity to have an impact on the squad. He was initially approached about the role when it was first created following regime change but it was only a couple of seasons later that he felt the time was right to return to Scotland following four years with Southampton.

As the football world continued to adapt and adjust to the Covid one around it, clubs and their prospective players found themselves in a new situation. The focus was still the same for

Rangers, though. It was quality over quantity and time was of the essence.

The deal for Ianis Hagi was the first one completed as his loan from Genk was turned into a permanent transfer. Jermain Defoe would also extend his stay following the expiry of his Bournemouth contract and the first new faces were those of Jon McLaughlin and Calvin Bassey, signed from Sunderland and Leicester City respectively to provide competition in the squad.

There is a strategy in the way that Gerrard and Wilson work but sometimes it is about how you react rather than how you plan. That was the case with the signing of Leon Balogun and Mark Wilson, a football writer with the *Scottish Daily Mail*, highlights the importance of being able to adapt quickly and adequately.

"They were confronted by a big issue before a ball had been kicked when Niko Katic suffered cruciate ligament damage in July," Wilson said. "Another significant signing had to be made, one that hadn't been part of the considerations during lockdown.

"Ross Wilson uses a phrase about being 'connected to the market'. And that was shown as Rangers solved the problem in a very efficient way. They assessed various options and talked about looking at young players from top Premier League clubs that had a bit of loan experience. But they quickly decided that Balogun was the man with the right profile and I think that was a key move when you look at the defensive record that followed.

"Katic had been an important player so you were trying to fill that number two or three centre-back position. While it hadn't worked out for Balogun at Brighton, he had good experience from the Championship, he had played in the Bundesliga and been to the World Cup with Nigeria. You saw straight away from his debut at Aberdeen that he hit the ground running.

"It wasn't long afterwards that Gerrard started to talk about him as a leader so it was a clever bit of cost-effective business to come back from a big, big blow like Katic being injured and helped create a defensive unit that was stronger over the course of a campaign.

"Balogun wasn't perfect all the time. He had a couple of difficult games in the latter part of the season and had to shift to right-back at times. But he brought a bit of pace, a strong personality and was another experienced guy who didn't seem in the slightest bit fazed by the pressure that confronted the squad. It was quite an understated move at the time but an effective one that delivered good value for money and that is to the credit of Wilson and Gerrard."

By the time Roofe and Itten had been added to the squad a couple of weeks later, Gerrard had the group he believed could take Rangers to the title. There was another step up in terms of the quality, but it was the character that would be just as significant this time around for Rangers and Gerrard had the right people as well as the right players.

It was captain Tavernier that would wear the armband, but Rangers had those who would lead by example and those who could be more vocal. That core of Tavernier, Allan McGregor, Connor Goldson, Steven Davis, Ryan Jack and Arfield have been pivotal over the course of the campaign and the influence of such inspiring figures cannot be overlooked as Rangers finally had that mark of champions that all successful sides must possess.

"What is interesting at a psychological level is that you start to look at different approaches," Dr Anderson said. "It might be that we bring in a seasoned pro or two and it could be the case that having someone like Steven Gerrard, in his own right, is the senior pro.

"Let's go away from Rangers for a second. The Tampa Bay Buccaneers won the Super Bowl after they brought in Tom Brady. It could be that all the other players see the behaviours of what this expert player does, they identify that they are the behaviours that will get you success and what they essentially do is copy them. That might not seem very psychological, but it is the influence top class professionals are having on your club.

"It could be that factor was at play at Rangers and the focus was about what we do repeatedly each day and we have got senior pros that are doing that. We reward that behaviour by giving praise, we punish it by moving on the players that don't do it and that becomes a very cultural behavioural idea.

"Not every player is going to buy into that, that takes a willingness and a lot of hard work. But it is not just that you buy one striker and he scores all the goals, you don't just get Gerrard and he wins you the league. What you are really doing is setting up a whole club that has good behaviours, helpful beliefs, a supportive culture, and if you repeat that over time then your probabilities go up."

Those that did not conform to Gerrard's methods or meet his standards did not last long at Ibrox. As he has enhanced the level of the squad technically, he has raised the bar mentally and the accusation of being weak can no longer be levelled at Rangers as they have overcome the odds and finally achieved their Premiership ambitions.

That ruthless streak is engrained in Gerrard's psyche. Peter Crouch, the former Liverpool striker, has told of how new signings at Anfield were written off after one training session by Gerrard and Jamie Carragher. Significant sums had been spent on them, but those that had come through the ranks and that defined the standards expected would deliver a quick and brutal judgement if necessary.

Gerrard would fire a pass at a player and expect them to control it instantly. A glare would greet those that failed and a similarly stinging ball would arrive from the boot of Gerrard soon after. It was only those who impressed first time or that improved to Gerrard's level that would earn his backing.

Such anecdotes provide an insight into the way that Gerrard operates and the demands he places on himself and those around him. The dynamics may have changed from team-mate to manager, but the way in which Gerrard seeks to improve and inspire those he works with remains integral to his work.

"Any relationship is a two-way thing and you have got two people talking in a relationship," Warner said. "In our mind model you have got four people talking because each person has got a human, logical brain and a more chimp, emotional brain.

"If each person in that relationship is both aware of their emotional triggers and each other's emotional triggers, they are more likely to be able to manage that relationship in an open and honest way. If you have got people who are closed to their emotional thinking or closed to the other person's emotional thinking, then you are likely to get a more fraught relationship because there is less understanding of the dynamic that is going on.

"We can only speculate but in any good management team that is operating where the manager is getting the best out of the team, there is likely to be a lot of emotional awareness going on in the form of an understanding of what each individual player needs and each player understanding the needs of the person that they are talking to, which is the manager."

The additions that Gerrard had made over time had put Rangers in their strongest position of his tenure and this squad was the most complete that had been assembled at Ibrox since the one which Walter Smith guided to the title a decade before. What Rangers couldn't do, therefore, was weaken it when they didn't have to.

There was a natural turnover of players as contracts expired, loans weren't extended and fringe players were allowed to leave. Supporters had an emotional connection and affinity with the likes of Ross McCrorie, Andy Halliday, Greg Docherty and Jamie Murphy, all of whom are fans of the club and were desperate to see it succeed. Like the rest of those that moved on, however, they were ultimately not at the level which Gerrard deemed necessary and the exits in all cases were for the best.

That wouldn't have been the situation with either Kent or Morelos. There is a realisation amongst supporters that the model of buy low, develop and sell high is one that Rangers must master if they are to thrive in the face of multi-billion-pound television deals across the continent. But that is easier said than done and it remains difficult to see top players leave, no matter the circumstances.

An offer of around £10million from Leeds United didn't attract sufficient interest from club or player to get beyond an initial approach. But the mark-up on Morelos, signed for just £1million from HJK Helsinki during Pedro Caixinha's hapless reign, could have been significant for Rangers as they decided to hold firm and hold onto their enigmatic Colombian.

"Of course, there is an element of a gamble in a financial sense but that is the benefit of having the investor base that Rangers have and we have seen that," Mark Wilson said. "But, in a way they had to draw a line in the sand regarding the value of the players and the value of how they saw the squad. If the Lille president is to be believed, he offered around £16million for Morelos and some people might have thought that was a fair price but Rangers clearly didn't and they wanted more and closer to £20million for him.

"There is a reasoning when you set your value and you decide where you are because this is not just about one window, this is Rangers setting their stall out in terms of knowing that they have assets and are not selling them on the cheap for years to come. Clearly there is an element of risk about it but it comes back to European football.

"It has not been as valuable this year in terms of the full houses, but once they qualified for the Europa League they were mitigating some of the losses. This season was just so huge, so how could you let players like that leave? It was clearly what they felt was right and if they had gone with just Roofe and Itten they would have been a bit short."

There had been a focus on the forward areas for some time from Gerrard and the signings of Roofe and Itten were the most anticipated of the window. Rangers had been over-reliant on Morelos for too long and while Defoe provided able back-up in terms of his numbers, Gerrard needed options that were contrasting stylistically, and he now had four very different but very effective strikers to choose from.

The support in the 4-3-3 system, which sees Rangers operate with two 10s in the forward areas, has come from Kent and Hagi, while the likes of Joe Aribo and Arfield are adept at playing in the midfield three or up a line. Gerrard had his blueprint and couldn't afford to go back to the drawing board just weeks into the campaign.

"Kent, I think, was always a bit of a non-starter, unless Leeds had gone to crazy money," Mark Wilson said. "Kent himself made it clear to Gerrard early on that he didn't want to go so that was a very different situation from Morelos. The Kent situation had come and gone fairly quickly in the end.

"Clearly Morelos was unsettled for a while, Gerrard talked about his head being turned and there must have been a temptation to cash in. I am sure they would have sold had Lille gone to a certain price but they didn't and Rangers had to draw their line about how they valued their players and how they will do that going forward.

"They needed more forward options, even after keeping Kent and Morelos and clearly Roofe brought that instant quality and experience. He was a guy you knew you could throw in, he had that bit of personality. Itten has shown enough overall and the business there was clever."

The main issues had been smartly addressed by Gerrard. The latest round of signings had undoubtedly improved the squad, but there was more to come from those that were already in situ at Ibrox and that factor has been just as important over the campaign.

The side that beat Willem II, for example, comprised of players from the previous season and it is clear who Gerrard trusts and who he feels he can rely on. Once that bond is broken, it is almost impossible to regain the ground lost.

That ability to learn on the job has been essential for Gerrard and he is unquestionably a more adept and well-rounded manager of players and games now than he was in those initial months of discovery at Ibrox. As he has grown, his team has evolved and improved exponentially with him and he is the father-like figure that has nurtured his side to the title.

"When Covid hit, Rangers, as a club, reacted better than a lot of others did and they were very stringent on how they were going to deal with it," Edgar said. "Maybe coming through that, it might be a cliché but they say that the night is darkest before the dawn, and it felt like that.

"That March was bad, it was utterly horrendous, but Rangers came out of it. They made a few signings, but there wasn't a head-turning one where you thought 'he is the difference' and it is guys that have been there – the likes of Goldson, Tavernier, Kamara, Davis – that have done it for us. I think going through that fire maybe strengthened them and going through that total collapse in form and morale allowed them all to learn something from it.

"The results just don't lie and it is not just the results, it is the way they have done it. We don't concede goals, we dominate games, there is at least one highlight reel goal every match it seems. They couldn't have been far off in March, it was just that we were just too close to see it."

The way in which Rangers signed players and retained players during that elongated summer window was indicative. There was clearly a conviction that this could be their season, but also a sense that it would be a case of ripping it up and starting again, most likely with a new manager, had these players and Gerrard failed for a third time.

As it transpired, their stock individually and collectively has never been higher. The medal was the most important thing this season, but money will always talk eventually and the sales will be self-fulfilling as cash is reinvested into the squad and the requirement for external finance is minimised.

"They have got numerous assets now that they can turn significant profits on," Mark Wilson, who has been with the Scottish *Daily Mail* since 2007 and previously worked for *The Herald*, said. "Borna Barisic was around £1.5million and there is a big profit to be made on him, even as one of the older guys in that sense.

"Kamara is the extraordinary case. It is slightly misleading to talk about him as a £50,000 signing because they had already agreed to sign him on a pre-contract and that was just to expedite it, but there is real value to be generated by him. He is a guy whose technical ability would make him suited to just about any league in Europe and he is a mainstay for Finland so there is huge profit locked into him, as there is with Morelos.

"In terms of Kent, they will not be faced with a losing money situation on him and Aribo is another one they will make money on. He has had two years of real development and there is potential and real value in him as well.

"The work there has been night and day compared to what preceded it in terms of building a squad that is not only effective on the pitch but that has the capacity for sales and reinvestment in the future."

The three years post regime change had seen the foundations relaid at Ibrox. Gerrard had two seasons of building and improving. Now it was time to complete the job, and 'The Journey'.

Ibrox was soulless without the supporters but the team had an identity and a personality which those watch-at-home fans could connect with. Every player that wears the jersey will always get backed and encouraged, but this group was more likeable, more relatable than many others that had been thrown together during the barren years and even just weeks into the season there was a feeling that it could be a special one for Rangers.

The ethos and environment were as important as those within it at Ibrox, as Warner can attest to. His clients come from the world of business and politics as well as football, motorsport and golf, while his work with Olympians and Paralympians allows individuals to gain insight into their minds and channel their behaviours in their pursuit of success.

"When you make what makes the team relevant in the minds of people, when you get what makes people feel like they belong clear and when you get what makes the team effective and unique clear, and make clear the traditions of the team, where it has come from, where it is now and where it's going, these are significant factors," Warner said. "When these factors become clear in the minds of everyone at the club, the research suggests that the individual members tend to perform better because effectively they are buying into what they are part of and therefore prepared to go the extra mile.

"It might not sound much, but in a game where it is someone making a run to get back and tackle or making a run to get into the box, that is the difference you can get from getting the social identity of the team right. If Rangers have worked hard on that and if Steven Gerrard has been the catalyst for that, then that may translate itself to an increased performance.

"If those messages around tradition, belonging, relevance, etc, are reinforced in a supportive way, then you can see how that could help individual players to commit more to what they are doing. It is all emotion based, really, and they feel like they want to work harder for the team and it creates a bigger sense of commitment."

Those feelings of unity and that desire to strive for a common goal are imperative in any successful side. Rangers looked like a title-winning team technically and tactically, but they had the feel of one as well and there was a camaraderie and resilience about them, traits which had been nurtured since the first day that Gerrard walked in the door.

It takes time to create the environment and the one in which Rangers operate today is elite in every way. Each manager will have their own identikit of how they wish to work and Gerrard would benefit from having the time to put his stamp on Auchenhowie and Ibrox.

He has referenced the work of those that have gone before them and Caixinha and Mark Warburton would put their own processes in place. During his stints as caretaker, Graeme Murty would do likewise. With respect to each effort, they are not at the level of Gerrard.

The task that faced Stuart McCall was arguably the most ominous of all and the Rangers that he inherited and the one that Gerrard has built are starkly contrasting. The 55th league flag was won on the weekend that marked the sixth anniversary of regime change and the first days of that new era continue to resonate strongly as staff and supporters analyse just how far Rangers have come.

McCall had been part of the legendary nine-in-a-row side of the '90s. It was, as Richard Gough put it, the team that drank together and won together and McCall's affable and infectious personality saw him fit in perfectly with a team full of larger-than-life characters.

When he returned to Ibrox in 2015, he was shocked and saddened by what he found as a squad bereft of confidence and a support deprived of hope stumbled from week to week. In many ways, his first task was similar to the one which Gerrard had to undertake, albeit in very different circumstances.

"Big Jim Stewart, who I know well, was on the staff," McCall said of his appointment as manager alongside long-time assistant Kenny Black as Kenny McDowall left a position he had held reluctantly since Ally McCoist's departure four months earlier. "As was Gordon Durie, Ian Durrant had been with the young ones, and I spoke to them, and Jimmy Bell, and got an idea of what the club was like.

"Of all my time in the game, it was the lowest atmosphere I have ever felt at a football club. In my 35-odd years, it was the lowest I had seen. The one good thing was the new board and I would never have gone in with the old board. It was because it was a new board and a new start for the club, but it was difficult for the supporters and the players and there was no atmosphere.

"The results had been poor, Coisty had left and that soured it a lot because he was popular with the players and then Kenny wanted to get out. The atmosphere was the lowest I had known at the club, all round the place, and Kenny and I said that our biggest job was to try and change the environment, try and get smiles on faces and lift the club."

It might not have felt like it at the time, but those first days and weeks under McCall saw Rangers draw a line in the sand. Mistakes were made along the way, but with the new board in situ there was a sense of normality around Ibrox. It has taken longer than expected and longer than it should have done but the transformation has been completed and Rangers today are a very different club at all levels.

The environment in which Rangers live, train and play does not just impact on those within the bubble, both in a Covid sense and more generally. The early months of the campaign saw changes in the way in which the club communicated and operated and that process was expedited as time elapsed. Press access was always subject to change given the Covid restrictions but what started as a departure from traditional media conferences ended up in a move away from established media outlets altogether.

Social distancing regulations limited access to the Ibrox gantry to rights holders only, with written and broadcast journalists relocated to the West Enclosure. It wasn't until the Europa League fixture with Lech Poznan in October that a more suitable and practical working area was established in a section behind the Directors' Box. Later in the campaign, access to the media room was reserved for selected journalists on each match day.

Questions at the pre-match press conferences held via Zoom were largely limited to one per person, and the same system was in operation after the game. The time spent with Gerrard was reduced, while access to players became almost non-existent for written media as Rangers sought to keep a firmer grip on who said what and to whom.

It was evident early on that this could be a wonderful story in the making but it became increasingly difficult to tell it to the world and relations between the club and some sections of the press would become strained as bans from media conferences and matches were commonplace. There was a definite shift in stance from Rangers but in a campaign of such success, their rapport with the press was of little concern to the majority of the support, and seemingly of little concern to those in positions of power and influence at Ibrox.

There is no reason why 'fan media' and the newspapers and broadcasters cannot co-exist and work alongside each other, but each party will have their own views on where that balance lay throughout the season. The disdainful, vitriolic even, way in which the press was spoken about by supporters online at times was as sad as it was worrying and those who sought to work professionally with the club found opportunities to do so frustratingly limited as the campaign unfolded.

Daily newspapers were denied accreditation for some matches, while press conference access became progressively limited. Towards the end of the campaign, it was scaled back even further as daily and Sunday desks were provided with RangersTV audio rather than given their expected opportunity to ask questions of Gerrard and his players.

The focus was on 'fan media' and club media as Rangers sought to monetise their content to an even greater extent. Given that there was no chance of censure from the Scottish FA or the SPFL, Rangers could control the output and seek to control the narrative, but if there is any club and any support that should be wary of a culture where questions and debate are stifled, it is surely Rangers. That is not to say that history will repeat itself, merely that it should serve as a warning and a reminder.

Journalists at local and national titles were well aware of the changing landscape but there was an opportunity to work with rather than work against that was missed as podcasts, blogs and social media channels grew in popularity and number. Edgar was granted press access alongside Mark Dingwall of the FollowFollow.com forum and fanzine as they became another conduit for the supporters to keep up-to-date at Ibrox.

"One, it is a privilege and I never take it for granted and it is not something that I get blasé about at all," Edgar, who founded the Heart and Hand podcast in 2010, said. "I am very grateful for it and every time I go in I make sure I enjoy it because it might be the last. If it is, I won't be huffy about it. I will be thankful that it happened rather than sad that it was over.

"One thing is that you can't talk to people about it because it is not fair. They don't want to hear about it right now, they don't want to hear your experiences of getting up and going to the game. For me personally, in terms of my mental health and everything, having this has been an absolute lifesaver and being able to get up to go to the game has given me a sense of normality in very unnormal times.

"It has been bizarre, surreal at times. I think where it really hit me was the game against Galatasaray. It was such a massive match, two famous names in European football, a Rangers team that were flying and big names like Falcao on the park. The referee blew the whistle and it was silent and you are thinking 'there should be 50,000 people in here going nuts, there should be Turkish fans in the corner letting off fireworks' and it was one of the strangest things I have ever experienced."

That win over Galatasaray would begin a month that would be defining for Rangers. The first weeks of the season had given fans reasons to be optimistic, but the ones that would follow allowed them to really dare to dream as Gerrard's side improved and impressed.

This season was the season for Rangers. If their time was going to come, then it had to be now and the business in the transfer market, their actions on the field and their words off it all fed into that feeling. Rangers were Ready.

FIVE

WINNING. It is the only ambition for Rangers, the trait that is in the history of the club and the DNA of its supporters. It is the word that Walter Smith most associates with Rangers but a feat that hadn't been achieved for too long. Until now, that is.

There have been moments over the last decade where Rangers have felt that they were on the cusp of achieving their ambitions. On the contrary, there have been many more where it seemed like they were as far away as ever as they peered across the Old Firm divide and wondered how, when and even if it could be closed.

Over 90 minutes at Parkhead in October, those fears were allayed. It was too early to say that Rangers were on the brink of history, but few matches during Steven Gerrard's tenure had given supporters as much optimism for the future. Indeed, few would have demoralised Celtic quite like this one and the changing of the guard would begin on that afternoon.

When Rangers had ended their long wait for a victory over Celtic in the December of Gerrard's first campaign, the emotions were raw. The strike from Ryan Jack didn't just earn three points, it would settle scores and induce feelings – everything from relief to euphoria – that supporters hadn't experienced against their age-old rivals for too long.

Gerrard and his players would get caught up in the moment and it was understandable why they did so. The same can be said of their win at Parkhead in his second season as Ryan Kent and Nikola Katic scored in a 2-1 victory that was Rangers' first there since 2010.

Gerrard would roar into the camera at the whistle and the scenes as he and his players celebrated with the band of supporters tucked away in the corner told their own story. It was a day to savour but one, like the win at Ibrox a year previously, that would ultimately prove futile in terms of the Premiership title race.

Those moments were unique for their own reasons and they felt like marker posts being reached on the road to recovery. When Gerrard's side won 2-0 in October, the whole occasion and significance was very different, and not just because this was the first Old Firm game to be staged behind closed doors as this famous fixture lost its most unique selling point. It was still more than a game, but it felt more akin to any other as the most important ingredient of the unique concoction that makes this derby was removed from the recipe.

That factor surely came into play at the final whistle. Rangers only had themselves to celebrate with, but Gerrard's look was of determination rather than joy this time around. He had won the battle that day, but he knew he needed to win the war in the Premiership.

Victory was marked with fist pumps and pats on the back. In his post-match interviews, he spoke of Rangers remaining humble and how he would refuse to allow them to get carried away. The challenge was for Rangers to go the distance and there was a different vibe around Gerrard's side, even this early in the campaign, which suggested that they could do just that.

Rangers had to prove that they were champions rather than challengers this time and that related to Gerrard as much as his players. Gerrard would easily come out on top in a game of 'show us your medals' but he needed a success as a manager to add to his past glories from his playing days with Liverpool and he too had a point to prove in the title race.

The character of a player is as important as the quality of one, especially at a club like Rangers. The same can be said of the manager and that is a situation that legendary Ibrox boss Smith can attest to. When it comes to understanding the range and scale of pressures one is under and the traits required to succeed, there is nobody more aware than the man who delivered nine-in-a-row and then three Scottish Premier League titles on his return to Ibrox, the last of which was the one that Gerrard was trying to follow this season.

"It takes a strength of mentality to manage any football club and the higher the level you go to the harder it is," Smith said during an extensive interview with friend Jim Traynor, the respected former journalist, broadcaster and head of communications at Rangers, on the Essential Scottish Football Podcast. "I know a lot of friends of mine have managed clubs in the lower divisions and they always look and say 'I wish I could manage Rangers'.

"It is a difficult task, but it is a great job, a rewarding job when you are doing well. When you have the difficulties and are not achieving what a lot of people think you should be achieving, even if you are winning titles year after year, you take those difficulties. They always drive you on.

"I always like winning. At Rangers, I was once asked for one word to describe Rangers, and they are winners. That is what the club have been, they have been winners. Like everybody else, you can't win all the time, but overall they have been winners and they are back to that now and they have won again. That is a significant step forward for the club."

The task of managing an institution like Rangers is not one that can be taken on alone and the burden must be shared with those you trust. Smith fulfilled that role as assistant to Graeme Souness during his Revolution in the '80s before he assumed the position and went on to finish what had been started as a ninth successive league title was won in 1997.

On his return to Ibrox ten years later, Smith was joined by Ally McCoist, Kenny McDowall and Ian Durrant in the dugout. European glory may have ultimately evaded them in 2008, but it was a period of cherished domestic glories that would prove to be the final ones that supporters could savour before the collapse that saw Rangers embark on a fight for survival rather than silverware.

The appointment of Gerrard was a moment where Rangers came out swinging, where they had the look of heavyweight contenders once again. The Liverpool legend was the figurehead, but this was never going to be a one-man job and, like Smith, Gerrard would surround himself with sound football minds. More importantly, they were good men.

Gerrard would speak of the importance of his backroom staff on the day that he was unveiled in May 2018 and he has regularly thanked them and praised them for their efforts in the years since. The deal for Gerrard was the most important one that Rangers secured, but none of the progress made in the first two seasons or the triumphs enjoyed in the third would have been possible without those that he calls friends as well as colleagues.

"I'm a human being so I'm going to make mistakes going forward," Gerrard said when he was appointed as manager. "I've made plenty in my playing career and I've made many this season as a coach. But I see mistakes as opportunities to grow and learn from. I believe in the staff I'm going to be bringing to share this journey with me.

"I'm not perfect but I will put people around me to support me, to complement where I need a bit of help and guidance. As a team of people, we will park the egos up and front it together. We believe we are the best people to take this opportunity forward."

That was a key consideration for Mark Allen. His job was to appoint a manager, but the former director of football knew Gerrard had to be part of a team and the first names – those of Gary McAllister and Michael Beale – were obvious ones to come on board.

McAllister had shone in the twilight of his career alongside Gerrard in the Liverpool midfield. It was a partnership that would yield five medals in England and Europe and the friendship formed then would lead McAllister to Ibrox many years later.

He would be joined by Beale. His route to Rangers has been unconventional but fascinating. His playing career was over before it started after he failed to make the grade at Charlton, where Jermain Defoe, Scott Parker and Paul Konchesky were his contemporaries. But Beale has long been top of the class when it came to coaching and his methods on the training field and philosophy in how football should be played have marked him out as one of the brightest minds in the game. He is an obsessive about football, a coach who takes as much satisfaction out of improving a veteran as a protégé.

A decade at Chelsea saw Beale work under the likes of Jose Mourinho, Carlo Ancelotti and Guus Hiddink and he can take credit for nurturing the talents of Mason Mount, Callum Hudson-Odoi and Tammy Abraham. A move to Liverpool saw him help Trent Alexander-Arnold and Harry Wilson along the road to stardom and his own stock was rising as quickly as those under his tutelage.

Beale had started out as a coach charging kids a couple of quid to play a version of futsal in his local church hall and he would find himself immersed in a new world as he travelled from South London to South America. An eight-month spell at Sao Paulo alongside Rogerio Ceni – football's highest-scoring goalkeeper with more than 130 goals to his credit – followed before he returned to Anfield. The rest, as they say, is history and Gerrard would make the call to Beale as the then Under-18s boss at Liverpool accepted the position of Rangers manager.

"Gary McAllister has a wealth of experience having played the game on both sides of the border," Allen said. "He was an international with a proven pedigree, he had a real knowledge of Scottish football and knew what it was all about and he was someone that could help Steven settle in Scotland and become accustomed to the Scottish football environment. Gary was perfect for that role.

"Michael was perfect in terms of the technical part of the session and he can aid Steven in so many ways when it comes to preparing the team for, for example, coming up against a low block and if the team would have to overload in certain areas.

"He had the technical know-how to design the sessions and plan the sessions that Steven would want for a certain day. That would allow Steven to take a backseat, in that regard, and analyse what was going on to really decide what he was looking for and how he wanted the session to shape up. Michael is capable of designing that session and taking that session and he has got a terrific way of working with the players and other coaches."

Gerrard had the former team-mate in McAllister and a coach in Beale whose reputation went before him. When it comes to Tom Culshaw, the relationship went even further back and two childhood mates are now champions with Rangers.

Culshaw's grandparents lived on the same street as the Gerrard family home in Huyton and a friendship was formed, partly through their love of football, at Cardinal Heenan High School. Gerrard and Culshaw shared the same dream, but only one would get to live it with Liverpool.

Culshaw was also a contemporary of Jamie Carragher and Michael Owen but he would fail to make the grade with the Reds.

Disillusioned with the game, he worked for a friend's tarmacking firm before embarking on a coaching career – which included a spell in Spain – that would lead him back to Liverpool.

Gerrard would promote his old friend to the Under-18s and there was no doubt that a move to Ibrox would follow. His title of Technical Coach sounds wide-ranging but his remit is simply to improve players and that has been achieved, most notably this season in terms of Rangers' defensive record, but his work on set-pieces at both ends of the park has also been integral to the successes.

One part of the Gerrard jigsaw was already in place at Auchenhowie and he would retain the services of goalkeeping coach Colin Stewart. The final one that he brought with him from Liverpool was Jordan Milsom. Gerrard had identified Rangers' deficiencies in terms of pace and power even before he was approached to become manager and the work of Milsom has allowed Rangers to be fitter and stronger than the opposition as they have advanced physically as well as mentally, technically and tactically over the last three years.

"We then looked at set-pieces and one-to-one coaching for those players who wanted to work on technique or free-kicks, for example, and we needed a specialist in that regard," Allen said. "And that is why Tom Culshaw was brought in. So there was a logic and a reasoning to the team that came in with Steven and he could then really excel in the management of the whole thing, which is the management and organisation of the team.

"A very important factor, if we wanted to play the kind of game that we wanted to play at Rangers – in terms of being attractive, exciting, playing out from the back and through the thirds with lots of possession – then we needed the athletic performance to be at a certain level. We had to have the right levels of training and match that style of football to the training sessions so that is why Jordan Milsom was brought in."

There was an obvious lure of the Gerrard name for the Rangers board and the Rangers fans ahead of his arrival but the appointment would have been doomed to failure had the appropriate blend of skills and experiences not joined him at Ibrox. That backroom team have been with Gerrard every step of the way and, quite simply, he and Rangers would not be where they are today if it were not for their efforts alongside the man who carries the ultimate responsibility but who shares the workload and the praise equally.

When Gerrard was named as the William Hill Scottish Football Writers' Association Manager of the Year later in the campaign, he was quick to thank and praise the work of those around him. There was a clear pride in the pictures of him with his prize, but one of the entire coaching staff together spoke volumes. From day one to trophy day, it has been a team effort.

"I'm delighted to receive the award," Gerrard said. "I receive it collectively with my staff. I think that goes without saying because we are very much a team here.

"I think we have achieved the success we have this season as a team of staff and I thank all of you guys in the press for voting for me and I certainly cherish the award."

Rangers were not the first club to come calling and to offer Gerrard a route into management and he had rejected a position at MK Dons two years previously before returning to Liverpool and assuming an Academy coaching role. The timing wasn't right for Gerrard and he would decline the offer after holding talks with chairman Pete Winkelman.

The conversation with Dave King was very different, though. By that stage, Gerrard had learned on the job, albeit at youth level, and he admitted that the opportunity with Rangers just felt different and felt right.

His stature in the game certainly helped him get the job but he knew it would count for nothing once he was in it. He is wiser for the mistakes that he has made over the three years and the input from those that he trusts both personally and professionally has been central to his development and ultimately to his success.

"All the pieces fit together and they have all got their certain strengths that complement each other," Jordan Campbell, a Scottish football correspondent for The Athletic that has written extensively about Rangers during Gerrard's reign, said. "I think that was important for Gerrard when he was thinking about taking the job because it was a big decision for him obviously and he had to make sure that going into his first position he surrounded himself with the right people.

"He is also quite modest and self-aware and he doesn't think he is the best at everything in the world. He knows he has the experience of being at the top level and what it is like to be a winner and he has that aura about him where he will naturally command a dressing room. But he doesn't have 20 years' experience coaching on the park, like Michael Beale has got from Liverpool, Chelsea and Sao Paulo. Gerrard heard great things about him at Melwood when he was there as a coach.

"I always remember when Gerrard came in and he said 'I know how I want it to look' and he knows what he wants his team to look like.

"If you look at them all separately, you can clearly see how they fit together and Gerrard is not one of these ex-players who has been at the top of the game and thinks he can just walk straight into management and succeed. He is aware that he will need to learn and improve and he knows he couldn't fail. To succeed, he had to have those kind of characters beside him."

It has taken until the third season for Gerrard to achieve what he was tasked with and deliver the Premiership title but boxes have been ticked along the way. Each one – whether it was qualifying for the Europa League or winning an Old Firm fixture – has been momentous for Rangers and the respective accomplishments felt like steps forward as the barren times of the so-called 'Banter Years' faded in the memory of a support that could strive for the future rather than be restrained by the past.

Overcoming Galatasaray to reach the Europa League for a third successive season was a significant moment for Rangers. Given how notable their results on the continent had been in the first two terms under Gerrard, there was a sense of expectation that Rangers would complete the hat-trick but the feat should not be taken for granted.

It was a result that reinforced the assertion that this side had something about it that Gerrard's previous two didn't. A renewed and more defined drive had been evident in the opening weeks of the campaign and that 2-1 victory over the Turkish giants – earned thanks to goals from Scott Arfield and James Tavernier – ensured momentum continued to build.

The win at Parkhead a fortnight later was even more significant in that regard. Ross County had been beaten in between to ensure Rangers would arrive at Parkhead top of the table. By the time they left, they had opened up a four-point advantage and, despite Celtic's game in hand, laid down a real marker of their intentions in the title race.

One of the central elements in the way in which Rangers play is the idea of control and that applies to their phases with the ball and without it. Old Firm games have been won by wider margins, but few had been this comfortable and emphatic in terms of Rangers enforcing their style and their blueprint on the fixture.

Two goals from Connor Goldson were the difference on the day yet the victory could, and should, have been more resounding as Celtic failed to register a single shot on goal. It was a performance that felt like the culmination of all the hours on the training ground and in the analysis suites, the perfect example of Rangers' evolution and identikit as a team.

"It is massive," Goldson said as Rangers announced themselves as credible title challengers. "Old Firms are always massive games and we knew we had to start well and score first and defend well at times because we know they are a good team. I thought we did everything right today. We controlled the game well, defended well, defended our box well and limited their chances and got two goals.

"We have worked on it for two years now, we have played against some top teams with the same shape. The new lads have bought into it and it has always seemed to work for us in big games. We know what we are doing, we have been doing it for a long time and in training for a long time and I think it worked. We limited them to not many chances."

That defensive structure that Goldson has been such an integral part of was the foundation upon which Rangers would go on to build their Premiership bid. Gerrard had produced extraordinary individual moments as a player, but his team is about the collective and their style is defined by the way in which they operate as a unit rather than relying on certain individuals to win matches.

The 4-3-2-1 or 4-3-3 formation has been honed over time. It provides Rangers with a level of rigidity when required, but the system and the options Gerrard has in his squad allow him to be flexible depending on the opposition or the occasion and that has been beneficial throughout his tenure as Rangers have been able to overcome the likes of Galatasaray, Braga and Porto whilst dominating domestic encounters.

Old Firm matches are characterised by their frantic nature, by the incidents that make heroes or villains in a split-second. That win was different, though, and it was a performance and a result that had been a long time in the making for Gerrard's Rangers.

"That style you see now is the philosophy that we spoke about when we discussed Steven taking the job," Allen said. "First and foremost you have to understand the league that you are playing in, so the first task was to sit and analyse Scottish football in terms of the tactical, technical, physical and mental requirements, if you like. What is this league all about?

"Then you decide how to augment it. We knew we could play in that way, but we needed an athletic and robust kind of player to play like that in Scotland and that leads into the profiling that we put together for each position.

"So we think about what we were looking for from players when we had the ball, when we didn't have the ball, when we were in transition and then looking at the physicality needed for each position. That was all part of the recruitment strategy."

There can be a tendency in the game these days to over-think and over-analyse and the parlance around football has changed. The fundamentals remain the same, though. As Bill Shankly put it: 'Football is a simple game based on the giving and taking of passes, of controlling the ball and of making yourself available to receive a pass. It is terribly simple.'

There is a clear method in the way that Rangers operate as the blueprint devised by Gerrard and his staff has been developed and refined. Gerrard is a man and a manager who values old-school ethics in terms of camaraderie, commitment and dedication, but his side play a modern style that has shades of Jurgen Klopp's Liverpool as emphasis is placed on the full-backs to provide width and an attacking outlet and the front three interchange regularly to ensure Rangers carry as much threat as possible.

The approach is defined as 'own the ball, own the pitch'. In possession, it is about Rangers enforcing their style on the game, while they seek to dictate the flow to the opponent when they don't have the ball.

It has become second nature to Gerrard's side over time. The instructions are clear and concise and Rangers look to control matches by protecting the middle of the park as the two No. 10s and striker position themselves narrow to limit passing options, forcing teams to go wide. In that scenario, the central three shift across simultaneously to either the left or the right and that allows the more attacking players to stay high in their positions.

If you know where you are going to win the ball back, then you know how you will be able to attack from that situation. Energy is not expelled tracking full-backs into your own half and the two playmakers find themselves in areas from which attacks can be launched as the front three interchange positions and roles with regularity. That fluidity is key to the approach and Rangers are, even from a neutral's perspective, an entertaining and exciting watch when at their best.

The process by which this setup is worked on is labelled 'the human tactics board' and it is refined towards the end of the preparation period for each match. It is at that stage where the 'pressing victim' – essentially the opposition player that will be targeted when he is in possession – is identified and trigger words are used to avoid the requirement for lengthy instructions to be passed onto the field of play.

"The way they work on that in training is to use mannequins and they are called 'walk through drills' where they set up in their shape and they have the opposition set up how their analysts have identified that they will line up," Campbell said. "They walk through it, so someone will have the ball and pass it left and the whole shape moves left and it is about working on distances and making sure they are moving at the same speed as the ball.

"When it comes to pressing victims, they will have ten blue mannequins and one red mannequin and that is who they are going to target, so it is drilled into them that when he has the ball that is when Rangers press.

"Rangers are coached to within an inch of their life under this management and it is very structured even when they are on the ball as well. You can see that in the way that they play, everyone knows their role inside out and it is almost second nature.

"They were almost on auto-pilot against Celtic and because that game was so slow, it didn't feel like an Old Firm game, you could watch the organisation of the team. There were no gaps anywhere and that was a big thing that stood out to me."

It is impossible to remove the emotion and sense of occasion from an Old Firm fixture but that day at Parkhead provided a unique opportunity to watch both sides from a different perspective. It was evident that Rangers were no longer at a disadvantage in terms of the ability of their side and it was they who had the platform to go and play courtesy of the knowledge imparted in them and the belief formed by earning results in Old Firm fixtures and European encounters over the previous two seasons.

As Celtic relied on ad hoc interventions that would never arrive, Rangers played in patterns and with precision and they didn't need the crowd to inspire them to produce single moments of magic. Rangers, both on that day and overall this season, looked better coached and managed than Celtic and victory in that tactical battle was indicative of how the campaign would unfold.

"It was almost like Subbuteo," Campbell said. "It was what Rangers had gone through on the training ground transplanted onto the pitch. Every moment was as you had planned it and it was unique to watch.

"I don't know if that's because it was behind closed doors and people watched more intensely. That game is usually blood and thunder and the tactical side of it is given a secondary thought but I think people were shocked that Celtic barely laid a glove on Rangers and Rangers barely got out of second gear.

"Dominant might not be the right word but it was controlled and even when they didn't have the ball they were just forcing Celtic into areas where they were comfortable.

"Goldson said afterwards it was two-and-a-half years in the making. The rare thing with Gerrard is that in modern football you don't really get three seasons to build on the one idea. He is reluctant to use the word 'philosophy' but to all intents and purposes it is a philosophy and it is a base for them to work from. In the domestic game you maybe don't usually see it to the same degree as you did that day, but you do see it in Europe."

It is one thing having the masterplan, but it is quite another putting it into action. It was becoming evident that Gerrard had slotted the two pieces together and that this season was going to be the season for Rangers. Quite simply, it had to be.

Previous wins over Celtic had been greeted with emotional celebrations but counted for little apart from brief bragging rights. That wasn't the case this time, though, and a win over Livingston, with Joe Aribo and Jermain Defoe the scorers, a week later ensured Rangers capitalised on their Old Firm victory.

During his two spells as manager, Smith had stressed the importance of the games before and after the Celtic fixtures. Defeat ahead of the derby would see pressure to win it mount, while a loss after it would either compound the misery or see ground gained immediately given back.

That was the difference this time around for Rangers and Gerrard's side were developing the mark of champions that had been missing in previous seasons. The plaudits would befall Gerrard at regular occurrences, but he sought to share the praise and downplay comparisons with those in whose illustrious footsteps he was aiming to follow at Ibrox.

"Walter is someone I have the utmost respect for," Gerrard said as he stood on the brink of matching Smith's title-winning achievement. "He is an iconic figure at this club, a successful manager. It is an unofficial mentorship, if you like – I don't even think Walter knows he is doing it.

"I've had the pleasure of his company around lockdown, it's been more difficult during lockdown. But he is someone I have spoken to a lot on the phone. He has a real connection with the League Managers' Association and has been a big help to me.

"I bounce a lot of stuff off him and he always has plenty of time for me and my coaches. So I don't even think he knows he is being a mentor but he has been fantastic for me."

Any talk that mentioned him and Smith in the same breath was quickly dismissed and the two would speak regularly as the legendary manager became a source of counsel to Gerrard. Those conversations remained private, but they were invaluable to the man who was seeking to become the first boss since Smith to deliver the title to long-suffering supporters.

There was a natural link to be made between Gerrard and Graeme Souness given their respective associations with and affection for Liverpool. Souness would join Smith at Ibrox for the Galatasaray game and the sight of two heroes and the man who was aiming to become one was inspiring for those supporters that watched on RangersTV.

"Steven has had to work a wee bit harder to get a group of players together and work with that group of players," Smith said of the comparisons that were made between Gerrard and Souness, whom he himself replaced as manager when Liverpool came calling in the search for Kenny Dalglish's successor towards the end of the 1991/92 season. "There have been differences but essentially you are looking at two players who achieved iconic status at the same club and then turn themselves to management. You have got to say that Steven has handled it extremely well.

"He handles the media, which in Scotland isn't the easiest place in the world to work. There is a level of intensity when you are at Rangers and Celtic with the media that doesn't make it easy and I think Steven has handled that extremely well.

"Like everything else, he will have his disappointments but he has built up and built up steadily and nearly every player that has been brought in has improved his standard of play, even at Rangers. Since they have come to Rangers, every one of them has improved, they have fitted into the team and I think they have had some quite remarkable results along the way."

That evolution individually and collectively was now set to pay dividends for Rangers. There was no chance of anyone within the club getting ahead of themselves, but the relentless manner in which Gerrard's side operated contrasted to Celtic and their campaign would go from bad to worse and end in disaster.

Everything was in place at Ibrox and Rangers had the manager, the staff and the squad to go on and become champions. As they sought to make history, it was events of yesteryear that kept supporters in check as reminders of the two failures under Gerrard continued to sit at the back of minds.

There would surely have been times when that was the case for the players as well but Rangers appeared unburdened by what had gone before. It wasn't a case of third time lucky, but more of learning from their mistakes and righting the wrongs.

"As you build up, it is not always just about football," Smith said during a fascinating hour-long conversation with Traynor. "To get themselves [in a position] last year, they had a better start to the season than the season before, so there was improvement right up until the break came. After that, they came back and didn't get as good results after that and it possibly cost them at least to be challenging for the championship towards the end of the season.

"Whatever reasons it is, it is very difficult to say from the outside, but for most of the guys it was possibly the first time they had been in a club that was chasing a championship. To gain that consistency over a season takes a lot of mental toughness in every player and it is something that if you play for Rangers and Celtic you have to develop. You have to develop a mental toughness to come and play.

"It is not easy, it is not easy for any player to come in and play in Scottish football. Steven and his staff will sit down and say 'what can we do?' and obviously from the outside we don't know if they have done anything different this season, we can only again judge by results.

"Judging by the results, whatever they have done, the performances of the players have been better. They have reached a good level just now, and that means that they can actually play down a level and maybe not play at their best but still have the mentality to go and win games. They look as though, to me, they have developed that this season."

Whenever former players or current pundits assess the job that Gerrard has done with Rangers, the way in which he conducts himself in public invariably arises. It is one thing having the tactical nous to be a successful manager, but the best ones speak just as impressively in public as they do on the training pitch or behind the closed doors of the changing room.

No manager has been as adept at using the media to his advantage as Sir Alex Ferguson. Gerrard and Sir Alex had been fierce rivals during their respective careers with Liverpool and Manchester United but a mutual friend, journalist and author Donald McRae, would unite them in later life. Gerrard joked he 'wouldn't dare' send the first message after numbers were exchanged but the greatest manager in the history of the game became another sounding board for a man whose stock was rising all the time.

"It's very high praise and I'm extremely flattered," Gerrard said after Ferguson lauded his 'magnificent' job and 'fantastic' press conferences during an interview with *The Guardian*. "He's an iconic figure in the game. Through no fault of our own we became big, big rivals at Liverpool and Manchester United, the two biggest clubs in British football. We were massive rivals for many years and he's someone that even though he was a rival I looked up to him immensely because he is such an iconic figure in the game and what he achieved in the game is up there with the very best who have ever lived.

"So I'm really flattered and humbled by his words and I'll let you into a little secret, I've had a couple of conversations with him. Since I've retired, we've parked our rivalry up and he gave me time on the phone to bounce a few things off him, a few questions to do with the management up here at Rangers.

"He was fantastic in those conversations and at some point moving forward I'd love the chance to sit down with him and have a coffee. He's agreed to that and that's fantastic from his point of view because he doesn't have to give his time, especially being a rival. But I think that goes to show what type of man he is – he's not just the iconic manager we all know."

It was not just in the Premiership where the fortunes of Rangers and Celtic would differ and diverge in the aftermath of the Old Firm fixture and their respective campaigns in the Europa League would play a part in emphasising the gulf between the sides this term. As Rangers continued to forge their reputation on the continent, Celtic's standing slumped.

On the night Neil Lennon's side lost at home to AC Milan, Rangers were victorious away to Standard Liege. As Celtic earned one of only four points they would accumulate with a draw in Lille, Gerrard's side beat Lech Poznan thanks to an Alfredo Morelos header.

That goal put Rangers on course for progression and would ultimately help them win Group D. It was one of the most important of the European campaign, yet it was dwarfed in terms of style and impact by the one which Kemar Roofe scored in Belgium seven days previously.

It was described by Gerrard as a 'moment of genius' and 'probably the best goal' that he had seen live. The praise couldn't have been higher, but the strike couldn't have been better.

A Tavernier penalty had already all-but won the game for Rangers. In the closing seconds, Roofe made sure in the most remarkable fashion with a goal that would go viral online and attract attention around the world.

Everything – from a sodden pitch to the distance from target – was against Roofe but his vision and ability trumped all. The ball was won just yards outside his own box before one challenge was held off, another evaded and a third skipped by as Roofe moved into what only he believed was shooting range just yards from the halfway line.

Nobody would call for him to have a go. The voice in his head said otherwise, though, and keeper Arnaud Bodart could only watch on helplessly as a wondrous effort dipped over his head and into the back of the net.

It was a moment that supporters had to admire and applaud no matter their affiliation. For nine-in-a-row legend Mark Hateley, it was one that was appreciated even more given the audacity and excellence from a player who had already shown why Gerrard was so eager to bring him to Ibrox in the summer.

"Before he even struck the ball, I was so impressed with the seconds leading up to the execution of the strike," Hateley said. "The conditions were ridiculous and he gets by two or three players, moves the ball three or four times and he stays on his feet on what is an unbelievably difficult pitch.

"You are looking at a player that has got the vision, that has got the balance and the strength and that has got both feet working. Then he has the vision to look at the goalkeeper and know what to do next. I have watched it countless times and he looks at the goalkeeper several seconds before he shoots. He knows, he has looked and, like all great players, he has got the picture in his head of where he is, where he is going, how he is going to get there and what the final outcome is going to be.

"That is a snapshot but that is what great players do and that is what I took from that goal. It is strength, balance, vision and technique. That is a great player and if you keep him playing game on game, he will only get better."

The strike from Roofe effectively ended the goal of the season competition there and then but the award for best player would become a far more difficult decision to make as several of Gerrard's main men moved through the gears.

October would end with Rangers once again making strides forward on the pitch. Off it, there was a further sign of the progress that had been made in a business sense as the Ibrox board welcomed a new money man to the table.

For three decades, Rangers had only provided an emotional investment for Stuart Gibson. He had left Paisley in 1987 to move to Australia and chase a dream but the days of visiting his grandmother in the shadow of Ibrox or attending games with his father were never far from his mind as he made his money in the Far East.

The impact of Covid-19 would delay Gibson's involvement with Rangers but a £5million share purchase saw him become the fourth-largest shareholder in RIFC plc. This was not the start of a takeover bid or a power trip but merely a lifelong supporter doing his bit for his club.

Gibson is co-founder and co-CEO of ESR, a logistics platform that raised around £1.3billion in its Initial Public Offering to shareholders in Hong Kong in 2019. He operates in China, Japan, South Korea, Singapore, Australia and India and would speak exclusively to me for an interview in the *Herald* and *Glasgow Times* just weeks after his seven-figure investment.

A £1million deal in May was a sign of his commitment and the balance would follow a few months later. Gibson was a guest of the board at the game with Bayer Leverkusen and would meet King on the flight to London as he headed back to the Far East alongside his family.

When asked about a seat on the Ibrox board, he joked that he was content with a lunch in the Blue Room and his passion for the club was evident. This was about doing his bit because he could, whilst also giving his young twins a link to his homeland and his boyhood heroes. Later in the season, a further £3million investment saw him increase his stake to 10.86 per cent.

"To be honest, I am happy with the composition of the board," Gibson said during an extensive conversation as he also charted his business career that saw him ultimately oversee the launch of ESR alongside Ibrox shareholder George Taylor, the lead investment banker for Morgan Stanley. "You have got some lifetime Rangers fans in there with their hearts in the right place and they will make sure that some of the atrocities that happened ten years ago will never happen again.

"And you have got some fairly unemotional, completely objective business heads in there, like Julian (Wolhardt), who want to see the club have commercial success. That has to translate into winning stuff on the pitch, which puts money on the balance sheet, which means we can put more money on the pitch.

"I don't think I can offer anything to be quite honest. I am going to take a few years to get to know the board a bit better and hopefully they will like me and we will continue to get along. With regards to joining the board, I just don't feel qualified, to be honest."

Gibson has no aspirations of a seat at the top table but he had made a habit of being in the right place at the right time. His start Down Under came with Sir Alfred McAlpine at a luxury resort in Broome, Western Australia, before a move to Bangkok saw him interviewed by a fellow Scot that was overseeing a highway project for a Japanese firm. A mutual love of Rangers sealed the deal for Gibson.

Five years in Colombo during the Sri Lankan Civil War brought business opportunity but personal toll. During a period where acts of terrorism and suicide bombings were frequent,

Gibson realised it was time to move and a year in Amsterdam preceded the switch to the Far East that has allowed him to live the dream.

He likens his key moment there to 'working for Coca Cola, finding out the secret syrup and then going and starting a company called Pepsi' and ESR is more infrastructure than real estate. In effect, he is the landlord for the likes of Amazon and Alibaba and his network of associates and partners is as vast as the continent where he operates and lives.

It is a market that Rangers will look to target and tap in to in the coming years. His money was most welcomed at Ibrox, but Gibson's contacts book could be just as valuable for Rangers.

"I would like to think I can help," Gibson said. "When you look at the Premier League matches and you look at the hoardings all around the pitch, whether it is Man City, United, Chelsea, Liverpool, there is a lot of Chinese advertising and Chinese money in the Premier League.

"Rangers are as big a club as any of these guys, certainly when it comes to filling stadiums at the very least. I think they are a highly undervalued club in that regard, and I think some Chinese sponsors would get that undervalued status of the club.

"I will make it a point to try and reach out to some Chinese or Asian money that might have an interest in football. That is probably what I can offer, to be honest, and maybe introduce them to new investors and sponsors."

Rangers were once an impossible sell. Now the story and the opportunity speaks for itself as the club, in both a sporting sense and a financial one, revel in their achievements and their glory at the end of a historic season.

Rangers are winners once again and success should breed success at Ibrox. Nobody could say it publicly at the end of October, but the evidence was becoming overwhelming as the Old Firm sands shifted in Rangers' favour and Gerrard's side continued to establish themselves as a force on the European stage.

Rangers had found themselves on the brink in a very different sense just a few years before as the dark clouds hung over Ibrox. Now they stood on the edge of a new era that would have the silver lining of success at long last. They would be winners once again.

SIX

RANGERS SUPPORTERS had followed anywhere and everywhere as Steven Gerrard restored the club's reputation on the European stage during his first two seasons in charge. In the third, his players would have to do it on their own as Coronavirus denied fans a chance to follow near and far during a campaign that was very different but just as memorable.

The ghosts of that night in Luxembourg still cast a gloomy shadow over Rangers when Gerrard was appointed as manager, but that embarrassment has been consigned to history. From the farce of Pedro Caixinha, Rangers have become a force under Gerrard and it is progress and not Progres that is now associated with a club who have re-established themselves on the European stage at a remarkable rate.

The priority has always been to return Rangers to top spot in Scotland, but that ambition could not have been achieved had it not been for their exploits in Europe. The challenge of competing on three domestic fronts and embarking on a continental campaign is far from straightforward, but the manner in which

Gerrard's side have performed at home and abroad has been admirable.

Gerrard had such an affinity with European competition as a player and those occasions gave him some of his ultimate highs, the most memorable of which, of course, was that night in Istanbul when he became a Champions League winner. That ambition is beyond him at Ibrox, yet these matches under the floodlights provide the kind of thrill that Gerrard needs, the competitive rushes that he is accustomed to, and his first three seasons as a manager will live long in the memory given the emotional rollercoaster that he has been on.

The Europa League has been a significant proving ground for Gerrard and the experiences have undoubtedly helped mould him into the coach that he is today. It has taken time for some to adjust to and appreciate, but he is now Gerrard the manager rather than Gerrard the former player.

Gerrard the person is just as impressive. In those first months of his time at Ibrox, the journalists that covered Rangers had the opportunity to get to know Gerrard, and to watch him at closer quarters was enlightening. There was an undoubted aura about him, but he was professional and composed, an elite operator off the park as well as on it.

Crowds would wait for him everywhere he went. Some wanted shirts signed, others wanted a selfie taken. Many just appreciated the chance to be in his presence and catch a glimpse of him as he stepped on or off the team bus.

When Rangers travelled to Skopje, North Macedonia, to face FK Shkupi in his first away trip as manager, he would have to fend off questions about Liverpool at his press conference, politely reminding those in attendance of the position that he now held and the reason why he was sat in front of them in the first place. Requests for photographs and signatures from the local journalists were accepted in good grace, even if there was an unprofessionalism about the way in which the Macedonian media operated. It is all part of being Steven Gerrard, though.

Incidents such as those were prevalent wherever Gerrard went. On each occasion, he obliged and was always courteous with his time. A crowd would gather to cheer him onto the bus following the victory over Osijek in the next round as supporters ignored the fact that Gerrard had landed the first blow in knocking their side out of the Europa League.

The victory over Maribor was an early indicator of the kind of team that Gerrard was building as a goalless draw ensured qualification. It was resolute, it was determined and it was the kind of performance that supporters and Gerrard loved as Rangers showed real character.

The bonds with his players were strengthening with every week, but those under his command were not the only ones that wanted his time and attention as fans and club officials, almost anyone within a near radius in fact, sought their own Gerrard moment. It is life as Gerrard has always known it and it is hard not to admire the way in which he deals with the expectations that his name and presence bring.

"You knew straight away that looking after the first team in terms of the safety and security was going to be different going forward," David Martin, the Rangers head of security that has accompanied Gerrard on trips across the continent, said. "Everywhere you go with him, people want a piece of him and that is the same at home and abroad.

"The first season when we were in Europe, we had a good run, and we used to laugh because it happened two or three times when we travelled to different countries in the Europa League. You would get the coach to the team hotel and invariably there would be a few dozen, or more, fans waiting at the door of the hotel waiting for Steven Gerrard.

"I used to laugh because he would get off the bus and people would produce Liverpool strips for him to sign and people wanted autographs and selfies. And while he is doing that, the first team squad would have to walk round about him and into the hotel and nobody paid a blind bit of notice to them. I used to think that was quite funny, but he is just used to it."

By the time Rangers landed in Russia a couple of weeks later, Gerrard was on the brink of his first major achievement as manager. Many of the supporters that made the journey, and most of the press that did likewise, had never heard of Ufa as a place, never mind had any insight into their capabilities as a team when the draw was made.

A 1-0 victory at Ibrox had given those that travelled enough hope that Rangers could qualify for the group stages. That would prove to be the case, but only after a remarkable evening that saw Ovie Ejaria's goal cancelled out, Alfredo Morelos and Jon Flanagan sent off and Rangers put under sustained pressure for the closing stages as nerves were frayed and hair was greyed.

Gerrard had once again been mobbed wherever he had gone. In a soulless city of more than one million people, he was the most famous face there and he would have to fight his way through a throng of supporters that had filled the hotel lobby before he could conduct his pre-match press conference at the end of a long day.

It had been an eventful one, too. On landing in the Republic of Bashkortostan, Gerrard had been ushered into a side room by a Russian military official. It was a move that wasn't exactly part of the UEFA protocol, but the request that followed was familiar to Gerrard as the door opened and a handful of Liverpool shirts lay waiting to be signed.

After the game, Gerrard would speak with the band of Scottish journalists in a corner at the end of a corridor having left the local media scrum behind. It was a chance to reflect on an achievement that has been defining for his tenure and he would make his way through another boisterous crowd before beginning the journey home having secured group stage football at the first time of asking.

Having now accomplished that feat in three successive seasons, Rangers have proven that they are more than comfortable at that level. They are a side that thrive rather than survive in the Europa League and back-to-back runs to the last 16 of the competition are hugely significant achievements as co-efficient points and pound coins have been collected with regularity.

It has been a case of success breeding success. It was in November that Rangers would draw twice with Benfica and all-but secure progression from Group D as they improved and impressed on the European stage once again. That achievement was just the latest point in their evolution and Mark Wilson, a football writer with the *Scottish Daily Mail* who has covered Rangers extensively in recent years, believes the triumphs of today can be traced back to the deeds of those early weeks of Gerrard's tenure.

"Ufa was one of the strangest games that Steven Gerrard has taken charge of in Europe given that Morelos and Flanagan were both sent off," Wilson said. "It is difficult to speculate, but the whole course of his tenure might have been different had they not got through that night to get that first group stage qualification.

"To see it out with nine men so far away from home was a pretty extraordinary feat. You do wonder what would have happened if Rangers hadn't got that result and I put that down as one of the most important games of Gerrard's entire tenure, just because of what it allowed him to build afterwards in terms of financial income and a belief in where they were heading.

"There was a sense of achievement at Rangers for the first time in a long time that night. That one sticks in my mind because it was a real launchpad for Steven Gerrard's tenure and what happened afterwards."

The core of the team that were successful on that nerve-shredding but satisfying night in Ufa have been with Rangers every step of the way on their European journey. Mistakes were made in the months that followed and a place in the knock-out rounds eluded them, but that first campaign re-established Rangers' name on the continent.

The season would end in frustration both domestically and in Europe, but Gerrard had shown enough to prove that he had Rangers on the right track. Qualifying in the first season was a bonus, in the second it was expected, but at the third time of asking it was demanded.

That feat can never be taken for granted, yet Rangers have been ruthless during their three preliminary campaigns and taken care of each challenge that has been put in front of them. Some, like St Joseph's in the second term or Lincoln Red Imps this time around are naturally easier than others but Midtjylland and Legia Warsaw were far more formidable opponents, as were Willem II and Galatasaray.

Both of the runs that would take Rangers to the last 16 would begin in Gibraltar. By the time Rangers travelled to The Rock in the summer of 2019, the security staff were well aware of the demands on Gerrard's time and the requests that would come from clubs that weren't accustomed to having a legend of the game at their front door.

"He is the consummate professional, there is no doubt about that," Martin said. "Don't get me wrong, I have seen the other side a couple of times as well where he has had enough. You get them coming up to the coach. It was in Gibraltar and they had their Island Games at the same time so there were loads of folk hanging about after the game and I think he had done enough.

"He had been upstairs and signed umpteen strips and the directors wanted strips done and people take liberties at times. They would come to myself or Robin Howe and ask if it would be possible to get a couple of things signed and we would say that we would sort it. You take them into the boardroom and they produce a dozen more strips to be signed. He takes that kind of thing in his stride and he is very good at it.

"I do remember him telling the driver in Gibraltar that day to shut the door and get us out of there. But, equally, you always have to be careful when you have everyone carrying phones with cameras.

"He is always acutely aware of that. I have seen occasions where the security staff have said that we are just about to head off and maybe you are waiting on a couple of players getting on to the coach.

"Steven will pick a wee kid out of the crowd and bring him on to the coach for a photograph and he is very good at that. That always goes down well, as you would imagine. He is very accommodating with supporters and I can't think of him and I can't remember him ever losing his cool, to be quite honest with you."

After starting the campaign with a 4-0 win over St Joseph's in his second term, Gerrard would guide Rangers to the group stages as they returned to Luxembourg and avoided a repeat of their ultimate embarrassment before those admirable victories over Midtjylland and Legia. The moment that Morelos scored the late winner against the Poles saw Ibrox erupt and is one of the most evocative goals of the Gerrard era. Even today, the footage still raises the hairs on the back of the neck.

From pot four, Rangers would finish second to progress to the knock out rounds. The draws away to Porto and Feyenoord were the highlights in Group D but the best would come in Portugal in February. In these Covid-impacted times of no crowds and no travel, the sights and sounds that come to mind as one reminisces about Braga are depressing to recall.

Braga were two goals ahead and seemingly too good after an hour at Ibrox. Come the end of the tie, Gerrard's side had produced a rousing recovery and a perfect performance to record a result that stands amongst the finest of his managerial career.

The brace from Ianis Hagi and a sublime individual effort from Joe Aribo elicited a visceral roar, the likes of which would have reverberated around Ibrox so often this season had circumstances been different. A week later, an away support that was a couple of thousand strong marched from the city centre to the stadium that is draped on the side of a rockface and serenaded Gerrard's side throughout a 1-0 victory, earned thanks to Ryan Kent's second half strike.

Trips such as that jaunt to Braga and the earlier one to Porto were sorely missed throughout this Covid-impacted campaign as travel restrictions forced a rethink into how matches were watched and covered. The friendships formed, the stories told and the memories made will span careers and lives and this European term just hasn't been as enjoyable for either punter or press. It has ensured that the most unique experiences will shine brightly in the mind, though, especially when compared to some fraught evenings of late dramas and Zoom calls this season.

The Estádio Municipal de Braga – known locally as The Quarry – is one of the most picturesque and unusual grounds that Rangers have played at in quite some time. It was a venue that showed Gerrard's side at their best, though. Another collapse in the Premiership had seen concerns raised, but that night was further affirmation that Gerrard was onto something special with Rangers.

"If you talk about the football side and the tactical side, I think that was pretty much a note-perfect away European performance," Wilson said. "They had endured such a difficult first hour in the game at Ibrox before coming through it and all the problems they had faced at Ibrox, when Braga looked like a huge attacking threat, were solved in the week in between.

"Sitting watching that game from that very high vantage

point in the stand, it was pretty close to tactical perfection from Rangers that night and, to be honest, they could have won it by more against a team who were in excellent and formidable European form around that time. The Braga game, coming in the middle of a difficult domestic period for Rangers, they somehow produced this near perfect away performance that was pretty exceptional."

That night in Braga took Rangers to a new level in the Europa League. This season, they have reached similar heights and their achievements third time around are just as notable even if they ultimately didn't progress a round further than they managed at the second time of asking.

By the time November arrived, Rangers were already in dominant positions in the Premiership and the Europa League. The title race was far from over but Gerrard's side had the look of champions elect already and the 1-0 win at Kilmarnock was another sign this group had a resolve and spirit about them as James Tavernier's penalty proved decisive.

A 4-0 victory over Falkirk in the League Cup would round off the month. That came on the day that Celtic would lose to Ross County and supporters gathered in the car park to protest and call for the removal of the Parkhead board and the sacking of manager Neil Lennon.

It was all angst and anger in the East End. At Ibrox, Rangers were really motoring and Hamilton were beaten 8-0 and Aberdeen lost 4-0 as Gerrard's side hit top gear in the Premiership.

On the continent, there was obvious frustration. Wins over Standard Liege and Lech Poznan had put Rangers on the brink of qualification but two entertaining ties with Benfica ensured Gerrard's side would need to wait until the following month for top spot in Group D to be confirmed.

The first fixture was historic for Rangers and Alfredo Morelos as he became the club's record scorer in European competition.

His effort against Benfica – scored from just a couple of yards out as he converted a low cross from Tavernier – was his 22nd goal on that stage and took him clear of the tally of Ally McCoist that he had equalled by heading home the winner against Lech Poznan on Matchday Two.

Adding to a Diogo Goncalves own goal and fine strike from Glen Kamara, it should have been enough to earn Rangers a notable victory. They would have to settle for a point, though, as Rafa Silva and Darwin Nunez scored in the closing stages to ensure Benfica didn't lose at home in the Europa League for the first time in 24 matches.

"We were having a bit of fun about it and obviously kidding on, but I was delighted for him," McCoist, who is Rangers' record scorer with 355 goals, said. "There were some great performances and some great goals from him and the team over the season. Some of his goals have been great and his record is really deserved and warranted.

"It is no mean achievement and good on him. Congratulations to him for being able to beat that record. In terms of the overall one, he will need to play until he's 107 to beat that one! I think that one might be safe!"

There was a clear irritation at the final result, but it was a night where Rangers enhanced their reputation once again. The same, of course, was true for a man who has so often saved his best for such occasions as Morelos grabbed the headlines once again.

The striker has been no stranger to that phenomenon during his time in Glasgow. Adored by the Rangers support, Morelos is the man that opposition fans, and no doubt some players, love to hate, but his notoriety has been forged through comment and caricature.

His disciplinary issues cannot be overlooked, but the incidents that saw red flashed in his face or bans handed down from Hampden were largely earned as a result of idiocy rather than malice. Morelos was christened with the nickname 'El Bufalo' during his childhood in Cereté, a working class town in the north of Colombia, and Gerrard now affectionately refers to him as 'Buff' whilst speaking in praiseworthy tones about a player who has been the ultimate test of his man-management over the last three years.

Morelos would admit to 'difficulties' in the relationship between the two later in the season. That assertion was downplayed by Gerrard and there is a clear affection for the striker, despite the headaches that he has undoubtedly caused over their time together.

"The person who deserves the credit for transforming himself is Alfredo, not me," Gerrard said. "He did an interview recently talking about the difficulties we've had – I'm not aware of them, because it's not been a difficulty for me.

"I've said he's been a challenge because he hasn't always been perfect, but he's been an absolute pleasure to work with. He's smiling and it's probably the happiest I've seen him over the course of the three years.

"We want Alfredo to stay fit and healthy and help us finish the season as strongly as we can and I'm delighted for him that finally he's got a reward for all the goals he's scored and all the top performances he's put in.

"He's really proud to be a champion and a league winner here, and hopefully it's given him the hunger to go and achieve many more things with the team. It's not just about Alfredo. It's about the team and the team have been magnificent this year."

There are few who really know Morelos the man. He has never conducted a newspaper interview during his time in Scotland and chances to see him in person were usually limited to passing nods and smiles as journalists waited for his team-mates to speak in Mixed Zones after European encounters. It was only towards the end of the season that he started speaking to RangersTV.

Gerrard joked about Morelos singing 'Sweet Caroline' following the victory over Livingston in March, while Ross Wilson, the sporting director, later revealed that Morelos joined in the celebratory singing in perfect English as the Premiership title was won. A Morelos in form will always be music to the ears of Rangers.

There was a vacuum created around Morelos that was subsequently filled with comment and conjecture and supporters believed he was an easy target. When he became the subject of racist abuse, fans would rally round their man. There have been many moments where they have had enough of his antics, but there were few players in the squad for whom they were more pleased when the title was won and his goal against Benfica was celebrated as the achievement was lauded.

His journey from Cereté to Glasgow, via a stint with HJK Helsinki where he caught the attention of former Rangers striker Jonatan Johansson, is one of bravery and dedication. Johansson would never get the best out of Morelos during his short spell on Caixinha's coaching staff, but the legacy of bringing the forward to Ibrox is a lasting one.

Morelos has the same ambition of leaving his own mark in life, albeit in a very different manner, as he cares for those less fortunate than himself. Through a Foundation in his name, he seeks to help the most vulnerable in his homeland, giving children the education and the opportunities that he never had whilst his father, a fruit seller, and his mother, a housewife who looked after her three children, sought to raise a family amid the poverty of a town whose main industries are cotton and cattle.

Morelos would tragically lose his six-year-old sister when he was a teenager and a promise was made to his family that he would provide for them. He has done that, and more, courtesy of the talent that has seen him become a real prospect of South American football as he makes his name in Europe.

Morelos would return home during lockdown to aid the fight against Covid-19, providing protective equipment and food packages in Cereté and the surrounding areas. He is painted as a fighter, a man with a short fuse and a fiery nature, yet those that have seen his kindness and generosity have very different opinions of a man who continues to divide them in Scotland.

"Alfredo is a humble person with a good heart, and with the Foundation he wants to help children fulfil their dreams both in football and in school," Franklin Gonzalez, a director of the Alfredo Morelos Foundation, said. "For us in the Foundation, for the Colombians and more than all in our native Cereté, we were very proud on the day of Alfredo's representation abroad and in the selection for the national team.

"One of the anecdotes that I experienced with Alfredo is when I spoke with him for the first time via WhatsApp, I told him that I was a countryman of his and that I was willing to help him in whatever he needed here. I put myself at his command as a professional, and he replied, 'Well, I'll tell you anything.' He didn't tell me anything else and then after four months he contacted me and here we are, thank God.

"In 2020 we worked with the vulnerable population of our municipality. In the pandemic, we delivered more than 1,000 markets to the neediest people in Cereté and we provided psychosocial telephone support through the professionals of the Foundation to those affected by the situation of the pandemic."

The rise and rise of Morelos is an inspirational tale. His international debut against Venezuela in September 2018 was widely celebrated in his home town, where he hosts a charity match at the end of every season as players are decked out in the red, white and blue of Rangers.

For Karina Ruiz Beleno, a journalist with newspaper *El Meridiano*, the impact of Morelos cannot be purely judged in goals, or indeed medals. She is also involved with the Foundation and has become a link between Scotland and Colombia as she regularly posts social media updates that highlight Morelos' popularity on the hard, deprived streets where he grew up.

"The Alfredo Morelos Foundation seeks to contribute to improving the quality of life of children who live in vulnerable situations," Beleno said. "With this beautiful project led by Alfredo, what we want is that children, adolescents and young people are not immersed in drug addiction, prostitution or illegal groups, but that they have an opportunity to study, to be professionals, to have a decent job. We also seek that families are more united, that the love between parents and children abounds and that children fight for their dreams, their passions."

Those battling qualities certainly apply to Morelos. He arrived at Ibrox as an unknown, a £1 million gamble, and while his time has often been controversial, his scoring achievements speak volumes for his ability and his character.

He has tested Gerrard, of that there can be no doubt. Yet Gerrard has been good for Morelos, honing his game and cooling his temperament and he would finish their second campaign together as the top scorer in the Europa League.

For all the changes that Gerrard has made to Morelos' game, it is one away from Rangers that has perhaps had the most profound impact on the striker. In May 2020, his wife Yesenia gave birth to their first child and Gerrard has regularly referenced the way in which fatherhood has impacted on Morelos, a man for whom Glasgow became home from home.

"A child is the greatest joy that can happen to one," Gonzalez said. "And he tries every day to make the most of the moments with his family, being a very happy person and dedicated to his home, in the time he has free. Alfredo is a great human being, it is quite simple. And he has a gift of helping those most in need, that is what characterises him.

"In Cereté, people have great appreciation for everything he is doing for their children. They love him very much and are very grateful for everything he is doing in the social part and obviously the Rangers fans appreciate him a lot for everything he has given the club.

"The truth is that he has been at the club for several years and he has been happy. Football is very fast changing and market after market and clubs and players sometimes have to make decisions that favour both of them. At the moment he is calm and he was eager to be a champion with Rangers."

The fulfilment of that dream in March came at a time of the campaign when Morelos was in fine scoring form but there were difficult moments in the season. His record-breaking goal against Benfica was the last he would score until the victory over St Mirren in late December but his influence went beyond simply putting the ball in the net.

Gerrard would hail his star man as 'outstanding' following that 3-3 draw and express his hope that he was getting close to his best once again. The goals didn't back up that optimism, but Morelos was still playing his part in a Rangers side who were gathering momentum week after week.

The return fixture with Benfica at Ibrox was another case of an opportunity missed by Rangers as two late goals once again denied them victory. Scott Arfield and Kemar Roofe had given Gerrard's side what looked like a comfortable lead, but Tavernier's unfortunate own goal and a strike from Pizzi nine minutes from time ensured Rangers didn't qualify with two matches to spare.

The points dropped against Benfica weren't enough to deny Rangers a place in the last 32 and they would ultimately secure top spot in the section ahead of the Portuguese giants. The Europa League had brought progression season-on-season for Rangers and that achievement was another notable one as they finished Group D unbeaten.

Former Ibrox midfielder Alex Rae has seen Rangers every step of the way through his work with RangersTV and as co-commentator on BT Sport's coverage of the Europa League. The matches with Benfica would only serve to confirm the evolution on the European stage.

"They are making good strides and you can see that, not only with the results but in terms of the performances at this level as well," Rae said. "In Gerrard's second season, the European form was excellent, but to then go on and top the group, to score more goals and to finish unbeaten was really impressive.

"I think Steven will reflect on some excellent performances and certainly that was the case against Benfica. Some of the football that we played was excellent at times and the team and the management have a belief in their brand of football and believe that they can go and get results in Europe.

"They are a big threat away from home as well. You don't think it is going to be backs to the wall stuff, just because of the style of play and the personnel that they have. You always feel as if they can go and get a result."

That belief in their own abilities has been nurtured over Gerrard's three seasons in charge and this is a squad that are now capable of holding their own in the latter stages of European competitions. To reach that point in such a short space of time is no mean feat and it is testament to the work that Gerrard and his staff have put in with their players.

The rewards in a financial sense have been there in black and white over recent seasons but the benefits of exposure to European football have been more profound for Rangers. There is a defined style about the way in which Gerrard's side play and the roles and responsibilities are clear to those that he tasks with carrying out each duty.

Mark Wilson has been a regular follower of Rangers on their Europa League journey under Gerrard and believes the growth is clear to see. Rangers had to go back to the drawing board in the aftermath of the defeat to Progres and Gerrard's blueprint has been evident since his arrival.

"The football aspect of it is no less important and the Europa League became the ultimate testing ground, I suppose, for the tactical structures that Gerrard, Michael Beale and the coaching staff had been working on," Wilson said. "That, in turn, must have given the players so much belief when they were being given tactical game plans to go in against teams who, with all respect, are a higher calibre than the ones they face most weekends in the Premiership.

"They were achieving positive results time after time and that must have given them a huge amount of faith in where the coaching staff were taking them on the journey, but also in terms of their own personal development and being able to go up against these guys on an individual basis and come through matches against gifted opponents. That must have contributed to their own personal growth as well.

"If you had said at the point of the hideous embarrassment of Progres that within three seasons Rangers would be disappointed not to beat Benfica home and away, that would have seemed extraordinary. The journey since then has been remarkable. Gerrard has brought the club back to a position of respect in Europe and the consistency over those three seasons has been the most impressive thing about it. Rangers are now regarded as a team, certainly at Europa League level, that should be making an impact into the knock out stages."

When it comes to competing in the groups, and certainly when the latter rounds come around, Rangers are always going to have to punch above their weight in Europe. The finances available to Gerrard are dwarfed by some of their continental counterparts, but that doesn't mean that results can't be achieved and the way in which Rangers have gone about their business is a credit to the coaching staff and the squad that Gerrard has had a father-like impact on.

Successes on the European stage always carry their own significance and Gerrard has been looking to follow in the footsteps of those that have gone before him. It would be quite the achievement if he could go on and match the efforts of Walter Smith and take Rangers to their first final since Manchester in 2008.

It would be just as remarkable if he were to equal the feats of Alex McLeish's side from two years previously and secure a place in the knockout rounds of the Champions League. That campaign was wretched for Rangers domestically as they suffered early exits in both cups and finished third in the Scottish Premier League, but the European exploits were historic as they became the first side from these shores to reach the latter stages of Europe's top club competition.

That is a box that Gerrard can look to tick in time. Finishing top of their section this time around was an effort that should certainly not be played down.

"They have done very well and it has been great for Rangers over the last couple of season," McLeish, who won seven major honours at Ibrox and went on to manage the likes of Aston Villa, Birmingham City and Genk, as well as take charge of Scotland in two separate spells, said of Gerrard's exploits this term. "When I coached in Belgium, it was a real priority for the Belgian clubs to get as far as they could in European competition. Round about that time, English clubs weren't that keen on Europa League progression because of their Premier League commitments and that gave some nations an opportunity.

"Rangers have taken their opportunity in these three years under Steven and they have progressed really well and really impressively in the Europa League. They have shown a longevity that we hadn't seen for a wee while.

"They have taken on and beaten some formidable opponents and only came unstuck last season against a very strong Bayer Leverkusen side that are well established at that level. Rangers have been a team that has grown and they have improved with every game over the first two seasons and to finish top of the group this year was a terrific achievement."

It would take wins over Standard Liege at home and Lech Poznan away for Rangers' qualification and then top spot in Group D to be secured but the job was all-but done after those two incredible fixtures with Benfica. Between the draw with Hibernian on 20 September and the defeat to St Mirren on 16 December, those meetings with the Portuguese giants were the only two games that Rangers didn't win as they built real momentum through what was shaping up to be a famous season.

The task of putting together a title bid and competing in Europe concurrently is far from straightforward but the experiences of the last two terms were invaluable. The schedule was relentless for Rangers, yet it wasn't one that would hinder them. McLeish knows all too well how strenuous that challenge can be as an expectant support demand results at home and abroad.

"When we went to Porto in the Champions League and got that result that was so important to us, we perhaps had a weaker side than usual and we had a few younger players in there as well," McLeish said. "Instead of going all out to try and win the game, you can have a more patient approach and play a more tactical game. We struggled in the league that season overall but we did have a strong unbeaten run in the second half of the season.

"When you are at Rangers, or at Celtic, and in the Premiership, you have to go for it in every game and you have to win every game. We always went for it in every game, but we didn't win enough of them and we weren't as strong as you would expect from a Rangers side.

"But when it came to the Champions League, we didn't necessarily go all out for the win and we could approach games in a different manner, especially away from home. In that Porto game, we went there and got the draw that got us into the last 16 of the Champions League and Steven has been able to go away from home and earn important results in the Europa League."

The depth of squad that Gerrard had at his disposal during that run certainly proved beneficial but there were players – the likes of Allan McGregor, Connor Goldson, Ryan Kent and Tavernier – that he would turn to time after time. Such is the relationship that Gerrard has with his tried and trusted operators, there was never an issue when he asked anyone to dig deep for the good of the team.

Gerrard was a manager that players wanted to play for. That trait, that spirit and will to win, was evident during McLeish's tenure as well. Such characteristics must come naturally, though, and cannot be forced or manufactured.

"We were playing against Stuttgart and lost a goal just before half-time and I had a real dig at the boys," McLeish said as he recalled one of his early Champions League ties as Rangers manager. "This is when I learned a bit more about foreign players. I'm sure it was Mo Ross that lost the duel and they went 1-0 up and I went a bit ballistic.

"One of the staff came to me later on and said that Shota Arveladze had said to him, 'How can we play the second half when the coach kills us?' That just emphasised the difference between dealing with the Scottish lads and some of the foreign players and that was a good experience and lesson for me.

"You have to learn to deal with them a wee bit differently because of their personalities and backgrounds and it was a good education point for me. It just shows you how important man management is and that feedback was interesting.

"There are some players who you know you can have a go at and you will get more out of them and others where you have to give them a cuddle and say 'you are capable of much more than that'. That man management is so important in the game today."

Rangers had improved individually during Gerrard's tenure to date, but it was the collective efforts that were more significant and the Europa League showed them at their best once again. A place in the quarter-finals would eventually elude them, however.

That was ultimately one of few negatives in the campaign, and there were reasons to be proud given what had been achieved as Rangers once again surpassed their record from the previous season.

"The whole European run was excellent for so many reasons," Rae, who was part of McLeish's title winning side in 2005 and worked with him at Genk, said. "Financially it has been beneficial, the club is being recognised as a name again in Europe. Rangers had been lost to European football for a while but people are now seeing them getting results against Porto, Feyenoord, Legia and taking on a very good Benfica that are accustomed to Champions League football.

"They have played and beaten sides of a good standard and standing and it is great to be back on that stage. If you go into Europe, you want to make an impact and I can't speak highly enough about the efforts."

It cannot be said for sure, but the theory that Rangers would not have won the Premiership without their European endeavours carries significant weight. The funds that Gerrard has brought into Rangers through the extended runs have been reinvested in the squad, while the wisdom earned through competing at that level has raised the standards of each player that has been so integral to the title success.

From a co-efficient perspective, Scottish football owes a debt of gratitude to Rangers for succeeding whilst others have failed and the standing of our game has been emboldened courtesy of their efforts. This season was, of course, all about Premiership superiority but the feats on the continent cannot be overlooked or downplayed.

"I think it has been a foundation of it and Steven Gerrard was asked at the start of the group stages whether this was the team that the Europa League built," Wilson said. "He was very quick to agree with that and it falls into separate categories.

"There is obviously the financial aspect and you think back to season one and making the group stages and the funds from that helped in terms of being able to buy Ryan Kent the following year. Making the last 16 in season two saw them bank more than £20million and that obviously has an impact on being able to go into the market for Ianis Hagi, Kemar Roofe and Cedric Itten the following summer.

"Even though Rangers have continued to run at a loss over that summer and had to rely on the support of its investor base, those achievements in Europe and the financial rewards of them must have given those investors confidence that if they persist with supporting Steven Gerrard and backing Steven Gerrard that there will be rewards. It was already happening in Europe and if they persisted with that then they would get to where they wanted to be domestically."

Where Rangers wanted to be was exactly where they found themselves at the end of the month and they had once again shown different sides to their game. The victory over Falkirk in the Betfred Cup ultimately proved futile in terms of landing the silverware, but the Premiership successes against Kilmarnock, Hamilton and Aberdeen were anything but.

If the victory at Rugby Park was sluggish, the 8-0 win at home to Accies was scintillating as Tavernier, Roofe and Joe Aribo netted braces and Arfield and Brandon Barker also found the target. Hamilton were fortunate not to see the scoreboard tick into double figures, while Aberdeen got away with one a fortnight later as they only lost by four. Rangers were very much in the groove.

"It was a very impressive performance, a strong win and another clean sheet," Gerrard said in the aftermath of the victory against Hamilton that became his biggest as manager. "The thing that pleased me the most was the standards that we maintained from start to finish. I have been on to these players, probably on to them too much, about keeping standards no matter what stage the game is at. It pleased me at half-time that we carried on looking to score goals and win even more emphatically.

"It has been coming, we have threatened to do that. But the pleasing thing today was that we were very clinical. We suffocated Hamilton from start to finish, we stayed on them and never let them... we never took our foot off the gas and you could see the quality throughout the squad. I made five changes today, brought five subs on and it didn't affect our level of performance. That is the most pleasing thing for me."

Rangers would end November in the ascendancy but there were issues for Gerrard to deal with at the beginning and the end of the month. For the first time, Covid headlines were made at Ibrox.

The losses of Filip Helander and Nathan Patterson for the match with Falkirk were outwith Rangers' control. Helander would test positive after reporting for international duty with Sweden, while Patterson had to self-isolate as he was caught up in an outbreak whilst on Scotland Under-21 duty and several clubs would count the cost of the protocols designed to limit the spread of the virus during foreign travel.

The other incident was far more serious, though, after George Edmundson and Jordan Jones attended a house party in Glasgow following the win over Kilmarnock. Both were suspended during an internal investigation and subsequently given seven-match bans by the Scottish FA. They would eventually return to training with the Rangers squad but neither would play again as Edmundson moved to Derby County and Jones joined Sunderland, both on loan deals, late in the January transfer window.

"I think the important thing here was to get the players out of the isolation period, first and foremost," Gerrard said as he addressed the first real crisis of the season for Rangers and the actions of his players which brought widespread condemnation from sporting and political circles. "Then it was about sitting down with the players face-to-face to gauge a reaction to how they feel and where they were at.

"I spoke to them both individually and they were both very sad over the incident, they were remorseful, apologetic and full of regret. They first and foremost wanted to apologise to the supporters and their team-mates for their actions.

"In my position it was time to support these two players once I saw that reaction. It was the reaction I wanted to see. Now it's about me giving them the support and managing them to come back to top players because they are good players, we need them here to help and support us moving forward."

Both Edmundson and Jones may have been given a second chance by their manager but many supporters were less forgiving and the anger was palpable. Given what was at stake this season, and the serious ramifications their selfish actions could have had, calls for them to be banished were not that out of order.

As it transpired, Rangers didn't need either of them. They had created unwanted and unneeded headlines, but the furore was never going to derail a Rangers side that were well on track in the Premiership and the Europa League.

Coronavirus had denied supporters the chance to revel in another European campaign but it wouldn't prevent Rangers from more notable achievements under Gerrard's guidance. As fans follow followed from home, they had plenty to sing about.

SEVEN

ON A bitterly cold and utterly abject night in Paisley, Rangers missed the ultimate chance in their pursuit of silverware. Thousands of miles away, Dave King had just provided supporters with the opportunity of a lifetime to protect their club for generations.

A month which saw Steven Gerrard's side play nine matches across three competitions was always going to be hugely significant. Rangers, of course, had been here before but there was a more defined sense of belief and optimism amongst supporters as momentum was maintained and they had Betfred Cup success firmly in their sights, as well as crucial Premiership wins and another notable European scalp.

But the bigger picture must always assume greater significance than the snapshot. This season has been historic for many reasons on the park, yet the proposition that was put to fans off it was just as important as King and Club 1872 agreed a deal that would see the former chairman sell his major shareholding in Rangers International Football Club plc.

It was that stock, which King had accumulated over many months in the build-up to the EGM vote in March 2015, that allowed him to win his battle for control alongside John Gilligan and Paul Murray. He had given his fellow fans back their club, now he wished to ensure Rangers was forever safeguarded and that the events of 2012 could never be repeated.

King was not just the saviour that rode to the rescue whilst supporters were fearing for the future of their club under the previous regime. He had invested £20million of his business fortune during Sir David Murray's reign as Rangers spent lavishly and chased European glory whilst enjoying domestic supremacy. It would, of course, all come at a cost.

Murray had been a dominating figure in Scottish football and business, but Rangers became a burden that had to be removed. Under pressure from the banks and with the fall-out from the use of the Employee Benefit Trust scheme weighing heavily on his shoulders and his wallet, he would sell to Craig Whyte for £1 and events would spiral out of control. Whether he was duped, as he claimed, or not is an irrelevance but the damage caused as a result of that transaction is incalculable in human terms and eye-watering in a financial sense.

Administration followed on Valentine's Day in 2012 and within months Rangers were under the ownership of a consortium headed by Charles Green and playing Third Division football.

The ins and outs of those murky days have been through the machinations of the Scottish legal system but supporters still don't know the full story of what happened to Rangers and why. Maybe they will never know, and maybe that is for the best.

The fall and rise of Rangers is the story of a lifetime and a career from a journalistic perspective. It dominated lives rather than just office hours and the lexicon of the sports desks changed as financial jargon and money matters dominated the agenda.

For some time, it was Jim Traynor and Keith Jackson who

would lead the way with their coverage in the *Daily Record*. Whyte's tenure at Ibrox would come to an ignominious end but that wasn't the final act in the drama as Green's arrival started the next chapters of a complicated but compelling story.

"We worked in tandem on that," Traynor, the former *Record* sports editor, said. "We played Whyte off against the Blue Knights and Paul Murray. We played one off against the other.

"There were days when Keith would have a great line from Paul and it would be a good back splash, or sometimes even a front page one. But we always wanted better and so there were times when Whyte's people would try to provide that stronger line. It would be necessary then to make sure Whyte was fully aware of what he was saying so that he couldn't come back when the story ran and claim he had been misquoted. It wasn't necessary to do this with others, Paul for instance, but with him you had to be sure.

"So, if he had a better line, it was back over to Paul to further the cause of the Blue Knights. That's why the *Record* was always ahead of the pack with this story.

"After a few months of stringing him along Whyte actually offered me a job but I had permission from the editor of the paper to continue squeezing information out of him before backing Paul, who was clearly always the one to be trusted.

"The *Record* and Jackson exposed Whyte and brought him down and even though my relationship with Jackson disintegrated they should have had more credit for having done so. But the real credit lies with the Rangers fans to be honest."

The past cannot be changed, but the future can be shaped and that is what King has sought to do from the moment he chose to take a seat at the table once again. His message of 'never again' was one which he spoke about to those close to him right at the outset as he decided, reluctantly and initially against his will and judgement, to enter the fight for his boyhood club. All in, he would write cheques for another £20million.

Right and below: This is where 'The Journey' started. In July 2012, Rangers fans travelled to Brechin City for a Ramsdens Cup first round fixture and saw Ally McCoist's side require extra time to earn a 2-1 victory. Rangers were the same club, but their challenges were very different in these uncertain and unique times. *SNS*

Left and below: There are few men who have given greater service to Rangers than Sandy Jardine and these two moments – as he unfurled the Third Division flag at Ibrox and marched to Hampden with thousands behind him – summed up his influence and significance to the club. Jardine would help ensure Rangers survived in 2012 but he would lose his battle with cancer before he got the chance to see them crowned as champions once again. *SNS*

Title 55 would not have been possible without the day, six years earlier, that John Gilligan, Dave King and Paul Murray won control of Rangers following a lengthy and at times bitter battle for control. From this moment on, it was a matter of when, not if, Rangers would win the title once again. *SNS*

Supporters had sung about 'Going for 55' during their Championship winning campaign under Mark Warburton and the line became a slogan that permeated their trials and tribulations in the years that followed. This card display preceded a 1-1 draw at home to Hamilton Academical as Rangers faltered on their return to the Premiership. *SNS*

The signing of Joey Barton summed up Mark Warburton's second summer at Ibrox and set the tone for a disastrous first season back in the top flight for Rangers. This 5-1 defeat in the first Old Firm game of the term highlighted the gulf across Glasgow and neither man would remain in situ much longer. *SNS*

This was the beginning of the end for Pedro Caixinha as Rangers manager. The defeat to Progres Niederkorn was arguably the worst in the club's history and the Portuguese was fortunate to emerge from it with his job. He wouldn't last long. *SNS*

Steven Gerrard watched on as Rangers lost 3-2 to ten-man Celtic at Ibrox and saw their ambitions of stopping seven-in-a-row ended. Within weeks, he and Andy Scoulding, Rangers' head of scouting, would be working together as Gerrard was appointed as manager. *SNS*

Graeme Murty's second spell in charge came to an ignominious end as Celtic followed up a 4-0 win in the Scottish Cup semi-finals with a 5-0 victory that sparked a title party at Parkhead. Murty was relieved of his duties shortly afterwards as the Rangers board found themselves under increasing scrutiny from disillusioned supporters. *SNS*

The beginning of a new era. Steven Gerrard delivered his famous message of 'let's go' and was greeted by a crowd several thousand strong as he was appointed as Rangers manager. *SNS*

The victory over Ufa was the first milestone achievement of Gerrard's tenure and perhaps one that further successes would not have been possible without. James Tavernier, Kyle Lafferty, Andy Halliday, Ryan Jack and Ryan Kent would feature on that nerve-shredding evening in Russia. *SNS*

The Old Firm fixtures had become ones to fear rather than excite for Rangers but two wins – one at Ibrox and one at Parkhead – changed their mindset and the dynamic of the derby. Rangers ultimately wouldn't capitalise on either, though, as Ryan Jack earned the win in December 2018 and goals from Ryan Kent and Nikola Katic sparked emotional celebrations 12 months later. *SNS*

There was an ominous look and feel about Steven Gerrard following the Scottish Cup defeat to Hearts at Tynecastle and Rangers were now zero from six in terms of silverware under his guidance. The loss to Hamilton days later piled on the pressure before Covid struck and ended the season. *SNS*

Rangers had started a defining season with a renewed purpose and victory over Galatasaray ensured qualification for the Europa League group stages for a third consecutive term. Scott Arfield opened the scoring and James Tavernier also netted in a 2-1 win. *SNS*

The goal of the season competition was ended in an instant as Kemar Roofe scored from his own half in the win over Standard Liege. Steven Gerrard hailed it as the best goal he had ever seen live. *SNS*

The Premiership title wasn't quite sealed with a kiss at Parkhead but a Connor Goldson brace was a sign of intent from Rangers. This was one of the most controlled derby wins in recent memory. *Getty Images*

A night of mixed emotions for Rangers as a point was earned but two were dropped in a 3-3 draw with Benfica. It was historic for Alfredo Morelos, though, as he became the club's record scorer in European competition. *Getty Images*

Rangers had a potential treble in their sights but suffered their first defeat of the season at the worst possible moment as Steven Gerrard's side were eliminated from the Betfred Cup and the Saints went marching on to Hampden. *SNS*

Right and below: Rangers and Celtic paid tribute to the victims of the Ibrox Disaster on the 50th anniversary of the accident which claimed the lives of 66 supporters. Hundreds more were injured on 2 January 1971 and the Old Firm were united in condolence as Rangers were unable to hold a larger memorial service due to Coronavirus restrictions. *SNS*

Rangers took a significant stride towards the Premiership title with a 1-0 win over Celtic. Joe Aribo got the congratulations, but it was a Callum McGregor own goal that ended Celtic's faint ambitions of winning ten-in-a-row. *Getty Images*

Come March, title 55 was won. Victory over St Mirren at Ibrox moved Rangers to within a point of the Premiership and Steven Gerrard and his players would celebrate with thousands of supporters that packed Edmiston Drive before and after the game. *SNS*

Steven Gerrard and his players had been greeted by a sea of smoke at Ibrox as supporters welcomed them ahead of the St Mirren match. The scenes of celebration were an outpouring of emotion at the end of ten long, hard years. *SNS*

Those party scenes lasted throughout the weekend as fans gathered in George Square and Celtic were held by Dundee United. As Covid regulations continued to grip Scotland, the celebrations were lambasted by police and politicians. *Getty Images*

A momentous month would end on a sour note for Rangers and the game as Glen Kamara was subjected to racist abuse during the defeat to Slavia Prague. Rangers – as a club and a support – rallied round the midfielder following the incident that sparked debate about racism in sport and society. *SNS*

Rangers saw their dreams of a double ended prematurely as St Johnstone emerged victorious at Ibrox. A penalty shoot-out defeat ensured there would be a sense of an opportunity missed for Steven Gerrard's side this term. *SNS*

A 4-1 Old Firm win was the final show of superiority from Rangers during a dominant season. Kemar Roofe scored twice as Alfredo Morelos and Jermain Defoe also netted and Steven Gerrard's side ensured they were unbeaten against Celtic this season. *SNS*

The picture that Rangers fans had waited a decade to see. Steven Gerrard's side rounded off the season with a 4-0 win over Aberdeen before captain James Tavernier lifted the Premiership trophy. *SNS*

Left: In three seasons, Steven Gerrard had transformed Rangers from hopeful contenders to deserved champions. The man that was a legend in Liverpool had become a god in Glasgow. *(SNS)*

Below: Fans had flocked to Ibrox to celebrate together as Rangers ended their wait for silverware. The league was won and 'The Journey' had been completed. *Getty Images*

His previous investment hadn't given him any real control at Ibrox. It was Murray that called the shots and that had the overwhelming shareholding. King, in effect, was powerless and others such as Alistair Johnston, himself a former chairman, and chief executive Martin Bain could do nothing to prevent Rangers being snatched from their control. Sadly, their warnings would prove prescient.

The arrangement with Club 1872 is King's way, then, of aiming to ensure that lightning can't strike twice at Ibrox. The fan ownership organisation was formed with the amalgamation of the Rangers Supporters Trust and Rangers First following regime change and the deal with King was transformative in terms of their ambitions to own and control a meaningful stake in RIFC plc.

Chris Graham had worked closely with King through the years that culminated in him returning to Ibrox as chairman. Now he would advise Club 1872 on the £13million blueprint that they hope will one day take them beyond the 25 per cent plus one share threshold to effectively give supporters a veto on major boardroom decisions.

"It was probably the outcome of a series of conversations after the talk of him deciding that he was going to step down as chairman," Graham said. "That would have been around November time, prior to the 2019 AGM, and we knew that he was thinking about stepping down.

"I think initially he thought he would say at the AGM that he was stepping down and that he would say he wanted to find a way of passing on his shareholding to the fans, but without necessarily being specific about Club 1872 or how he was going to do that.

"Although he announced he was stepping down at the AGM, he didn't leave until March 2020 and everything went a bit quiet, having had initial discussions around the AGM the previous November.

"It was Dave that initiated the conversation again and it was very much an exploratory question around whether Club 1872, or more broadly the fans, would be able to take on the shareholding. He asked about the level of support we could get and he wanted to do something after explaining the situation with his family and not being sure what they would do with the shares.

"It was kind of a series of discussions, but it was certainly initiated by Dave in terms of saying there was going to be an opportunity there, that he wanted to move the shares on and he was very clear that he wanted the fans to have the chance to buy the shares. He doesn't want a situation where the fans don't have a say over the club or what is going to happen in the future."

There was an initial scepticism amongst some sections of the support over the worthiness and the timing of the King deal. Some feared it would cause an unnecessary distraction that would hinder Steven Gerrard's side on the park, while others were uneasy about funds from fans going to King rather than into Rangers as the board guided the club through the financial storm created by the Coronavirus pandemic.

King would downplay suggestions of a rift between himself and the board that he had departed in March. He had remained in close contact with Johnston in the months since, with their shared love of golf a usual source of conversation. King would join Gary Player for the ceremonial opening of The Masters in November 2020 and has regularly caddied for the South African, while Johnston – the vice-chairman of management behemoth IMG – has a collection of 30,000 books that he will ship from his home in Cleveland to St Andrews as the Royal and Ancient establish the world's most comprehensive collection of golf literature at a library named in the exiled Scot's honour.

On the night that King would discuss his plans with a handful of journalists over a Zoom call, he informed Rangers of his intentions out of a sense of decency and courtesy. The news would leak online before Club 1872 officially launched their membership drive but that did not diminish the significance of the announcement and opportunity as fans were given a chance that they could only have dreamed of a decade previously.

"I think the board recognises, quite rightly, that I'm no longer on the board," King said at a press briefing conducted in home offices and living rooms rather than the grandeur of Ibrox. "I'm the same as any other shareholder in the sense I shouldn't get access to inside information. My relationship with the board in terms of contacts since I stepped down has been fairly remote.

"Having said that, I know the individuals. I did chair that board for a long time so I know they are going to be sympathetic, I think, to what I'm trying to do and sympathetic to working with Club 1872. Everyone recognises that without the supporters we wouldn't be where we are today. I had an impact because I put some money into it, but it wasn't just about people with money.

If the take-up and buy-in from Club 1872 members was sufficient, the initial three-year timeframe to complete the transaction would be shortened and King would lose more than £2million on his shareholding. As it transpired, additional funding requirements at Ibrox saw the King agreement renegotiated as fans' cash was initially invested into Rangers instead.

And the club would later launch their own share offering – aimed at raising £6.75million – in an attempt to bolster the balance sheet ahead of their title defence. That would give individuals their own stake in their club, but the disparate nature of that arrangement would offer supporters no real voice when it came to influencing matters at Ibrox.

There is an important difference between fan involvement and fan ownership. At a club the size of Rangers, it is wholly unrealistic to suggest that the supporters could effectively run the business on a daily basis and that has never been the ambition for Club 1872. Their model is one that seeks to represent rather than rule and Rangers would still be operated by the executive team that is now well established at Ibrox even if fans owned the major shareholding.

King expressed his belief that the directors would be open to having a Club 1872-appointed director on the board. While that individual would still be bound by the regulations and protocols of any plc, supporters would at least have their voice heard around the table for the first time. That shareholding and that ability will be, he hopes, King's final gift to his fellow fans.

Club 1872 set a target of increasing membership numbers to around 20,000 to ensure they can complete the purchase over the next three years. A 'legacy membership' donation of £500 could be paid as a one-off or in instalments in an attempt to raise the £13million required to purchase King's entire shareholding.

"That was his real focus, and we went back and forward a few times to discuss how we would raise the funds and make sure that the base of support was there," Graham said. "That was when we started to talk about the legacy idea so that there was always that base of thousands of fans who would contribute this one-off amount to buy them in the first place and then look after the shares.

"It went back and forward like that and then Covid intervened. We had an idea of launching around March time and then that was put back because we didn't know what would happen with Coronavirus and we decided to delay it until the summer.

"We were into season ticket time and there was that pull on people's money, so it went on from there until the actual launch and when we thought was the best time to present it to people. The discussions did go on for a long time."

It was in the days before the launch and the announcement that the latest accounts for RIFC plc were released. The AGM, so often one of the key dates of the campaign for Rangers, was held virtually on 15 December as Covid restrictions put paid to the usual gathering at the Clyde Auditorium in Glasgow.

Recent meetings had been polished and professional and a far cry from those held under the previous regime. One had famously been dubbed 'the winter of our discount tent' as the then board set up base camp in a tacky marquee on the pitch, but the distance between the stage and the supporters didn't protect them from unfriendly fire. It was an event that encapsulated an era and a time that is thankfully long gone at Ibrox.

The meetings at the Armadillo were far more serene and sedate affairs and the approval ratings for both boards could not have been more contrasting as Rangers returned towards something that resembled normality. King had announced his intention to step down on that very stage the previous year. There was an emotion in his voice as he spoke and the ovation he received from the floor was fitting given his efforts since returning as chairman and for some time before.

His replacement, businessman and motor mogul Douglas Park, has a very different persona and his address to shareholders to begin the 2020 meeting was brief. The King speeches were always detailed and lengthy, but this year it was John Bennett, the vice-chairman, who stepped forward to speak with real eloquence about where Rangers had been, where they were and where they are heading and those two numbers – a 55th title and the 150th anniversary – featured prominently.

There was no chance to gauge the mood of the room, of course, but there would have been few critical voices on the day. There were cautionary readings of the accounts as operating losses increased from £11.6million to £15.9million but an 11 per cent rise in revenue to £59million was indicative of the progress being made on and off the park. Covid had caused only part of the damage it could reap financially thus far and two factors – on-field success and the backing of supporters – were again crucial to Rangers as Europa League participation brought in £20.7million and season ticket and hospitality revenues increased by £1.2million and £0.7million respectively.

"Completely different personalities," Traynor said of King and Park. "If Dave thinks he is right and Douglas believes he is right, I'd say you would have longer to talk things through with Douglas than with Dave.

"Dave, when he believes he is right, doesn't waver. I am not saying he didn't take advice because he did, but when he believed, not only passionately believed but intellectually believed that he was right, that was it.

"I am not saying he is intellectually superior to Douglas. If you look at Douglas' business empire, my goodness that requires an intellect beyond us.

"But Dave's arguments were always immensely logical, profound and solid and you just wouldn't play poker with him. One of his strengths is that no matter the pressure he is under, even when the club were making bad appointments like managers or a manager bringing in the wrong player or money being squandered, he never once blinked.

"You never thought he was under pressure. Not once. You could look at some of the other directors and say 'they are struggling here, they are feeling this, they know this is wrong'. Not with Dave. Not once in all the crises that Rangers faced during that period did I see him flinch or waver or show any doubt or weakness.

"That is one of the remarkable things that I will always remember about Dave. Never showed a weakness, never showed anger, even though there were times he must have been seething inside at some of the things a manager or player or a director had said or done. He never showed it publicly. He just dealt with it.

"Even when Rangers were struggling and falling way behind in the title races the whole place just felt better and sharper when Dave King arrived. Unfortunately, he couldn't be in Glasgow often enough because of his business commitments in South Africa but the whole place just felt better, even when it wasn't going right on the pitch, when he was there."

In these joyous times that supporters are living today, it is easy to forget just how far Rangers have come at all levels in what is still a relatively short period. Just months after he returned to Ibrox, King signed off the 2015 annual report that showed revenue of only £16.5million and a loss of £9.9million and the financial gulf to Celtic was as cavernous as the sporting one. Neither could have been closed without the other thriving.

The deficits that have been run each season since regime change have been calculated risks and Rangers would not be in the position they are today without the goodwill and financial generosity of their investors. A further £23.6million worth of loans were provided to Rangers to the year end 30 June, 2020, while another £4.5million was signed off post year.

In total, the commitment from investors stood at £57million at that point and history should look upon those individuals extremely favourably indeed. Park and Bennett had played a crucial part in the process, while others such as George Letham and George Taylor had been hugely influential for some time. The likes of Julian Woldhardt and Barry Scott were more recent money men and Stuart Gibson, a Far East-based businessman, had come on board with a £5million cash injection in October.

None of that investment should be taken for granted and Rangers cannot be a hobby that supporters expect someone else to pay for. Each individual will have to determine in their own mind whether it has all been worth it but the reliance on external finance has to be lessened for Rangers over the coming seasons as they move towards self-sustainability. The years of reckless spending are over and there will be no bombast like that of the Murray era with claims of spending a tenner for every fiver that Celtic spent.

Rangers do not need to indulge in that kind of rhetoric these days in order to convince supporters to put their hands in their pockets. That process of handing over their hard-earned cash is still done with remarkable consistency and the manner in which fans have re-engaged with the club has been pivotal in terms of the growth of Rangers in a sporting and financial sense. Those same punters are now being asked to dig deep once again, but the cause is even more meaningful than the bottom line on season ticket sales or MyGers memberships.

"We are hoping to capitalise on that feelgood factor amongst the support and there is that sense of pride and achievement that we supported the club and rebuilt the club," Laura Fawkes, a Club 1872 director, said. "I don't mean Club 1872, although we have played a part in it, I mean the fans as a collective alongside the board, the players and staff.

"There is a sense of achievement and we are hoping that sense of achievement will instil a confidence in the Rangers support. If we have done that, if we have come back from the brink and achieved this 55th title, we can do anything we set our minds to.

"People across Scotland, the UK and the world were thinking that Rangers would never do it and that the club was ruined. But we have done it and that should give the Rangers support confidence that we can achieve significant fan representation and ownership.

"Dave has always been really clear on that and we have been looking back on old footage from years ago when Dave was talking about fan ownership. He was always very open and welcoming of Club 1872 and he is on the record saying that he couldn't have achieved what he did without the support of the fan groups.

"It wasn't Club 1872 at that time but this is where we are now on that journey. He has always been very supportive of the fans and acknowledged the part that the support played in it."

The deal with King is the second transformative arrangement that Fawkes has been involved in during her term on the Club 1872 board. A lifelong Rangers supporter, she has been a firm advocate of fan representation for many years and would join Club 1872 in 2016 following an initial involvement with the Trust and Rangers First when she raised concerns over The Offensive Behaviour at Football and Threatening Communications (Scotland) Act 2012.

The following year, Fawkes was part of the deal that saw Club 1872 purchase half of the shares owned by Mike Ashley through MASH Holdings Limited. The remainder were bought by Wolhardt as he came to the table for the first time and Rangers fans were the second-largest shareholders, behind King, in the summer of 2017.

The issues between Rangers and Ashley were not resolved there and then but the share sale was a retreat from a man who has forged, or perhaps bulldozed, his own path in business. Attempts to sell his controlling interest in Newcastle United have proven to be unsuccessful but Ashley's influence at Ibrox was very much on the wane in those days as King claimed a small but significant victory.

It was another piece of the jigsaw being put into place. King has been responsible for more segments than anyone else over time, but he was able to step down as chairman and step back from the board in March 2020 with the knowledge that his efforts hadn't gone to waste. King has always played the long game in business, in his high-profile litigation with the South African tax authorities and at Ibrox and foresaw that it was only a matter of when, not if, Rangers would be champions again.

"I knew this wasn't about a quick fix and move on and I know the extent to which Dave is still engaged in this," Fawkes said. "He keeps on top of everything and he wouldn't have stepped down when he did unless he felt Rangers were on the cusp of the title. He would have seen that as a project unfinished.

"I believe he stepped away at a time when he knew we were on the cusp of that and that is why he chose to come to us when he did and make the offer to pass the shares on. That is not some vague feeling that he had, that is based on all his experience at Rangers.

"I remember a reporter asking me a while ago if I thought the club would be in better shape if we had a hands-on chairman and not this absentee chairman. Dave was physically removed from Scotland, but he knew everything that was going on and was very much in control of what was going on.

"Based on that time as chairman, he had the real sense and confidence that we were going to achieve what he set out to achieve and that was stabilising the club and then winning 55. None of that would have been possible without him."

That opinion is shared by Traynor, yet he has to give credit to those that backed King emotionally and financially. Those key individuals were, of course, hugely significant, but the support of the Rangers fanbase was what really saved the club and ultimately allowed it to become the re-established force of today.

Traynor had spent a brief spell as director of communications during Charles Green's tenure but instead of finally getting the time to get closer to his own team, Airdrie, his focus would soon shift to ousting the Ibrox regime. Conversations with King convinced him to provide his assistance, while an e-mail from Park containing details of his financial commitment to the club demonstrated the strength of desire those two individuals had to make things right again at Rangers. More than a year would pass before their battle was won.

That time with King allowed Traynor to develop a relationship with him on a professional basis and friendship on personal terms. Few know him better and King is content to let others assess his contribution to the cause.

"In all my conversations with him he never once said anything that suggested he believed he had done more than anybody else, or that he was special in saving Rangers," Traynor said. "Not once. He was always hugely grateful to the supporters and those who backed him, like Douglas, like John Gilligan, like Paul Murray and George Letham and John Bennett. He was always grateful to them.

"He always put the fans first. I know that sounds like a dull cliché but he did. He couldn't have done it without them and he never lost sight of that truth. At the crack of dawn just about every morning when season tickets were up for sale he would look at the rising numbers and praise the supporters for their loyalty and belief. With him they came first and I must say the commitment they showed towards their club was remarkable. I believe it is unsurpassed and I just can't think of any club in this country that could attract such loyalty and sacrifice. What so many of them did to save their club should never be forgotten or downplayed."

Given what he invested into Rangers emotionally and financially, there could be feelings of regret on King's part that he had to watch a historic campaign from afar rather than being able to travel to Glasgow and really feel part of it. He has been separated from the city of his birth since the 1970s, but his head and heart have always been at Ibrox.

The list of villains in the Rangers tale makes for harrowing and chilling reading for supporters but those who ensured the story had a happy ending will forever be held in high esteem. Some had tried and failed but that wasn't an option for King, who felt at the time that the Scottish business community should have done more to force the changes he knew were necessary and was later successful in achieving.

Fans found themselves staring into the abyss, searching for information and hoping for salvation for so long. No other support has endured as much or shown such levels of loyalty. It can often be a bit clichéd and insincere when wins are dedicated to the fans, but that sentiment is certainly the case when it comes to Rangers.

"Ibrox was a special place to be at that time," Fawkes said. "It is engrained in Rangers fans and Walter Smith said that one word he associated with Rangers was winning. That is in your DNA as a fan, you expect to be winning titles. You had that, but you also had this uncertainty and there was a coming together, this knowledge that we were in a different place. I suppose it was getting in touch with who we were as a support. There was that feeling when you went back to Ibrox.

"It was this really interesting mix of emotions and attitudes and a coming together of the fanbase. It was a difficult time for the support, but it was special as well and there is this real feeling now that it has been worth it. That is a strange thing to say now because people ask if you could go back and change it, would you? It has been really unpleasant, of course.

"It has been bittersweet, but I think the pleasure that we get, the sense of satisfaction and the sense of pride that we get from winning 55, I am not sure that I would go back. There are aspects of it I would change, but I think the emotions right now make it worth it."

Football and life don't owe anyone anything, but those that made the dream a reality have earned their gratitude and ordinary supporters deserve their moments of euphoria. It was said that if Rangers played on the streets then they would support from the pavements and the sentiment is fitting. Society has seen the benefits of vaccinations in dealing with Coronavirus, but success was the ultimate drug for Rangers supporters as the pain of the last decade was flushed out of their system.

"Dave is right to give credit to other people because it was a group effort in terms of the finances, in terms of different people needing to buy the shares to force the EGM and move everything forward," Graham said. "It was a group effort. But there is absolutely no question in my mind that it wouldn't have happened if he wasn't involved.

"I don't think there was any one person who had enough profile with the support, enough gravitas and enough will to actually see it through if he hadn't have stepped up when he did. I just don't think it would have happened.

"There had been various attempts at it before from very well-intentioned people. Even guys like John Bennett who are now involved, he had been part of the Blue Knights, Paul Murray tried very hard to get the club back into the hands of the fans. That is to their credit, but it took somebody of Dave's wealth, but also experience and personality to get it over the line or it just wouldn't have happened.

"That is my feeling on it. When he became involved, it gave everyone a hope and a focal point that things were going to move forward. It had been quite disparate, there were a lot of people having different conversations, but he just grasped it and took it on and made it happen. I don't think it would have happened without Dave's involvement."

There are different parameters by which success can be judged in football. At Rangers, the main one has to be silverware and in that regard King ultimately failed. During his tenure on the board, he would only see Rangers lift the Petrofac Training Cup and the Championship in Mark Warburton's first season and the years following their return to the top flight were barren.

The success that Gerrard's side would go on to achieve this term would not have been possible without King, though. He may not have been chairman when the title was won but having reverted back to a role solely as a supporter in an emotional sense rather than a financial one, he would take as much pleasure and satisfaction as his fellow fan.

The announcement of his deal with Club 1872 began a month that brought a real low but also significant signs of promise. A 4-0 win away to Ross County was followed by a 2-0 victory in Poland as Lech Poznan were beaten, top spot in Group D was secured and Gerrard could add another achievement to his CV at Ibrox.

Ticking boxes is all fine and well, but it is winning trophies that matters most. Just a week later, that ambition was over for a seventh time as Rangers were beaten by St Mirren in the Betfred Cup. It was a result that few would have backed with the tournament sponsors as Gerrard gambled with his team selection and lost it all.

The previous weekend, Dundee United had been taken care of at Tannadice on a day that was notable for two moments. The first was a stunning free-kick from James Tavernier as he scored from around 30 yards to add to Connor Goldson's opener and give Rangers the cushion that would prove crucial in the end.

The second was an incident involving Alfredo Morelos that would see him suspended for the St Mirren match just days later. The Colombian's ill-discipline had cost Gerrard in previous seasons – most notably in the League Cup semi-final defeat to Aberdeen as Gerrard was left with only the hapless Umar Sadiq to play through the middle – and Morelos was absent as the Saints marched on to Hampden on a night where the wretched conditions mirrored Rangers' performance and mood.

Once again, the striker only had himself to blame. At first glance, his aerial duel with Mark Connolly looked borderline between yellow and red and referee Steven MacLean would book Morelos. Post-match, Gerrard insisted there was no elbow involved and a broadcast journalist was bizarrely banned from the following interview with Tavernier after rightly addressing the incident with Gerrard. Two days later, Rangers would accept a suspension after Morelos was issued with a Notice of Complaint by the Scottish FA.

Gerrard refused to be drawn in depth on the issue after the St Mirren game. To be fair, there were far more pressing matters at hand as Rangers suffered their first defeat of the season at the worst possible moment.

It was a classic cup tie, but a catastrophic one for Rangers. They were ahead through Goldson and then level with seconds to spare when Steven Davis equalised after two goals from Jamie McGrath. In a phase of play that mirrored the worst of his first two seasons, Gerrard's side couldn't manage the game and a Conor McCarthy winner in injury time signalled the end of their cup campaign.

The dust invariably settles but that process takes considerably longer where Rangers are involved. The emotions between the two respective camps could not have been more contrasting. As Jim Goodwin, the St Mirren manager, dared to dream of cup glory, Gerrard knew an opening had been slammed shut as Rangers failed to capitalise on Celtic's exit to Ross County in the previous round.

"To call it a crazy night would be respectful to us," Gerrard said. "Look, we haven't performed well and I'm responsible for that. I made all the decisions, the tactical and personnel, I tweaked certain things.

"This is one where I'll take the blame, I'm responsible for it all – because the players have been absolutely first class since the first day of pre-season. We've had an awful lot of praise as a group, defensively and offensively. But tonight we just weren't at it. And to concede the three goals in the manner that we did is obviously disappointing.

"But I'm responsible for it. So, we have to take what's going to come our way. It'll be a bit different for us, in terms of the season. I'll demand that we react in the right way. I'm bitterly disappointed because it's an opportunity missed.

"We can't allow the disappointment to spiral. At the moment emotions are running high, after a setback like this. But you have a choice in these situations. And you find out a lot about the group, about players.

"I know what I'll be doing. I'll be trying to react in a positive way. Of course it will sting. It will hurt. But it's my job to pick them up and make sure they go again."

There were moments in Gerrard's first two campaigns where he deviated from his own philosophy of not getting too high when Rangers win or too low when they lose. Given the pressure he was under and the way in which he is programmed – to always push, to always succeed – that was only natural, especially when you consider his relative inexperience as a manager.

That night was different, though. He seemed more hurt than angry and he was measured in the way he addressed the team selection and the performance. In the face of such crushing disappointments, it takes a certain kind of character to be able to pick themselves up, dust themselves down and go again the morning after the night before.

In this age of social media, breaking news and instant reaction, a calm and considered response can be hard to come by. The condemnation of the result was as vehement and intense as was to be expected from supporters and the concerns over the mentality of Gerrard's side came to the fore once again.

In many respects, they were fair. This was a team that had been nearly men too often over the previous two seasons, but the questions were answered emphatically on this occasion.

"I think it was inevitable because it had happened twice before in his first two seasons in charge and they were fair questions to ask,"

Andy Newport, a sportswriter from the PA Media Group, said. "At times, this team had proven that it can demolish the opposition in this league, it had proven it could go toe-to-toe with Celtic and come out on top and proven that it could get results in Europe.

"What it hadn't proven was that it had staying power and that it could go the season. When that happened, they were fair questions to be asked. But what I will say is that they came up with the answers pretty quickly and the game against Motherwell was a big one for them."

Gerrard wouldn't have been caught off guard or taken aback by the headlines that followed in the days after the St Mirren defeat. The analysis had to be condemnatory because of the manner of the loss but there was a sense of perspective as well and Gerrard has become increasingly adept at finding and conveying those messages, both in good times and bad.

He would take the hit for the result on that occasion. It wasn't the time, nor was there the need, to call out his players in public and Gerrard would carry the burden ahead of that Motherwell match that proved to be a defining one for Rangers.

"At the end of the day, he is responsible and he picks the team and at that point Rangers were two wins away from a cup final and three from his first trophy," Newport said. "There would have been fans thinking 'name the strongest team, get the trophy in the bag', but he has obviously got a bigger picture and he needed to see the title out.

"Gerrard would have backed those guys to perform. The buck stops with him but I think he was maybe trying to shield the players. The players hadn't let him down, it was one blip. Yes, it came at the worst possible time and at that time they could probably have afforded to lose a league game rather than a cup game and still got what they wanted out of the season.

"It is just unfortunate that it has come at the point where it cost them a trophy. The players, the way they had performed to that stage, that night has to be forgiven because the way they recovered from the lows of last season and kicked on and became this formidable side is very impressive. I think it was only fair that he took the blame for that one given that the players hadn't let him down at any other stage through the season."

The old saying regarding the next game being the most important one has been repeated ad nauseam in pre-match press conferences and post-game interviews once again this season, and not just at Rangers. At that time, though, there was a feeling that the match with Motherwell could make or break the campaign for Gerrard. The cliché in that moment carried real weight.

The wounds of previous failures may have healed, but supporters still had the scars of seeing two promising seasons crumble in similar ways. There had been a renewed optimism and drive around Rangers since the start of the campaign and the days after the defeat to St Mirren would determine if this was a squad that had the mark of champions.

Had Ibrox been full, it would undoubtedly have been on edge. When Callum Lang gave Motherwell the lead six minutes in, the pressure from the stands would have gripped and squeezed like a vice in the minds of Gerrard's players.

With no boos at half-time, no growls that could become howls, Rangers could stick to their task free from increased demands and two goals from Kemar Roofe either side of an effort from Cedric Itten won it. Motherwell had set up with two banks of five in an attempt to stifle and frustrate Rangers, but Gerrard's side found a way to earn a victory that assumed more significance than just three points.

That afternoon was telling for Rangers. Another 1-0 win over Hibernian the following week was a sign that they had a resolve about them at long last and victories against St Johnstone and St Mirren either side of that afternoon at Ibrox ensured the momentum that had been built prior to the Betfred Cup defeat wasn't shattered by one result.

The win at McDiarmid Park was the pick of the three in terms of the performance as goals from Roofe, Glen Kamara and Ianis Hagi earned a comfortable, controlled victory. It was an eleventh successive league win as Gerrard's side maintained their 16-point lead over Celtic and the decisive Old Firm fixture at Ibrox was now looming large.

Rangers had become a team of several faces. The narrow 1-0 wins could be fought and scrapped for, while on their day they were able to operate with an elegance that was so far above the level of their opposition. Nothing, of course, is won at Christmas, but Gerrard's side were showing that they could have the title wrapped up by Easter.

"The Motherwell game was a big test of character and everyone was thinking back to the last two seasons and the slip-ups that occurred around that time of the season," Newport said. "People were thinking, 'Is this the start of another wobble that could allow Celtic back into the title race?' They found themselves a goal down to Motherwell and the way that they dug out that result was so impressive.

"That was a point in years gone by where they might have cracked but they stayed so calm, they stuck to their plan and moved the ball wide, moved it into space and didn't get desperate. They got their rewards with three goals in the last 15 minutes and that allowed them to kick on leading into January where they only dropped two points from a run that included an Old Firm game and trips to Pittodrie and Easter Road.

"That was a testament to the fortitude that this team has got, but the result against St Mirren did give them a kick up the backside, if you like, and a reminder that there was still work to be done. They lost the chance of a Treble but part of me thinks it is too early for this team to be doing things like that. They are still developing, they are still improving and as impressive as they have been this season there is still more to go. Getting the league was the most important ambition for them this season and that is what they will be remembered for ultimately."

Rangers were a side that were ready to win something, but not win it all. While they were proving themselves as likely champions in the not-too-distant future, Celtic were savouring triumphs from last season as victory over Hearts secured the 2019/20 Scottish Cup and a fourth successive Treble. The last 12 trophies available in Scottish football had resided at Parkhead, but the next one is always the most important one.

As Celtic fans took to the streets and the car park to demand the sacking of Neil Lennon and the removal of chief executive Peter Lawwell and Dermot Desmond, the major shareholder, Rangers kept calm and carried on. The Celtic fans that broke Covid regulations and defied pleas to stay at home were powerless to force change and the way in which the momentum and power shifted across Glasgow was extraordinary.

There are lessons to be taken for both sets of supporters here. For nine years and a historic haul of trophies, the Celtic hierarchy could do no wrong. But by the time the tables had turned, the people who paid their wages had no influence to show for their backing and that is why the deal that King laid out with Club 1872 was so important for Rangers.

This season was all about the present but as Rangers look to the future, the past cannot be forgotten. Nothing lasts forever. No group of fans should be more aware of that and more mindful than those that endured for so long but that now enjoy these glorious times thanks to the efforts of so many.

Supporters will be eternally grateful to the current Ibrox board and those who view themselves as custodians of the club, but that doesn't mean that the status quo will remain and the fanbase know to their cost how quickly things can turn when your destiny is taken out of your hands. One seat in the boardroom can be more powerful than 50,000 in the stands and those that fill them now have the chance that their Old Firm rivals could only dream of.

The focus has rightly been on title 55 and where Rangers are heading. But it would be negligent and reckless to forget where the club and the support have been. Events on the park through December shaped the immediate future, but it was the one right at the start of the month that was truly momentous.

King had famously spoken about Celtic's position being like a 'pack of cards' three years previously. Those at that briefing inside the Members Lounge at Ibrox left with their dictaphones full and their back pages taken care of and King, as usual, made for thought-provoking and debate-inspiring content.

His detractors would foolishly mock the man rather than analyse his message but even he couldn't have envisaged the rate at which Celtic would spectacularly implode. The self-entitlement from supporters was staggering as they realised that 'The Ten' wouldn't be won and the achievement they had spent so long talking up and using to disparage Rangers would be denied by the very club many insisted would never be a threat to their dominance.

Rangers fans were entitled to enjoy the fall-out. What a refreshing change it was to be on the other side of the story. After a decade of share announcements and court cases, a time where financial results carried as much weight as sporting ones, these were joyous weeks for a support who could focus on the football, a love of the game and of their club. Two opportunities were now within their grasp.

EIGHT

IT IS said that football is the most important of the least important things in life. It matters, of course it does, but only in context and perspective. A reminder of that can often be welcome and useful and one is provided every January for Rangers supporters as they commemorate Absent Friends.

The last decade has undoubtedly been tumultuous and harrowing for fans to live through but they are not the darkest times in their club's history. Rangers have suffered on and off the park but their trials and tribulations in a sporting and business sense are incomparable to the weeks that followed the Ibrox Disaster and the loss felt 50 years on puts recent hardships in an alternative light. It is easy to get caught up in the emotion and lexicon of the game, but there must always be a reminder of the true tragedies that unfold around us and that has been felt as deeply as ever during a pandemic that would change and take too many lives.

The build-up to the Old Firm fixture in January was typically feverish from press and punters alike and the significance of the contest in terms of the title race could not be downplayed. Yet there was a more sombre tone to the coverage in the days ahead of the New Year meeting and a very different feeling around Ibrox in the hours before kick-off.

The absence of supporters played a part in that, of course. On a crisp morning in Glasgow as the winter sun bathed the iconic red brick in a warming glow, there was no sense of excitement or tension in the air and the crowds that gathered were there to pay their respects rather than support their team. An occasion that was so important to Rangers' future was put into context by its past.

It was on that day in 1971 that 66 supporters lost their lives in the Ibrox Disaster following a crush on Stairway 13. A 1-1 Old Firm fixture was nondescript as Colin Stein equalised in the final seconds after Jimmy Johnstone looked to have won it for Celtic. Had fate not played its hand, the derby draw would have been lost in the mists of time.

Instead, the fog that enveloped Ibrox as darkness fell would be the backdrop to events on a scale that hadn't been seen before in British football. Until the Hillsborough Disaster in 1989, the accident on Stairway 13 was the worst loss of life in a stadium on these shores.

The thought that anyone could go to a football match and not return home is difficult to comprehend, especially today given the safety of our stadia and the security operations that are in place whether the crowd is 500 or 50,000. The game can provide so many moments of sheer adulation but those of tragedy resonate even more strongly and unite supporters no matter the colour of their scarves.

The recollections of Ibrox, Heysel and Hillsborough are very different for Derek Pickup. He will never forget, though, and he remembers to this day. His cousin, Nigel, was the youngest victim of the Ibrox Disaster. In a tragic twist of fate, Derek was present when 39 Juventus fans were killed at the 1985 European

Cup final and he would survive the crush in the Leppings Lane end four years later as Liverpool lost the 96.

Pickup mourns the deaths, each one so heart-breaking and cruel, no matter the time that has passed. As he consoles his mother, Dorothy, he can only admire her strength of character to deal with the pain and the worry on each occasion.

It was young Nigel, just eight years old and attending his first ever match, that was at the forefront of their thoughts in January as Rangers supporters and the survivors remembered those that went to a game and never returned. It is a cruel destiny that Derek is all too familiar with.

"My mother is exceptional, she is 87 and still got her faculties," Pickup told me in an interview for the *Herald* and *Glasgow Times* that was published on the weekend of the anniversary. "But her life has just been tainted and marked by football tragedies and losing people at football. When we lost Nigel in '71, it had such a massive impact on the family. Nigel is buried with my dad, my uncle and my grandparents.

"I went to Heysel in '85 and Hillsborough in '89. After Heysel, my mum said I was never going to another football match. We had lost Nigel and she said I wasn't going again.

"I used to be in the Merchant Navy and when I was home on leave, I used to go to whatever games I could. I was stuck behind the goals at Hillsborough. Jon-Paul Gilhooley, the youngest victim at Hillsborough, he lived 12 doors down from my mother. She has had so much involvement with football tragedies, there is probably nobody else on the planet who has had to deal with what she has.

"At Heysel, we didn't have phones and at Hillsborough we didn't have phones so my mum was watching it on the telly and didn't know what the outcome was going to be."

It is perhaps natural given the differences in time and circumstances that the Ibrox Disaster doesn't have the profile of those events at Hillsborough, but the lives lost and touched by the tragedy remain just as worthy to remember. The disaster is as important a part of Rangers' history as its most famous players and celebrated triumphs and while the coverage made for uncomfortable reading and viewing, it is essential that supporters of today understand and appreciate the events of yesteryear.

Many would find it hard to comprehend and the personal recollections emphasise the grief as well as the fear as survivors talk about the life being squeezed out of them, only to be saved with seconds to spare. Steven Gerrard would need no briefing into the impact that such devastating days have on clubs, communities and families and the Liverpool legend spoke from the heart as his pre-match press conference naturally switched between past and present matters.

When Gilhooley was killed at Hillsborough, the man who would go on to captain the Reds lost his cousin. Five decades on, another link between Merseyside and Glasgow was strengthened as Pickup arranged for flowers to be laid at the statue of John Greig that stands as a tribute to the 66 at the corner of the Main Stand and Copland Stand.

Front and centre of the red, white and blue-dominated display was one with the letters 'LFC'. Facing out onto Edmiston Drive was a photograph of Nigel and his father, Joey. Nigel would spend New Year in Scotland and travel to Ibrox with a family friend. The 1-1 draw between Rangers and Celtic would be the first and last game he would ever see.

"Nigel, it was his first ever football match," Pickup said. "Eight years of age and he never came back. You couldn't make it up, it is such a sad, sad story.

"He was a Liverpool lad, but because he emigrated to Canada a lot of people on Merseyside didn't make the link and they didn't realise. He was the initial link between the two clubs and Nigel's tragic story will never be forgotten.

"You just think of the excitement on his face at eight years of age. Someone says they have got you a ticket for an Old Firm game, you are going to your first ever game. The feelings for him must have been immense, but he would never come back. Jon-Paul was ten when he went to an FA Cup semi-final and he never came back. It is just so, so sad and both lads will always be remembered."

Ten years previously, Greig and legendary Celtic captain Billy McNeill had laid wreaths as an Old Firm encounter at Ibrox marked the 40th anniversary of the disaster. Plans for a fuller ceremony, similar to the one which was held in Glasgow in the aftermath of the tragedy, had to be postponed due to Covid restrictions and the array of flowers, cards and tributes at the foot of the Greig statue was significantly smaller than it would have been had supporters been able to pay their respects in the manner in which they wished.

Some survivors still find it difficult to talk about those fateful moments and the stories of those that are able to put the pictures into words are chilling to hear.

The opportunity to work with Derek Johnstone on his column for the *Glasgow Times* was a personal and professional privilege and a Rangers legend has become a friend over more than a decade of covering every high and low along the way at Ibrox.

One conversation just before Christmas was different, though, as DJ recalled his memories of 2 January 1971. Months earlier, he had written his name in Rangers folklore as, aged just 16, he scored the winning goal in the League Cup final against Celtic. It was the start of a career that would see Johnstone become a Gers great. He would win the European Cup Winners' Cup in 1972 and two Trebles under the guidance of Jock Wallace and has served as a club ambassador alongside his extensive media work in print and on the airwaves.

The story of his Hampden winner was a remarkable one that is unlikely to ever be matched but another Old Firm encounter provokes very different memories. DJ had returned up the tunnel that day ultimately satisfied with a point from the derby. As he replayed the action in his mind whilst submerged in one of the deep baths that dominated that section of the dressing room, the commotion outside grew louder as sirens wailed and vehicles negotiated their way through the crowds on Edmiston Drive.

Johnstone was on the end of a quip from Greig as he asked 'have you not got a home to go to?' after the Rangers captain had received treatment in the physio room. When Greig returned, his manner was far more serious as the scale of the devastation just yards away began to hit home.

"I went through the door into the dressing room and on the floor on the left-hand side there were five or six black bags," Johnstone said. "The door opened and an ambulanceman came in and said he didn't realise there was anyone still in. He told me it was madness out there and to get myself away.

"I asked what was going on and he explained what had happened and that the supporters had been crushed. As he is telling me this, on the floor in the dressing room is the black bags covering the poor people that had died. It was horrific and they kept bringing bodies in as I was getting changed."

By the time manager Willie Waddell reaffirmed Greig's message to get himself home, the death toll had sadly risen. As DJ approached the touchline, a glance to his right brought into view the scores of bodies lined up side-by-side and the efforts to save those that had been pulled from the mangled barriers that had collapsed under the weight of thousands of supporters.

Unable to get a taxi and with the queues for the subway far busier than usual that long after the whistle, Johnstone would end up walking along Paisley Road West to return to the city centre. The death toll has as profound an effect on Johnstone today as it did the moment that he saw the newsflashes and he would return to his family to seek solace and comfort.

"It hit me that hard that I went home to Dundee," Johnstone said. "I had only just turned 17 in the November and I didn't want to be in Glasgow on my own that night so I got the train back to Dundee and went home. My mum didn't know anything about it. She hadn't seen it and my brothers had been out, so it was only when the news came on later and the pictures came through that they saw the tragedy that had unfolded."

There is a heart-breaking story behind each of the victims and a tale of survival related to those that were hospitalised or emerged from the chaos and confusion. The passing of time hasn't diminished the grief for those that lost fathers and sons, uncles and nephews. One family would lose a daughter and a sister.

Margaret Ferguson was the only female victim of the Ibrox Disaster. Aged just 18, she had been told not to travel to Ibrox by her father and, after leaving the family home in Falkirk, she would never return.

Just weeks earlier, she had chapped the door of Stein to hand over a teddy bear for his newly-born daughter, Nicola. To Margaret, Stein was a hero for the club that she adored and the Barcelona Bear would later attend her funeral as Rangers ensured that they were represented at every service to pay their respects.

At just 17, it was a heavy burden to place on Johnstone's shoulders. Indeed, he was only a couple of years older than the five from Markinch that travelled together and died together. The losses of Bryan Todd, Ronald Paton, Peter Easton, Mason Philip and Douglas Morrison would shatter a Fife village and three of their Celtic-supporting schoolfriends would return home oblivious of their deaths after watching the match from the Broomloan Road end of Ibrox. The Old Firm were united in grief in the days after the disaster and they would again come together on the 50th anniversary as both clubs paid floral and heartfelt tributes to the 66 and the scores that were injured.

"All the players were given areas, like Greigy and Sandy Jardine in Edinburgh," Johnstone said. "There was nobody from Dundee but I was in Fife and went to the funerals of the five lads from Markinch. They were all from the same school, they played for the same team and they came through on the supporters' bus. They were only a couple of years younger than I was.

"The turnout that day was incredible, the streets were so crowded and it was such a sad day. I remember speaking to Greigy and was telling him how bad I felt and that I couldn't sleep, and he said to just think of the parents of those kids, of the brothers and sisters, the aunts and uncles and the grandparents of those five lads and of everyone that lost someone in the disaster. That sticks with me to this day.

"Some of the stories we had were terrifying to hear but the supporters were so glad to see us and we just had to do anything we could to help them get through it. It was a duty, it was us being part of the Rangers Family. These fans had given up their time and their money to come and watch us, so it was only right that we paid our respects to those that died and visited those that were in hospital."

Out of the darkness of the disaster, a new, modern Ibrox was built. Today it stands as a symbol of the club and a tribute to those that died on its vast terraces that swayed and sung in unison and support. The project to redevelop the stadium was driven by Waddell but it would be decades later before the safety of supporters was given due care and attention across the United Kingdom. By that time, tragedy had struck at Hillsborough and the Taylor Report would bring about long overdue structural and procedural changes that modern day fans perhaps take for granted.

This extraordinary season played behind closed doors has only emphasised how important football is in a social sense in

Scotland and the game continues to inspire, to offer an escape. Whenever fans next step foot inside their stadium, they should not take the surrounds for granted and Ibrox, like Anfield, will always remember those lost doing what they loved.

Had fate dealt him a different hand, Pickup could have suffered the same outcome as Gilhooley, who was the older cousin of Gerrard and from the same Huyton estate in Liverpool, on that harrowing afternoon at Hillsborough. There is an emotional tremble in his voice as the recollections from that day are recovered from the depths of his memory.

His first instinct – as it was at Heysel four years earlier as he spent the night in an Amsterdam train station – was to phone home and to let his mother know that he was safe. All of those that Pickup travelled to Sheffield with would make it back safely eventually. One was found out in the city, another walking on the M62 as the scale of the tragedy took hold.

"My mother has been gripped by football tragedies for years and I will never forget that day at Hillsborough," Pickup said. "I remember walking back up the hill going back to our cars, we didn't have mobile phones, and there were two telephone boxes. One was coins and one was cards and every time you walked by the cars it was 10 dead, 20 dead, 30 dead, 40 dead and we were all an emotional wreck.

"Nobody was using the booths for the cards, everyone was using the coins trying to phone home. I picked the phone up, reversed the charges, and my mother just went 'oh, God'. I said 'I am alright' and then I shouted to the other lads to use that booth, reverse the charges and phone home. We waited around for hours afterwards. There were 16 of us that went in a van and 13 came back, but the other three lads went astray. It was a sad, sad day."

It was on the 20th anniversary of Hillsborough that Pickup thought it was time to alert the Merseyside public to the loss of another one of their sons in a football tragedy. The story of Nigel's death resonates just as strongly in Glasgow and a group of Rangers fans would travel south to place a commemorative plaque on his grave at Yew Tree Cemetery in Huyton a decade ago.

His father Joey now lives in a care home in Toronto. On his 80th birthday, Derek made the journey across the Atlantic to gift a signed Liverpool shirt. It was fitting that the 50th anniversary of the Ibrox Disaster was marked by an Old Firm fixture as both clubs united in commemoration of the 66 that were killed and the almost 200 that were injured on Stairway 13.

A banner in honour of the victims of Hillsborough and Ibrox was also on display. At a time of isolation, the Rangers Family was together in spirit that afternoon. As Rangers remembered, those bonds broken in death half a century ago were stronger than ever in the minds of those who will never forget Ibrox.

"I phoned Radio Merseyside and they had me on," Pickup said. "They said that they were unaware of Nigel, they didn't have any clue that he was the Liverpool link to Ibrox and the youngest to pass away in a football disaster.

"I always thought that Ibrox was a forgotten disaster and I said that on the radio, that there was a generation of people who didn't know anything about Ibrox. They think of Bradford, Heysel and Hillsborough as the three tragedies.

"I got a few calls from Rangers fans and a few lads phoned me about a year later and said they wanted to put a plaque on Nigel's grave on behalf of Rangers fans worldwide. I couldn't believe it, it was fantastic. Those lads came down and put that plaque on Nigel's grave.

"The Scottish lads said that Rangers didn't do anything for the disaster for 30-odd years and it was somewhat overlooked. We have the Hillsborough Flame at Anfield but Ibrox, for some reason, never really got due recognition for so long.

"Nigel's dad Joey was brought up in Huyton, just a mile away from where Steven Gerrard was brought up. All the brothers were brought up in the area where Gerrard is from. His dad used to drink in the local club and the manager of the club used to give Joey his tickets. Maybe Steven doesn't even realise how close the links are."

Like Liverpool had to in the aftermath of Hillsborough or Bradford following the dreadful fire at Valley Parade that killed 56, Rangers had to move on and get back playing football. Within 18 months, the club had won its most illustrious crown as Dynamo Moscow were beaten in the Nou Camp and the European Cup Winners' Cup was lifted.

The squad that played that fateful day at Ibrox was tight-knit and remained together for many years. They would savour the triumphs that would follow in their careers but never forget those who paid the ultimate price whilst watching them in action.

"It wasn't great, it wasn't great," Johnstone said of the weeks after the disaster as Rangers returned to action. "Usually the dressing room is full of laughter and pranks, but there was nothing like that and it was just so quiet between the lads and in training. We just had to get on with it, but it took a toll and nobody will ever forget it. Football went on and we just had to do what we could for the victims, the survivors and the fans.

"You think back and wonder what life would have been like for those that died. They never got the chance to grow old, some never got the chance to have a family and take their kids to Ibrox. Their families have been grieving all this time.

"Every year they will have gone to the cemetery or the statue at Ibrox and remembered. It is something I will never forget, the families will never forget and Rangers and the supporters will never forget."

It is so often the situation that adversity brings out the best in people and that is the case when it comes to the Old Firm. It is a rivalry that is unique – one that is a concoction of sporting animosity, politics, history and religion – yet one which captivates like no other. On that day, there was decency and decorum that was befitting of the anniversary but the competition on the park would then take centre-stage.

Neither support may like the fact, but both clubs need each other to drive them on and challenge them. The allegation towards the Celtic board this season is that they have been complacent and under-estimated the fight that would come from Rangers. They have been accused by their own fans of self-inflicting the wounds which have denied them ten-in-a-row and the pressure on manager Neil Lennon going into the Old Firm encounter was fierce. It was even worse after a 1-0 defeat that all-but ended their chances of winning the title.

It was a tale of two McGregors. Rangers keeper Allan produced a Man of the Match performance and namesake Callum, the Celtic midfielder and captain for the day, scored the own goal that left Lennon's side 19 points adrift at the top of the table. The fact that they had three games in hand offered faint hope, but that solace was found only in the minds of the overly optimistic. The title race was over.

The criticism of the Rangers performance afterwards was well founded. This wasn't the controlled, swaggering showing of October but once again Gerrard's side proved that they could win in different ways. This one had the hallmarks of the nineties about it.

There were times during their own run to nine-in-a-row under Walter Smith that Rangers had to rely on the excellence of their goalkeeper to win big games. Andy Goram would be the scourge of Celtic and the highlights reel from his saves in the derbies alone makes for extraordinary viewing as he earned the reputation as the best keeper in the club's history.

Rangers have always been blessed in that department. Chris Woods preceded Goram at Ibrox, while Stefan Klos would later follow. When it was time for McGregor to stake his claim, he grabbed it with the authority which he now shows between the sticks. Had he not returned to Ibrox in the summer of 2018, he would have been viewed with real affection by supporters. Now he is the best goalie since The Goalie.

A handful of saves early on at Ibrox – including one world class stop to deny Leigh Griffiths – kept Rangers in it as Gerrard's side struggled to assert themselves and find any rhythm. When Callum McGregor inadvertently diverted a corner into his own net with 20 minutes remaining, the game and the title were gone for Celtic and won by Rangers.

"He is up there with the best of them," Jim Stewart, the former Rangers goalkeeper and coach, said of McGregor. "Someone asked me not long ago about the comparison between him and Andy Goram and, for me, he is on a par with Andy Goram. I know a lot of Rangers supporters will argue the toss over that.

"Allan did his bit previously, left for well-documented reasons and then got the chance to come back to the club. He could quite easily have had an easy life and seen out his career somewhere, but he decided he wanted to come back because he still felt that he had something to give the club and an in-built desire to win things again. That is one of the things that drives him on and he obviously felt that he had unfinished business with Rangers."

The four years that Stewart spent at Ibrox as a player were relatively barren for Rangers as Greig and then the returning Wallace struggled to contend with the old challenge of Celtic and the emergence of the New Firm in Aberdeen and Dundee United. His time at Ibrox as a coach was very different, however, and he played his part in the final successes that Rangers would enjoy before their downfall.

Throughout those silverware-laden seasons with Smith at the helm, McGregor was a dominant presence on and off the park. Since his return, his importance in both regards has grown exponentially and he is a player that leads by example and that inspires those around him with his words as well as his actions.

The saves in the Old Firm game stand out due to the high-profile nature of the match and the importance of the win but such moments permeate the campaign. McGregor's position as number one was briefly challenged by Jon McLaughlin at the start of the season but it is his place amongst the legends that has been secured in the months since.

"That is not a negative to Andy at all that people are having that debate," Stewart, the father of current Rangers keeper coach Colin, said. "When you look back at his Rangers career, he had periods where he was absolutely unbeatable and he was at a level where he was contributing to the fact that Rangers were the top team in the country. His level of performance for many seasons was just incredible.

"Allan is the same at the moment and when you look at the Old Firm game, he wasn't overworked, but the saves that he did have to make went a long way to Rangers winning that day. He gave them a platform to come through the stages where it was awkward for them and they won the game."

The place that McGregor now holds in the hearts of supporters and amongst the pantheon of Ibrox greats has been hard earned. In 2009, it looked as though his Rangers career was over and he wouldn't get to toast the triumphs that he has after the infamous 'Boozegate' affair on Scotland duty.

The first mistake that McGregor and Barry Ferguson made was to indulge in a lengthy drinking session at Cameron House following Scotland's return from a World Cup qualifier in Holland. The biggest one was to ignore the message from Smith to accept their punishment.

The images of the pair making V signs on the bench against Iceland days later must still embarrass them to this day. Time won't diminish the shame, but it has had an effect on McGregor and boss Gerrard now speaks of him as being amongst the best professionals he has worked with during his career.

From such lows, it is remarkable that the keeper has scaled the heights he has. He was told he would never play for Rangers again, but now his importance cannot be questioned.

His early years in the first team saw him make front page headlines as often as back page ones. The stories of celebrity scandal made for prime tabloid copy and McGregor rarely speaks to newspaper journalists even all these years on. The writers that he snubs were not responsible for penning and splashing the tales from his youth, but they have had ample reason to praise his performances and professionalism once again this season.

"I think it is a testament to him to come back and play again at this level," Stewart said. "He has always been the type of person that looked after himself, although some people think differently. He is the first into the building doing his work and that hasn't changed from the first time that he was there as a younger player.

"It is testament to the coaches there and obviously his desire to become a top player. He has realised what he had to do to maintain that level and he is still doing the same things.

"He was fully committed. He did things and you were thinking 'what reaction are we going to get?' after something made the press. But Allan's preparations and performances were never affected, and you wouldn't say 'he lost a poor goal because of the headlines in the press'. He had an ability to shut exterior things out and focus on the game and when you look at him now he has certainly maintained that level of focus when it comes to preparing for matches."

There have been various moments throughout the campaign where Gerrard has had the opportunity to lavish praise and plaudits onto McGregor. They will be taken with gratitude by the man himself, yet his mentality is such that personal rewards mean nothing without team triumphs.

That mischievous side to his character remains, too. After finding himself cited and retrospectively punished by the Scottish FA, McGregor used his time in the stands to email the Compliance Officer with a list of incidents that he witnessed whilst watching Gerrard's side in action. His point was made and a request soon arrived at Ibrox from Hampden to ask the keeper to desist as he became a one-man complaints logging machine.

Many players speak of a winning mentality, but McGregor's actions prove what makes him tick and the empty grounds have given those privileged enough to be there many an opportunity to laugh at the way in which the keeper roars at defenders or lambasts referees. He is older and wiser, but certainly not calmer.

"He will always say that the next victory is the most important victory and the things that he has done previously are there and now on the back-burner," Stewart said. "His desire to be in a team that wins a championship again has been uppermost in his mind. He clearly wanted to come back and help Rangers win the title again and you have to say he has been such an important part of that. His performances have been excellent, but the standards that he has will have helped the squad throughout the season. He will celebrate winning it, but as soon as the final whistle goes he is onto the next challenge and looking at the next thing to win."

Once the title had been secured, McGregor's focus would shift to safeguarding his own future. Gerrard had expressed his hope that the keeper would extend his stay at Ibrox for another season and the news he and supporters had waited anxiously for arrived in early April.

"It was monumental," McGregor said in an interview with RangersTV as his new contract was confirmed and he reflected on the title win. "Obviously I know a lot of Rangers fans all over the world and just what it means to them over the last long period of time not to have won anything.

"To me as well and all the boys in here, I know what it meant to them, and the manager and all the staff and everybody in the club. It was a massive occasion. It didn't give me a new hunger, I have always been hungry.

"I thought about that day for the last two-and-a-half or three years. It has maybe overtaken my life a wee bit and I thought about it too much actually. I don't know if that is healthy or not. But we have done it and it was a special occasion."

The days and weeks after the Old Firm win saw Rangers do their best to play down their impending title success and Celtic do their utmost to blow their chances of making Gerrard's side sweat. The ill-fated and ill-conceived trip to Dubai didn't help their cause and a record that saw them win just once in January ultimately ended their ten-in-a-row ambitions.

In contrast, Rangers had the mark of champions about them. Two points were dropped away to Motherwell in the middle of the month, but they would matter little in the grand scheme of things. A Cedric Itten equaliser preserved their unbeaten run on a day where the performance was mixed and the end goal almost unavoidable to speak about.

"It's going to be a challenge because the reality is there are big prizes to play for," Gerrard said. "It's impossible not to realise where we are as a group and what's at stake. But it's important that we stay focused and don't get ahead of ourselves and stay focused on each challenge. That's where we are trying to keep the boys in terms of their thinking and the preparation.

"After a fantastic win no one's getting too high and if we have a bump or don't get the result we want it's important to stay calm. We haven't managed to stretch our lead today but at the same time we haven't lost anything either. You've seen two sides of us today, a first half showing that wasn't us and wasn't good enough but the second half was an awful lot better."

Gerrard had his players almost programmed to repeat the 'one game at a time' mantra. It might not have made for blockbuster press conferences, but the message had stood Rangers in good stead and it was understandable why the mindset was so important.

Had Rangers stumbled at Pittodrie the weekend after their Old Firm win, the questions over their mentality would have returned once again. Rangers had been here before and beaten Celtic only to crumble in the weeks that followed and that was now their challenge to overcome. Rangers wouldn't falter and Gerrard was destined to take his place amongst the Ibrox greats.

"Most of the people watching football just now couldn't go back as far as Symon and Waddell and then on to Wallace," Jim Traynor, formerly of *The Herald* and *Daily Record*, said. "Their places are secured in Rangers' history and the Scottish football story book. Souness was a remarkable turning point for Rangers and Scottish football, and Walter Smith? Outstanding. You only have to look at the way he conducted himself, what he achieved in both stints and especially in the second as Rangers were under siege and buckling, yet he won the league and got to the UEFA Cup final. That was astonishing.

"Steven Gerrard is not up there with them yet but he has taken a massive step, what a massive step, in his first three years. He will deserve his place in Rangers' folklore as well, because he stopped ten-in-a-row.

"Now, you can argue if this ten would have been a legitimate one all season long if you wish but the record books will show they had nine titles. Celtic had no genuine opposition for a number of those titles and even when Rangers were back in the top division they were still lame. They were way behind in terms of the development of their players and the finances available.

You can argue until the end of time whether those nine titles were legitimate, but the record books show they won nine, even if a number of them were what could be described as 'extremely soft' victories.

"What no one can argue against is that Steven Gerrard deserves his place because stopping ten is a momentous achievement. So, of course he deserves his place in Rangers' history and all the glowing praise showered upon him."

The Motherwell match would be the only points that were squandered in a five-game sequence. Potentially difficult tests at Aberdeen and Hibernian were overcome, although the win at Easter Road would be at a cost as Alfredo Morelos was subsequently given a three-game suspension for a stamp on Ryan Porteous, the Hibernian defender. The needless actions of Morelos courted more controversy, but the valid and long-standing concerns that Rangers had over the process would later come to the fore once again.

The other match in the month was a 5-0 home win over Ross County. It wasn't just the most emphatic victory of that run, it was by some distance the most assured performance and the margin should have been greater. Rangers wouldn't be as free-flowing as that for some time but the points were all that mattered as the wins were racked up relentlessly.

It was clear that the only thing that could stop Rangers this season was Rangers. There had undoubtedly been further evolution in the side tactically and technically, but the mentality that was forged in the summer was now shining through. Rangers had long looked like a very different proposition and emerging stronger from January than ever before was an ominous sign for a Celtic side waiting for a collapse that would never come.

There was an attitude about the way in which Gerrard played the game with Liverpool and England and he needed his players to harness those same characteristics now that he was a manager.

For Dr Robbie Anderson, a managing director with Chimp Management and a member of the British Psychological Society, the focus on mental gains cannot be overlooked. Anderson has worked with Olympic athletes and oversaw psychology for England Rugby's National Performance Programme, preparing players for the 2019 World Cup.

"Sport is a performance industry, so top teams will therefore look at all the factors that contribute to performance," Anderson said. "Over the period of modern professionalism, sports have explored the physical conditioning of athletes, nutrition became a massive factor, so why wouldn't you work on something as powerful as the mind?

"What you see is a lot of sports saying, 'If we are going to cover all the bases and give ourselves the best chance, why wouldn't we invest in psychology?' You could list the pressures that exist for any top professional, not just in sport, to meet the demands of their role. But when you put that into something like football, when you ordinarily have thousands of people watching you perform and then social media too, you can appreciate there is a performance psychology aspect to cover, but also just a need to keep this human in a great place. I think those two things are really pushing together now, for the right reasons. There is more willingness to address psychology in sport."

Before a ball was kicked in the Old Firm game, Rangers knew the opportunity that lay ahead of them over the next four weeks. Come the final whistle at Easter Road, they had seized the moment and maintained the momentum and the countdown was now on to the title as potential dates for the party were circled on calendars.

There were many contributing factors to the failings of Gerrard's side in the first two seasons but the manner in which the initiative was so quickly lost after the break was clearly a starting point for any post-mortem. Those long weeks in lockdown provided Gerrard, his staff and his players with the chance to re-evaluate and the time has been extremely beneficial.

"Teams who are able to voice problems and talk about them and try and find solutions are more likely to succeed," Dr Anderson said. "In any relationship that is important. A team that has got to the halfway point and it hasn't gone well, that could be through chance first time around. When it happens again, you have to, by the nature of professional sport, review what is happening.

"Making the same mistake twice or thrice is often just not accepted in sport. A good team will have plans in place to address problems that can arise, but also if it does start to turn sour, they are going to talk about it, pull together and galvanise. Often we learn most from our mistakes; and that is a great strength of a team to say we have learned from our mistakes and push on."

There is no harsher critic of Gerrard than the man himself. There were times in his first two seasons where he appeared to take too much to heart and got caught up in the emotions, not just of the game but of what it all meant to himself and to Rangers, but he has been calmer and more composed throughout a campaign that has set his legacy.

By the halfway stage of the season, that ambition was coming clearer and clearer into view for Gerrard and it was a matter of when, not if, his side would be crowned as champions. After nine years of waiting, Rangers were now just weeks away.

There had, of course, been significant setbacks for the club and Gerrard along the way but their resolve was crucial to their success. It had been done the hard way, but there was never a doubt that they would get there in the end.

"Steven is quite a remarkable individual," Traynor said. "I wouldn't claim to know him well, but I worked with him and we had lots of discussions.

"A remarkable individual. So deeply focused on what he wants to achieve. And he's a bit like Dave King, unwavering in his belief when he feels he is doing the right thing.

"That is important in football because you always have people, in the media or amongst supporters, and especially on social media, who tell you that you got this wrong, that wrong, or that you shouldn't have said or done something. You need to have a profound belief in your own abilities and Steven Gerrard certainly has that.

"The longer he stays with Rangers, the more success he and they will enjoy. But the length of stay, that's the big question, isn't it?"

There was satisfaction to be taken from the position that Rangers found themselves in but a reluctance to acknowledge what that advantage would ultimately lead to. That was to be expected within the walls of Ibrox and Auchenhowie, but even those that would usually have been in the stands were hesitant to talk of the title as a job that had been completed.

Some pressed ahead and basked in the glory, while others were fearful of jinxing the whole thing, as if somehow their belief that Rangers wouldn't be caught would have an adverse effect on Gerrard's side. The mentality of the squad was undoubtedly more refined, but the mind of the football fan can be a funny thing to understand.

"There is no doubt that it is the scars of the last ten years, it is raw," David Edgar of the Heart and Hand podcast said. "Under normal circumstances, a team as far ahead as Rangers were, the fans would have been making the title party plans in January. But with Rangers fans, because we have had so many kicks and knocks over the last ten years, there was this feeling of 'I can't get ahead of myself'.

"For me, the Old Firm game at Ibrox was the turning point. A lot of the discussion was that the fans fancied us to beat them, that on football terms we were the better side, but there was this feeling that it wouldn't be like us to make it so simple and to go that far ahead.

"That is not what we have experienced for the last decade but then the team went and did it. Every time this season the team were asked a question, the response was magnificent. The St Mirren defeat in the cup was the case in point and after that they took 25 points from 27, including against Celtic, Hibernian twice, Aberdeen away.

"Rangers this season have always answered those questions, and the questions did exist because people were waiting on a January collapse, they were waiting on a bad result taking us a couple of weeks to get over because that is what had happened even in the first two seasons under Gerrard. But it is a huge sign of the growing maturity of the side that those situations didn't happen."

A month which started with the country facing more weeks of lockdown and restrictions on their lives would end with Rangers on the brink of ending their own Premiership purgatory. There had been a chance to reflect and remember, but the focus was now very much on the future as Gerrard's side closed in on the finest achievement in Rangers' history.

The questions had been answered, the doubts had been dismissed and the title had been all-but won. The league flag was coming home.

NINE

THE SEASONS as a player and a manager, the years as a husband and a father, have shaped Steven Gerrard into the man and leader that he is today.

When Gerrard speaks, people listen. There are times when those roles are reversed, though, moments when Gerrard is all ears as those around him open up on their personal and professional issues.

His move into management has asked different questions of him over the last three years. His qualities and characteristics are still the same, but there are unique challenges associated with that role compared to the one of captain that he performed with such distinction. In this Covid-impacted campaign, Gerrard has been tested like never before.

Footballers are creatures of habit. There are routines that they are accustomed to, ways of life that they have been brought up with and that they maintain throughout their careers.

The rewards for their efforts are markedly different depending on the levels that they reach on the park, but there is a method of working through a week that will be familiar across the board, no matter the stage on which they perform. This term, that pattern had to change.

Whenever players or managers speak of the difficulties which they face personally or professionally, the barbed riposte from many is that they should be able to deal with any issue because of the money that they are paid. The wages that Gerrard and his players take home are considerable when compared to those that have supported them this season, but that doesn't mean that they don't share the same concerns or anxieties as the man in the street.

Coronavirus did not infect on the basis of profession or pay packet, it didn't discriminate or single out any sector as it swept through society, taking too many lives and wrecking countless more. The risks and the fears were shared across the country during the toughest months that many citizens have ever lived through and managers, players and staff at clubs up and down the land were just as wary of the threats and consequences as anyone else.

There were various stages throughout the campaign where the importance of Covid in a news sense would rise and fall at Rangers. It was always there, though, and Gerrard would deal with it in the professional manner which staff and supporters had come to expect.

In April, Gerrard participated in a 'Team Talk' initiative as the Rangers Charity Foundation worked in conjunction with club sponsors 32Red. He would join more than 20 fans on a Zoom call ahead of his pre-match press conference and gave up half an hour of his time to listen to their stories and to offer insight into his own struggles at home and at work.

It was Gerrard at his best, at his most engaging and personable. Those on the small screens in front of him saw him as a hero, yet he seemed touched by their tales as they fronted up to mental health issues and revealed suicide attempts and devastating family situations.

As the United Kingdom stepped into the unknown during the pandemic, people from all walks of life had to come together and unite for the greater good. Gerrard would speak with compassion and authority and detailed the way in which his own home life had been impacted during the long, difficult months of lockdowns and restrictions.

"I've found it really challenging from a personal point of view with my own family," Gerrard said. "I've got four kids. It's very difficult to explain to a four-year-old and a 10-year-old that they're not allowed out the door to see their friends and family, that they can't go to school.

"Then I've got my older girls. One's just got a boyfriend [and] can't understand why she can't see her boyfriend. Then I've got a 14-year-old who has got to do home-schooling and can't get her head around that. So those are the challenges I've had to face myself along the way. I've had to listen to Alex nagging for a year about not being able to have her normal life.

"But along the way we made sure from a football point of view that we had loads of Zooms, where we gave the players the opportunity to talk. We tried to put some quiz activities on and some tactical and technical presentations, just to keep them involved and give them something to do and try to take them away from some of their own insecurities and concerns about lockdown.

"I think all of us were just a bit lost because none of us had an end date to work to. It was challenging for everyone. As a club, what I will say is we did everything to try to support the players and their families during what was a tough time for everyone.

"That goes for the youth academy and the Ladies' team. We did a lot of Q&As and made sure the first-team players went on to support the younger kids to give them some fun.

"We really connected as a club, from the Ladies to the academy to the first team, to make sure we were all active during the lockdown. We gave them training sessions as well to keep them ticking over from a health and fitness point of view."

The time and effort that Rangers put in at the start of the season in a football sense would certainly pay dividends come the end of the campaign. The summer of 2020 was a difficult and different environment in which to work, train and do business, but Rangers would handle it better than most from a sporting perspective.

The same can be said from a personal point of view. Gerrard would find himself in a unique situation, but this test of his man management and leadership was one that didn't trip him up and Rangers would benefit from having such a strong figure overseeing matters in the dressing room and on the training pitch.

When Jordan Jones and George Edmundson broke club and Government regulations in November, Gerrard was badly let down. Neither player was a regular starter for Rangers, but both had been given the opportunity of a lifetime to play at Ibrox and they would squander it in such selfish circumstances after attending a house party in Glasgow.

Gerrard was firm but fair in his assessment at the time. When he faced a repeat situation in February, the anger from outside Ibrox was even more palpable as three members of his first team squad and two Academy players – Brian Kinnear and Dapo Mebude – breached those same guidelines.

There would have been some fans who would have banished Nathan Patterson, Calvin Bassey and Bongani Zungu from the club and ended their Rangers careers there and then. The trio had seen the fall-out from the Jones and Edmundson incident but made the same mistake rather than learning from the misdeeds of others and their actions were reckless.

Gerrard could only condemn their conduct but he would fight their corner, too. Rangers would appeal the six-game ban, four of which were to be served immediately with two suspended, that was imposed by the Scottish FA. By the time a lengthy appeals process had come to a conclusion, Patterson had impressed enough to be spoken about as a potential Scotland internationalist, while Bassey and Zungu had returned to Gerrard's first team squad.

Gerrard would stress that the quintet had been dealt with in the same manner as Jones and Edmundson, while repeatedly hinting at a different set of circumstances between the two rule breaks. In the end, whatever mitigating factors Rangers put forward at their Hampden hearings, they were not enough to see their suspensions reduced come the end of April.

Rangers were not the first nor the last club to have to deal with Covid issues during a season like no other, but few managers were doing so under the pressure that Gerrard found himself in. His stature and his position ensure his words carry greater meaning than most and every utterance regarding each scenario was significant.

It is safe to say that Ally McCoist knows a thing or two about operating in unusual circumstances as Rangers manager. There was no 'how to' book, no manual to refer to, as he took the weight of the support on his shoulders during their club's darkest days and the way in which he handled himself was testament to his character and his mentality.

In comparison, a couple of players stepping out of line may seem inconsequential. He appreciates the way in which Gerrard would deal with each set of circumstances, though, as he once again led by example at Ibrox.

"I'll tell you what he has done, he has got an opinion on it and he stands by his decisions, which is what you have got to do," McCoist said. "I don't care what anybody says, you have got to do that as a manager.

"He has taken disciplinary action against players who have let themselves down and let the club down and rightly so. He had to do that.

"At the same time, you cannot bite your nose off to spite your face because his first job is to do what is best for the football club. He has done that and he takes that into account.

"You make decisions as a manager and some people will agree with them and some will disagree with them. The decisions you make as a manager have to be for the benefit of the football club because that is who you are employed by and what you have to look after. I think he has handled it really, really well.

"I think he has handled just about everything really well to be honest. I can only think of a couple of times where he has maybe dropped his guard a little bit.

"I think he gets the whole situation and he has got good support round about him in Gary McAllister, who knows the club and the game, and Michael Beale is a very respected coach, as are the other boys there with him. He has surrounded himself with good people. That is very important and has certainly helped him again this season."

The manner in which Gerrard conducts himself pays homage to the privileged position which he holds. It is only natural that decisions or statements will be disagreed with at times, but there is a class about Gerrard and he looks and sounds like a Rangers manager should.

It takes a certain kind of individual to carry that off. It is not a job for the faint of heart or mind and those that have failed at Ibrox have been unable to live up to the weight of history or the burden of success. Very few clubs in the world have such a mixture of pressures and the fact that one of the others resides in the same city only adds to the exclusivity and uniqueness of the role. Gerrard handles it all like a Rangers manager should.

"That is the biggest compliment that you could pay him," McCoist said. "That may sound like a strange thing to say, but I know you know what I mean. He just gets it. He gets the history, he gets the importance of the club to the fans, he gets the way he has to conduct himself.

"All of that is important. It is important to the Rangers supporters throughout the country and all over the world that they have a figurehead that they can respect and a figurehead that knows the importance of the position that they are in. Steven does that really well and he carries himself really well.

"You think of Rangers managers – like Walter, like Souness, like Big Jock – and they have all got something about them and they have got a respect from everyone. Steven has certainly got that as well. As the manager of the club and the figurehead of the club, I just think he has handled things really, really well."

The evolution of football from tactical and physical perspectives has changed the game significantly over the decades but the basics still lie at the heart of any successful side. Gerrard has assembled a group of elite individuals, but it is their cognisance as a team that has made them champions during a season where the challenges outside of the game were just as unrelenting as those within it.

The Ibrox dressing room today is a multi-cultural, multi-lingual environment and there are an array of characters within it. Some bonds will naturally be tighter than others, but Gerrard trusts his leadership group of experienced professionals – James Tavernier, Allan McGregor, Connor Goldson, Steven Davis, Ryan Jack and Scott Arfield – to effectively oversee the squad from within.

He still, of course, holds the pre-eminent position of authority and his man management has allowed him to get the best out of his group. The Covid-impacted world around them had the potential to unsettle individuals and spread into the collective and Gerrard would offer an insight into his relationships with his players during that enlightening Zoom session as he opened up to supporters. It was class, but expected.

"In life, there are certain things that are above football," Gerrard said. "None of us want to say that because we all love the club. Growing up at Liverpool and now being here at Rangers, football is a big part of my life. But as a manager, you have to deal with certain things that are above football.

"It could be a player loses a family member or a loved one could have a terminal illness, for example. These are things which fans and people on the outside don't see. It's my job to make sure that I'm as big a support as I can be.

"There are times when I have got to put football secondary and give them the support they need from a lifestyle point of view. They might need to be away from the game and get some family time. They might need ongoing support or someone to open up to in a one-v-one situation so they can get things off their chest.

"I want to be the type of manager who is always there for my players and my staff. It can't always be football. I need to be that care and support for them from a lifestyle point of view as well.

"We've had to deal with many things here at Rangers and I had to do it too with my younger kids when I was the Liverpool Under-19s coach. You just want to support them in any way, shape or form to try to get them back in a better place."

There are many ways in which lives can be impacted. The grand gestures attract the headlines, but it is the efforts that often go unnoticed by many that can have the greatest resonance for those in need and the role that football clubs can play in that regard should not be understated.

The work of the Rangers Charity Foundation was halted like the flick of a switch in March 2020. The light-bulb moments quickly started for Connal Cochrane. As Scotland was plunged into lockdown, Cochrane and his team of staff and volunteers felt it as much as anyone, but it was the knowledge that others would be struggling or suffering more that drove them to refocus and regroup.

The months that followed were far from easy, but the RCF continued to make a difference where and when it mattered most.

Life has changed in the new normal, but that willingness to work and desire to help certainly hasn't at Ibrox and the 7,000 people that were involved in the various programmes and initiatives – more than 20 of them, in fact – were at the forefront of minds.

The efforts from supporters have always been an integral part of the Foundation's efforts as they give up time and hand over money. That help is a two-way street, though.

The power of football and the affection that people have for their club is inspiring and it is certainly not taken for granted at Ibrox. Behind the plans and schemes, there is a personal touch to the work the Foundation undertake.

"One of the things we have been doing behind the scenes every week is responding to requests from people that are maybe going through a tough time or are terminally ill or suffering a bereavement," Cochrane, the director of the Rangers Charity Foundation told me as the *Glasgow Times* shone a light on the work of the staff and support network that sought to help those in need during the most difficult weeks of the pandemic.

"The Rangers Charity Dream Fund is something we have had in operation for several years now and we adapted that as well. As well as letters that came out from us on behalf of the club, the manager and players, we managed to produce a number of individual player videos to send out by WhatsApp to individuals that were going through a really tough time and we know that made a difference.

"One of those was a young man down in London who was initially in hospital recovering from significant treatment and was then back home. I was corresponding with him and his dad and sadly he passed away quite suddenly and tragically.

"It is just keeping that relationship, about letting people know that we are thinking of them and how they are and we will do whatever we can to send that message of support from the club that they love."

Throughout the months of uncertainty, confusion and fear, the Foundation were innovative in their approach as programmes were rethought and reintroduced alongside new endeavours to help those of all ages and in very different circumstances.

The Foundation from Home initiative saw more than 3,200 worksheets sent to children and to the 36 primary schools that the RCF partner with as well as being made available online. Focusing on health and wellbeing, all with a Rangers theme, they provided an educational resource and family activity during a time of concern for parents.

The hugely successful Football Fans In Training scheme was adapted so supporters could take part at home, while challenges for children with autism were delivered across four age groups every week as the Academy setup at Auchenhowie got involved to keep kids active and harness their love of the game. It was that affection for Rangers that allowed the Foundation to keep their Football Memories programme running as video packages were sent out to those suffering with dementia.

With the support of the Steven Gerrard Foundation, a £5,000 donation ensured that a daily food service was able to continue operating as young people and their families in Govan were given assistance with meals when they needed it most.

The same can be said of the programme that was run at Glasgow Royal Infirmary and the Queen Elizabeth University Hospital as a free tuck shop service was provided. With visitors under restriction, the supply of juice, snacks and puzzle books was a small thought that made a big impact to many that found themselves cut off from family and friends.

There has naturally been a focus on helping people through the pandemic, but the scope of the Charity Foundation is wider than ever as those with issues from addiction to unemployment are listened to and aided. The work has changed, but it will never stop.

"Maybe more than ever, the need in society is so great at the moment because of the way that people have been affected, particularly their mental health," Cochrane said. "It is important that, working safely, we are able to start helping people again.

"We feel a responsibility to do that, but we must follow guidance and do it as safely as we can. It is also about making sure that the Foundation stays as a unique support for people of all ages and that is an area that we have worked hard on for years and years.

"The public in general probably don't realise the unique power that football and Foundations such as ours and others all across the country really have in their communities. They will seek support from us when they might not do from other sources, even though that support is there. Having that hook might bring them out of their shell a bit."

That association with their football club was the only normality that many had in their lives and the good fortunes of Rangers would help keep spirits up as Scotland moved towards a full year under the shadow of Coronavirus. Few would have expected the nation to still be gripped by the disease come February and what had been dubbed as the 'new normal' at the outset had just become a way of life.

The testing regime for players was now part of the routine, as were the restrictions in the dressing rooms and eating areas as social distancing rules were enforced. Clubs would hire additional buses for match day travel and the Joint Response Group – a task force which consists of Rod Petrie, the Scottish FA president, chief executive Ian Maxwell, SPFL counterpart Neil Doncaster and Dr John MacLean, the Scottish FA Chief Medical Consultant – became a hugely influential body in the running of our game. As Scotland tuned in every day for the First Minister's briefing, football fans waited each night for the latest update from the JRG.

Club-wide tests were required to be carried out within seven days of the previous one, meaning tests can in theory be taken on a Sunday for a match the following Saturday. Midweek testing programmes were more common, however, as clubs sought to provide the most relevant results, whilst also giving them the necessary window to collate the information and provide it to the Scottish FA and SPFL, both of whom have a dedicated email inbox for negative test data.

Those results are then cross-referenced with a database of all individuals – everyone from the manager to the administrative personnel – that have been declared within the club's bubble. In the event of a positive test, the Scottish Government is made aware and close contacts are required to self-isolate once they have been identified and even a negative test within five days doesn't permit them to return to the bubble before their ten-day isolation period has been completed.

In such ever-changing and unique circumstances, it was clear that mistakes would be made but it can only be hoped that the lessons learned from these months never need to be put to use again. Football had to adapt to survive and those that covered the game did likewise as the press corps brought the news and views, the insight and analysis, from a campaign the likes of which the country had never seen before.

"During the Covid time, the one word that has been used repeatedly has been 'unprecedented' and that is exactly what it has been for us," Scott McDermott, the secretary of the Scottish Football Writers' Association, said. "I don't think anyone could have predicted just how much our lives would change, our working conditions would change, the nature of the job would change.

"Of course, it has been completely different to what we are used to, whether that is working from home, getting used to Zoom calls rather than face-to-face interviews and the whole match day experience for journalists is totally different.

"I am proud to be part of the football writing fraternity in Scotland and I think we have handled it well. From the SFWA point of view, we have tried to engage with clubs and press officers right from the start to ensure that these changes were as smooth as possible.

"In the main, while the bigger clubs have been a bit more difficult to deal with at times, most of the clubs have been really receptive and helpful and tried to aid that transition. It has been totally different."

The processes and protocols that journalists had to adhere to seemed to change from club to club and week to week at times. It was a new way of working, but everyone that did so had to be appreciative of the opportunity that they had to attend matches and speak to the key figures throughout what had been an extraordinary season for many reasons.

There were issues with Rangers along the way but Gerrard wasn't one of them. The time spent with him was limited, or taken away in some circumstances, but he was always an engaging and interesting interview whenever the opportunity arose.

The move to Zoom press conferences certainly suited some clubs and it offered them even greater control on who said what and to whom. They still allowed for copy to be filed and the job to be done, but the formal, procedural nature of them would weaken the personal relationships that journalists sought to form with their subjects.

"One of the things that has saddened me the most is that we have lost a bit of the rapport that we had with managers and players that you only get face-to-face," McDermott, a sportswriter with the *Sunday Mail*, said. "I would probably put Steven Gerrard at the top of that list.

"Going up to the training centre once or twice a week, I found Gerrard a really amenable, personable guy who was really down to earth and you were getting to know him a bit better and he was getting to know you. You were sitting with him for 20 minutes or so with the Sunday papers, you felt as if he was quite enjoying it and you would get a bit of chat before and after the press conference.

"You felt like it was going really well, like it was with Brendan Rodgers and then Neil Lennon at Celtic. You were getting to know Gerrard and getting that insight and sadly that has just been lost with the Zoom calls. It feels as if we have taken a backward step in that sense because they are so formal and structured and you can't get any sort of rhythm into the interview.

"You don't feel as if you are getting anything in-depth or any great insight and that has been tough for me. Rangers and Gerrard would be top of that list. It has been such a great story with them becoming champions and it would have been brilliant to feel part of that and to be at close quarters interviewing Gerrard every week but unfortunately we haven't been able to do that."

Only time will tell how clubs handle the transition from the 'new normal' back to life as we all knew it but there is a fear that Zoom press conferences and limited access could be here to stay. Some clubs have certainly been more accommodating than others throughout the pandemic but there is no doubt that the circumstances of this season have been trying.

The time spent with Gerrard was never a waste, though. Come February, the Premiership title was in sight but he remained level-headed about the opportunity Rangers had in the not too distant future.

There will be times when Gerrard disagrees with a line of examination or sees the headline before the question has been fully asked. It was evident in the way he conducted himself in public why he would be such an inspiring figure in private and the messages relayed throughout the season – on everything from Covid to refereeing standards – were absorbed by his players and his supporters.

"I don't think Gerrard enjoys the Zoom conferences either, I think he would rather be face-to-face and meeting people and speaking to them," McDermott said. "It has not been ideal for him, but he has handled everything really well, even away from Covid.

"When they were going for the league, it was hard to get any answer out of him about winning the title. It was frustrating for us at the time, but you can totally understand it and respect it given where Rangers have been, where he had been in the last couple of years, that he tried to play everything down and not get too high or get carried away.

"I think overall, when you look at Gerrard's performance this season, both in terms of his team on the pitch and how he has handled things off it, it has been very impressive. He has learned lessons from the first two years.

"Listen, I am sure he has made one or two mistakes that he might look back and think 'I shouldn't have said that or done that' but, in the main, I think he has handled himself really well and Rangers, as a club, couldn't hope for anyone better in terms of being that ambassador and leader as manager.

"One of the great by-products of taking the gamble on Gerrard the untried coach was that you knew from his time as a player that he had those leadership skills and that authority, that aura, about him. He has been talking in press conferences his whole career and as captain of England and Liverpool so that was one thing you were sure of and he has handled that side of it well."

The Gerrard name and the position that he holds naturally ensured there was greater significance attached to his words and actions throughout the season and Rangers' dealings with their Covid issues were the subject of much conjecture and comment. When it came to how the Scottish FA handled the cases of Rangers and others, most notably Celtic's ill-fated trip to Dubai in January, there was controversy alongside personal conclusions.

There will be a time and a place for Scottish football and its key stakeholders to analyse how it dealt with Coronavirus. Mistakes have been made at Hampden and at Holyrood but the season would be completed as champions were rightly and deservedly crowned in our four divisions and others paid the price for their failures on and off the park.

Nobody has won as a result of Covid but Rangers were victorious in spite of it. The sport would survive in the bleakest of times but there would still be acrimony at the end of it all. The game didn't exactly stand united, but at least our clubs didn't fall divided.

"I think, in general, football, football players and football clubs have actually done extremely well during this," McDermott said. "For us to go over a year with all the restrictions that have been in place, I don't think we can fully appreciate and understand just how different it will have been for players and coaches and staff with all the protocols that have been in place.

"We have had a few isolated incidents, like Boli Bolingoli, the 'Aberdeen Eight' and the Rangers incidents, but they do feel to me like isolated ones. Of course they were ill-advised and they shouldn't have happened but the clubs have responded well and Rangers especially were very swift in nipping it in the bud and ensuring the players didn't get back into the bubble and didn't train again.

"These incidents are obviously highlighted and they spring to mind for us in the media, but I think if you take a step back and look at the bigger picture, football in Scotland has done well with all the testing, the protocols that have been put in place between training and games. For it to only have a few isolated incidents, it has been handled pretty well.

"I think there have been mistakes made at Government level and authority level but in terms of the clubs and the game in general, I think it has been handled pretty well and we will look back in years to come and say 'that was a big ask for clubs and players and staff to get through that'. They made sure the game continued at a time when everything else was stopped and I think the game can be pretty proud of itself."

Rangers would handle the challenges of Covid better than most. Even when faced with the incidents in November and February, the swift actions to suspend and then punish the culprits avoided the situation becoming significantly worse and impacting on the rest of the squad.

That is what made the actions of Patterson, Bassey and Zungu in particular all the more unfathomable. Rangers had worked so hard and come so far this season and a setback with the finishing line in sight would have been unforgiveable.

Rangers had started the month with a 1-0 win over St Johnstone at Ibrox and another against Kilmarnock would follow. In between, points were dropped at Hamilton as a lacklustre performance attracted Gerrard's ire and he would admit that his side were fortunate to avoid defeat as a last-minute effort from Ross Callachan earned Accies a point that they more than merited.

It was after the victory over Kilmarnock – courtesy of a wonderful strike from Jack – that the breaches from three of Gerrard's players, plus Kinnear and Mebude, came to light. The issue would dominate the agenda ahead of the trip to face Royal Antwerp in the Europa League and that night in Belgium offered Patterson a chance to reflect on his actions.

A thrilling 90 minutes saw Gerrard's side somehow emerge with one foot in the last 16 after a 4-3 victory but the injury sustained by Tavernier overshadowed the occasion. Back home, Patterson could only watch on and ponder what might have been as the man that he had provided back-up for throughout the campaign suffered a rare injury.

With Patterson in exile, Gerrard had to turn to Leon Balogun to fill in at right-back. It wouldn't cost Rangers on that memorable night as victory was secured in dramatic circumstances – courtesy of a Joe Aribo opener and two Borna Barisic penalties either side of a fine solo effort from Ryan Kent – but it was clear that the Nigerian internationalist wasn't a long-term solution as Tavernier faced several weeks on the sidelines.

Balogun started the 4-1 victory over Dundee United a couple of days later. On the day that the Arabs became only the second team to score a Premiership goal at Ibrox, Jack made his final appearance of the campaign as he was forced off through injury.

He wouldn't return as his season was brought to a premature end and his dreams of representing Scotland at the European Championships were over. It was a cruel blow to a dedicated professional and the sympathy and disappointment in Gerrard's demeanour was shared by Steve Clarke, the Scotland manager. The only positive was that the surgery that Jack would undergo several weeks later was deemed a success as he embarked on the road to recovery.

"I'm hugely disappointed for Ryan as he deserved to be part of our squad for Euro 2020," Clarke said. "His performances for Scotland have been excellent, not least in the play-off final against Serbia when I thought he was outstanding at the heart of our midfield.

"I know how disappointed he is to miss out on the run-in to a memorable season – both with Rangers and with the national team at a major tournament this summer – but ultimately his long-term fitness is the most important objective for him now.

"We all wish Ryan a full and speedy recovery to enable him to get back to full fitness and playing at his best for club and country."

The loss of Jack was another injury issue for Gerrard to deal with. As he sought to cope with Tavernier's absence, he would bring Patterson back into the fold sooner than many expected and his impact was immediate.

Balogun only lasted 45 minutes of the return leg against Antwerp as Rangers went in tied at 1-1 on the night but ahead overall. Just 16 seconds into the second half, Patterson made a darting run down the right, burst into the box and finished emphatically.

From that moment, he and Rangers would never look back. A 5-2 victory on the night had to be seen to be believed and it was only once the adrenaline levels had dropped that the full scale of the achievement could be savoured as Gerrard's side reached the last 16 for the second consecutive season.

Patterson's goal was the second of the night after Alfredo Morelos had opened the scoring. Antwerp may have replied twice, but Kent and Barisic scored again before Cedric Itten completed the victory from the penalty spot.

"Listen, I have got to be honest and I want Rangers to progress," Alex Rae, the former Rangers midfielder and now a radio pundit and BT Sport commentator, said. "But I absolutely loved both fixtures. I loved it. If you are talking about entertainment and excitement, it had the lot.

"It was funny because I always felt that Rangers looked as if they were in total control throughout those two games, even though the first leg was 4-3 and the second 5-2. The first leg, we scored two goals in the last seven minutes and that came after at one stage thinking 'OK, we will settle for a 3-2 going back to Ibrox'. Then Kent scores an unbelievable goal and I think the European games really helped him because he hit the form that he had showed earlier in the season when he was contributing in terms of goals.

"You have the emergence of Morelos once again as well and he was pivotal in everything that happened in those two matches. I thought it was brilliant over there and after a 4-3 I thought we wouldn't get anything like that at Ibrox and it would be a stuffy, tight affair.

"It was anything but and to get through in that way was incredible. The script was written for Patterson to score it seems.

Barisic scored his penalty and then handed the other one to Itten, and I think that epitomised this group of players.

"He could have said 'no, I am taking control here', but he knew the importance of Itten getting a goal as a striker and I think that spoke volumes about the group in general that he was willing to hand that over.

"I remember doing commentary that night and joking that it was the first to ten wins. It was like the old days, you play until ten and then it is up the road for your dinner! It was a great spectacle and both legs were just incredible entertainment from start to finish."

Like so many occasions during Rangers' European campaigns under Gerrard, this one was a concoction of emotions and headlines. It was a crazy yet captivating match to watch and cover and the only negative was that Ibrox remained almost completely silent as Covid continued to ensure the gates remained bolted and fans were locked out.

Gerrard made his case for including his three Covid sinners in his squad as he reflected on an incredible evening. Patterson had learned a harsh lesson, but it ultimately proved to be the making of him in his breakthrough season.

"I was slightly surprised, I must admit, that they came back so quickly when they were selected for the European game, and Patterson obviously got on at half-time and scored," McDermott said. "But as the weeks have gone on and you heard more details about that particular incident, it looks like that wasn't as bad as a lot of things that have happened before it.

"That is why Rangers appealed the SFA bans, although they were ultimately unsuccessful there. Rangers obviously gathered all the information and of course it was a breach and of course Gerrard would have felt let down when he heard about it, especially after the Jones and Edmundson incident.

"The instant reaction was to say, 'How could they possibly do that after what happened with Jones and Edmundson?' It was just such folly to do it again and fall into that trap. There are clearly details that Rangers know about and that is why they appealed.

"Of course it was a mistake, the boys were silly. But it wasn't crime of the century. I don't want to condone it at all, but sometimes you need to take a wee step back and say 'how bad is this?' As much as it was unwelcomed from Rangers' point of view, when they have looked at it then it has not been as bad as people thought."

The machinations of the Scottish FA disciplinary process took some time to work through and it was late April by the time the Rangers quintet were forced to serve their bans. By then, Patterson's stock had risen even further and international recognition would soon follow. He was named in the Scotland squad for the European Championships and handed his debut in the victory over Luxembourg as his remarkable rise and rise took him up another level.

Gerrard had spoken of the impact that a suspension could have on one of Scotland's brightest talents but there was little Rangers could do. All Patterson had to focus on was his football as he deputised for Tavernier with such assuredness.

When Tavernier was injured in Antwerp, the initial fear amongst supporters was that his season could be over. That was never in his mind, though, and he would eventually return during the Premiership fixture away to St Johnstone as he ensured he was fit to lead Rangers out on the day the silverware was lifted at Ibrox.

It would have been cruel if Tavernier had been denied the chance to play on that emotional afternoon. He did miss several key fixtures as he recovered from a knee complaint but he was back for the trophy day and there are few within Gerrard's ranks to whom this title success means more.

Matt Polster had provided back-up to Tavernier during his stint in Glasgow. He arrived from Chicago Fire and would return to Major League Soccer ahead of Gerrard's third season to sign for New England Revolution. Rangers left a lasting impression on the American and he knows the significance of 55 for club and captain.

"The biggest thing is just to get the monkey off your back and a relief of pressure maybe," Polster said. "I'm not sure if that's what he felt like, but to finally get over the line and give the fans something to be happy about, I am sure he is ecstatic. I am happy that he has been able to get that done because he has been with the club for so long.

"Rangers is so special because of the fans and because of what they bring to Ibrox and what it feels like to step onto the pitch in front of them. That is special. For Tav, I don't want to speak for him, but he has been there for a long time and he has wanted to achieve something, like any player wants to achieve. He wanted to give something back to the fans that had been there for him.

"I think this will mean the world to him. He will be happy and there will be relief. Knowing him and knowing that group, winning that title is not enough and they will want to go and win it next year as well. I know they are happy and he is happy, but I am sure they are going to be pushing for more titles."

One of the hallmarks of Tavernier's game is his consistency of performance and selection. For all the qualities he brings to the team, especially in an attacking sense, his importance to a manager and a squad can be found in his robustness and it was an unusual sight to see team sheets without his name on them during his lengthy absence.

That reliability that Tavernier has shown throughout his Ibrox career would prove detrimental to Polster's own aspirations. He had immersed himself in Glasgow, but ultimately had to move on for the sake of his career as his friend stood in his way.

"I know that I was competing with him to play at right-back and it was tough for me to get into the team, but he was still that guy that I could talk to," Polster said. "In the States, we call each other 'dude' and he was my dude in Scotland.

"We had a really good connection and friendship but he had that with everyone in the group, he was able to chat with anybody and he is a calming presence on the field. He is a great captain and a great leader and I think he is going to push that team to go even further next year.

"You hit it right on the head and he has that respect and he is well liked. He demands a lot from the group and he demands a lot from himself. You can see that he is well liked and well respected and you need that to be a captain at a big club like Rangers. He is definitely the right man for that job, for sure."

Had Tavernier not suffered that injury in Antwerp, he would surely have gone on to sweep the board when the Player of the Year awards were handed out. He had scored 17 times in the first half of the campaign but his value to the team wasn't just measured in goals and assists.

This was the Englishman's sixth season at Rangers. He may not have been born into the ways of the club, but he had learned through time and he understood as well as anyone why the title that Rangers were chasing was as significant to the club and the support.

Nobody within that group had sustained as many blows as Rangers lurched between crisis and calamity in the years before Gerrard's arrival. His relationship with Rangers will continue into a ninth term after he signed an extension to his contract and Ibrox is now home for a man who had spent years bouncing around the English leagues in search of contentment.

"Definitely, John Greig was a good mentor when I was going through things in the early days," Tavernier said. "I would see him after every single game, have a chat with him. He'd normally give us some stick – he was always quick to do that!

"But he's such a great man, he was obviously voted the Greatest Ever Ranger, so he's someone you're always going to listen to and take advice from.

"The likes of Jimmy Bell and Disco [Davie Lavery] who have been here for such a long time have helped. Then there's my family and close friends. It's people like that who have really settled us in.

"Before I moved up here, you knew how big Rangers was. But you don't really realise it until you're actually in amongst it, you understand how quickly you need to adapt to it. All of those people gave me a great helping hand in doing that."

The words of advice from Rangers' most revered servant would have kept Tavernier going during his darkest days. From Old Firm humiliations to that night in Luxembourg, he had experienced some crushing lows at Ibrox but the highs were now able to be savoured.

His legacy will stand alone in Rangers' history. Whatever failures he endured or other successes he experiences, he will always be the man that captained Rangers to title 55.

"Rangers were the first club to really put their faith in me and give me that platform," Tavernier said. "So I've always said I will always pay Rangers back for that. And I'm loving what I'm doing at the minute.

"I'll just keep working hard and see what happens but, yeah, I'm delighted the club put faith in me – and the gaffer as well – to extend my deal. I'm really, really happy at the moment.

"I always had faith. A club of this magnitude, this size, you see the trophy cabinet and realise they're known for success. It's been a very tricky time since I've been here, a bit of a rollercoaster. But, every step of the way, there have always been improvements.

"And ever since the gaffer has come in the door, the improvements have stepped up massively. Not just the squad but around the place, everything has improved and it's put us on another platform. So that's why I'm delighted to extend my deal, because I can see the potential of where this club can be."

By the time Tavernier returned to action and signed his new contract, Rangers had won the title and been eliminated from the Europa League. In his second game back, more heartache would hit as Gerrard's side were knocked out of the Scottish Cup but Tavernier and supporters are no strangers to such travails and they will emerge stronger from those disappointments.

The world around them would provide context. In a season of such sporting achievement, the ills of society could not be overlooked and they would impact on Gerrard and his players like citizens across Scotland and beyond.

This campaign will never be forgotten thanks to the extraordinary backdrop against which it was played and the challenges that it provided. As Covid continued to grip the nation amidst hopes of a vaccine, Rangers stood on the brink of giving fans the ultimate shot in the arm.

In time, the decisions made by those in positions of power in Glasgow and Edinburgh throughout the pandemic will be debated and deliberated. Mistakes have certainly been made.

That was the case at Ibrox, too. In Gerrard, Rangers had a manager who would lead in adversity and actions would speak louder than words as the Premiership title came into view. Soon, it would be won.

TEN

RANGERS ARE champions. The sight of the words, the sound as they are read aloud, will elicit a range of emotions. No matter how often they are said, they will never lose resonance with a support for whom a 55th league title has become a defining moment in their lives.

On 29 July 2012, Rangers started what would become christened as 'The Journey'. On 7 March 2021, they completed it. Rangers are champions.

There are dates, times, places and people that will forever stick in the mind and provoke feelings of despair or euphoria. There have been more events at the wrong end of the scale for Rangers fans over the last decade, but one has now trumped the lot as they revel in a unique sporting story and the greatest triumph in their club's history.

The items within the Trophy Room at Ibrox signify past glories and encapsulate what Rangers is about, what makes it special. The cups, medals, artefacts and trinkets tell the story of Rangers' past, but the moment that the Premiership trophy was placed behind the glass this season carried extra definition for a number of reasons.

The task of putting the achievement and its significance into words and into context is no easy one. Unless you have been through it, it is hard to comprehend just what title 55 means and why it is so emotive and so cherished.

Football may only be a game, but Rangers is a way of life. Those that don't understand don't matter, those that understand need no explanation.

The decisions made by a manager that many have never met and the actions of players who many aspire to follow shape fans' feelings and wellbeing in a way that is as consequential as it is irrational. On a historic afternoon at Ibrox, all of those individuals would come together in spirit and mind to celebrate and to remember. Rangers are champions.

At his home in Portugal, Paul Murray would do likewise. It was six years to the day since he, Dave King and John Gilligan emerged from the Extraordinary General Meeting as the new board at Ibrox and became the custodians of the club, of their club.

He watched on as Steven Gerrard's side beat St Mirren – courtesy of goals from Ryan Kent, Alfredo Morelos and Ianis Hagi – and moved to within a point of the Premiership. The following day, Celtic were held to a goalless draw by Dundee United and their reign was over. Rangers are champions.

The day was always going to be special regardless of when Gerrard's side got over the line, but the fact that it came on that anniversary was fitting and it was almost like it was meant to be. The new era had started with a 0-0 stalemate at Cowdenbeath just hours after the EGM triumph and the crowning moment carried special significance for one of the men that helped make the dream a reality.

"I actually had a funny feeling that it was going to be that weekend," Murray, who stepped down from the Ibrox board in the week that Gerrard was appointed in 2018, said as he reflected on two momentous dates in Rangers' history. "I just felt that it was almost like fate.

"It was six years to the day and from that first match against Cowdenbeath. It was an incredible bit of symmetry in some ways and it was a great weekend.

"I am not ashamed to say that I shed a few tears and that I was quite emotional on the Sunday. I was the same on the Saturday because you felt that when we beat St Mirren, even though it wasn't mathematically guaranteed, that result and that match meant it was hard to see how we would lose it from that point. I watched the Celtic game on the Sunday and had this feeling that something was going to happen that day.

"The emotions I had was obviously a relief that it had been done but great joy and the main thing for me was pride. It was a really difficult ten years when you consider everything the club had been through.

"John Gilligan said some people viewed it as important to get the 55th title or stop ten-in-a-row, but that the most important thing of all was to give a title to a generation of young fans that had never seen Rangers be successful and give them a bit of pride in the club as well. I think that was really important and that is what Rangers have done this season."

Murray may have been hundreds of miles away from Ibrox in body but he was there in spirit as Rangers earned the victory that all-but secured their status as champions. In the home dressing room and on Edmiston Drive, the scenes told their own story as flags fluttered through the smoke from the canisters that were held aloft by a crowd a couple of thousand strong.

Rangers fans have had few reasons to gather in celebration over the last decade. Six years previously, they stood at the front door of Ibrox to protest at a reviled regime in what felt like the culmination of every rally or demonstration before that point.

Within weeks, their club was saved as Murray, King and Gilligan won their long-running power struggle.

The achievement of winning 55 is arguably the most important in Rangers' history. It wouldn't have been possible without that EGM victory, however, and it is harrowing to even begin to imagine what fate would have befallen one of Scotland's great institutions had those that cared for Rangers not ousted those that cared only for themselves.

The men that made it happen will never have a song sung or a stand named in their honour, yet their importance to Rangers cannot and will not be forgotten. Title 55 offers Rangers a chance to move forward but the past provides lessons as well as memories.

"You had the euphoria and the relief of the General Meeting on the Friday," Murray said. "Outside of the birth of my children, that was one of the happiest days of my life in terms of it being an incredible feeling to be so successful and to be so emphatically successful.

"I was actually chairman at the time, I had been installed as chairman while Dave was waiting for his Fit and Proper clearance from the SFA. We were still listed on the AIM Market at that point and I had to release a statement to the Stock Exchange announcing the result.

"I had a representative from the NOMAD sitting with me at Argyle House and we were checking over the statement to make sure it complied with Stock Exchange regulations. We were clearing off all the numbers and it was about 3 o'clock in the afternoon. He said he would release it and he sent the email.

"Within about 30 seconds you heard an enormous roar outside Argyle House from the fans that had gathered to wait for the result. It had gone to the Stock Exchange and been immediately released. I never knew that Rangers fans followed the Stock Exchange!

"It was incredible. Within 30 seconds you heard this roar and the fans then knew what we knew and that we had won the vote. That will always live with me."

The three men who were appointed as directors that day were not in office when the league was won but there are no feelings of what might have been for any of them. There was a time and a place for their input, whether that was financially or emotionally, and the satisfaction of seeing Rangers back where they belong, at seeing 'The Journey' completed after so many twists and turns, was the overriding emotion.

Others had tried and failed to win control of Rangers but it was King, Murray and Gilligan that won the hearts and the backing of the support. Names such as Bill Ng, Robert Sarver and Bill Miller – who all touted themselves as saviours but were never going to rescue Rangers – will be forgotten in time, as will the likes of Craig Mather, Graham Wallace and Derek Llambias. The figures behind Blue Pitch Holdings and Laxey Partners are now thankfully irrelevant at Ibrox.

The motives of so many that climbed the Marble Staircase were questioned but those of King, Murray and Gilligan, and of those well-intentioned individuals that have followed, never could be. When the final whistles were blown at Ibrox and Tannadice, all the time, money and effort that had been invested paid off. It was all worth it. Rangers are champions.

"It is a funny question to answer, because I don't think we would have won the league title without winning the EGM," Gilligan said. "Many people ask what was behind all this and what the end game was and I always believed it was to sell the stadium and rent it back, I think that is where the money was. It would have been a major struggle for us to compete again if that had happened, so getting control of the club was so important.

"It has taken five or six years to get us back and winning 55 or stopping ten-in-a-row means nothing to me. I mean that genuinely. What it means to me is that Rangers are now back as league winners, we are now back going into the Champions League and the club is now completely and utterly returned to a normal position of competing every year. Everyone focuses on 55 and stopping ten but, for Rangers as a club, this changes everything. That is us back, that is the final piece of the jigsaw.

"Naively I didn't think it would take as long. I have to say that I didn't think it would take as long. After a couple of months I started to worry it would and then as things went on we were under lots of pressure and we had some real low points and bad defeats in there.

"You always have belief, as a Rangers fan, that Rangers will get back, but there were certainly serious worries about how long it would take when you looked at what was happening at times. To finally win the title again was just wonderful and the Rangers supporters deserved that."

Every fan will have their own JFK moments from the last decade. Whether it be the night that the Championship was won against Dumbarton or the Scottish Cup victory over Celtic on penalties, the evening that administration was announced by Craig Whyte or the humiliating Old Firm defeats at Ibrox, Hampden and Parkhead, they can say 'I was there' for good or for bad.

Many would accompany their team every step of the way as the stories of yesteryear were passed to the supporters of the day and the passion for Rangers was kept burning. There are many factors that have been imperative to the achieving of 55, but nothing would have been possible had it not been for the loyalty of the Rangers supporters.

"I think there was a real danger of that," Murray said when asked if there was a fear that a generation of Rangers fans could have been lost had the club not been victorious once again. "I have got two sons myself and kids tend to follow successful teams. There is so much sport on TV just now and coverage that is way more than there was when I was growing up. Kids have got a favourite German team and a Spanish team and an English team, so there was a real danger of that.

"We have all said that the loyalty of the fans has been incredible and their loyalty to the club, to go down to the fourth tier and get 50,000 at matches, was absolutely staggering. Of all the things, I think that is the thing that saved Rangers and it was incredible how they stood by the club."

That fact has never been lost on Murray. Indeed, he has one other memory from EGM day that encapsulates those feelings and that sums up the significance of what he helped to achieve.

He was running on adrenaline through the press conferences that followed the vote and when he, King and Gilligan met then manager Kenny McDowall and staff at Ibrox and Auchenhowie. His next conversation was an unexpected one.

"It was about 6.00 p.m., 6.30 p.m. in the evening and I was driving through to Edinburgh to see my son in a play at school," Murray said. "I was emotional all day and just completely exhausted. I stopped at Harthill for a coffee and to have five minutes to myself and calm down before I went on. I was sitting with a coffee, reading the paper and I felt this guy standing over me and this presence on my shoulder.

"I looked round and this guy must have been late 70s, maybe even older, and he had tears in his eyes. He said 'Mr Murray, I want to thank you.' He was an old guy, but he gave me a really big bear hug, and at that point you realised just what it means to people. He was just so delighted. It was a great day."

The one that followed was anything but for Rangers. Just hours after the EGM win, the new board made the trip to Cowdenbeath and witnessed what Murray recalls as a 'dreadful' game as McDowall's side, low on confidence and with no chance of catching Hearts in the Championship, were held to a goalless draw by a side who had lost 10-0 to the Jambos the previous weekend.

There are stark contrasts between then and now throughout this story of recovery and redemption and events six years apart encapsulate just where Rangers were and where they are. In the mud, the wind and the rain, Rangers were at ground zero at Central Park and post-match conversations were cut short to allow the awaiting stock cars into the stadium to utilise the track that surrounds the pitch.

Murray didn't get involved with Rangers for a second time to sample the glitz and glamour. His motivations were to help rather than hinder and he had experience from a stint on the board under Sir David Murray and then Alastair Johnston to put to good use as Rangers embarked on a rebuilding job that would ultimately take six long and difficult years to complete.

By that stage, Murray had stepped down once again. He had left the board in protest when Whyte purchased Rangers and his warnings at the time would sadly prove to be accurate as the club survived a brush with death.

When he left again, just days before Gerrard was appointed, it was for a very different reason. His time had come to a natural end. The three years of clearing up legacy issues off the park and overseeing false dawns on it had taken a toll and the moment was right for one of Rangers' saviours to become just a supporter once again.

"I had been thinking about it up until that point and it wasn't a decision that I took lightly," Murray said. "I had been through a lot and I just felt it was time to go. We had a couple of quite heavy defeats and I think that is something that people have to realise.

"When you are on the board, you are a director as well as a fan and I think John and I found that difficult. Dave was a bit more detached, he was living in South Africa and wasn't here a lot of the time. John and I went to all the matches and were the public faces for a long time and you took that responsibility personally. Maybe we shouldn't have done that, but you felt responsible and took a lot of weight on your shoulders.

"I decided that I was going to step down. I knew that Steven was coming in and I didn't want in any way to confuse the whole thing by me going after he joined. That would have looked really odd. I think I resigned on the Tuesday of that week and then Steven came in on the Friday and my position was lost amidst all the Gerrard stuff, which was fine and certainly suited me.

"I just slipped away and Barry Scott resigned the same day. There was a bit of coverage at the time but it got completely lost in the Steven Gerrard news, which was obviously more important. It was one of these things.

"There was nothing sinister about it. I had decided to go and it happened to be that week and in the end it worked out OK. I slipped away and Steven came in and that was the main story."

The departure of Murray from the Ibrox board left only King as the last man of the three still in position. Gilligan had stepped down the previous May and it would be March of 2020 by the time that King resigned as chairman as he was replaced by Douglas Park.

Like Murray and Gilligan, he would watch on from the outside looking in throughout this momentous and historic campaign, but King still had his finger on the pulse with what was happening at Ibrox. Gerrard no longer worked for him, but King would support the manager that he appointed through the most important months of his tenure.

It had been a matter of when rather than if Rangers would win the title for some time. The focus that had been evident since the start would pay off and King had to credit Gerrard for the success and the manner in which it had been achieved as 55 was secured. Rangers are champions.

"I had a communication with Steven in January and I said to him that he had done a fantastic job of keeping the team focused on one game at a time," King said. "It was vital that he continued that, and that wasn't advice that he didn't understand, he got that already. He had increased media attention saying that Rangers had won the league and what we had to absolutely avoid was any of the team members thinking that was the case.

"I said to him that this team would go down as legends. This club is 150 years old and there will never be a title more memorable than this one and it will stick in the mind because of where we have come from.

"I said this would be the greatest title in 150 years, so his team had the option of being a great Rangers team that won the league, stopped ten-in-a-row and, more importantly, signalled the re-emergence of Rangers as the major football force in Scotland.

"Alternatively, they would go down as the team that blew it. Either way, they would go down in history. It was vital that everyone focused on three points at a time, one game at a time and went down in history for the right reasons. That is where they are and it is absolutely phenomenal."

For many of the supporters who celebrated at Ibrox or in George Square, in isolation at home or with friends and family, this title win will not be their first. They will have heard the stories of the great side of the 60s and been told of Jim Baxter, been regaled at the tales of the Barcelona Bears or of the Souness Revolution that sparked the nine-in-a-row glory days.

More recent times have seen victories earned thanks to big-money signings under Dick Advocaat or dramatic triumphs overseen by Alex McLeish and Walter Smith. Title 55 doesn't outshine Helicopter Sunday or Rangers' 50th league flag in terms of drama, but it is arguably ahead of nine-in-a-row in terms of meaning for the club and the support.

The pictures of a tearful Richard Gough raising the trophy at Tannadice in 1997 were the images of a childhood or the highlight for an older generation. It is as iconic a moment as the header from Brian Laudrup that won the Scottish Premier Division and one which still resonates strongly to this day.

In years to come, it will be the images of this season that will fulfil that particular role. It is these wins, these scenes of celebration that will evoke such wonderful recollections after Gerrard and his players earned their place in Ibrox folklore. Rangers are champions.

"I hope they realise what they have achieved and what that achievement means to so many people," Gough said. "I think this title was one of the most important titles in Rangers' history because of what it means to the club, and the fact that Celtic were going for ten-in-a-row.

"Now, there would be a lot of asterisks on those titles because Rangers weren't in the league and the ninth one got given, it wasn't finished. There are a few asterisks there and Celtic had a free shot at the title and ten-in-a-row, but if you were a betting man at the beginning of the season, a lot of money would have gone on Celtic to achieve that because, on paper, it looked like they had a proven team and they had the results in the past years.

"I think Steven and the players have been remarkable. I played in many great teams over my nine championships, but we never went through the season undefeated.

"In most of my titles, we won it with three or four games to go and we probably gave up a couple of defeats because it is difficult when you have won the championship to motivate yourself to the same level in the games that are left. For Rangers to have won the championship this season as soon as it has been done before is terrific."

Those legendary sides that Gough captained with such distinction are some of the finest ever to pull on the famous blue jersey. Their names and their deeds are recalled with fondness and affection to this day and they have been joined by contemporaries who have now become greats in their own right.

The success will not be as sustained, but the achievement of 55 stands alone and it has been done in the most unusual of circumstances as Covid has denied Gerrard's side a chance to take the acclaim of the Ibrox crowd.

Thousands would gather on Edmiston Drive hours before kick-off against St Mirren as Gerrard, his staff and his players were given a heroes' welcome. With flags and banners all around, fans sang their songs of celebration and were swept away by the tide of emotion whilst the blue sea inside Ibrox remained empty.

They would return following the 3-0 victory and the party would begin all over again as players took it in turns to appear at the windows, some holding beers, some taking scarves from the crowd. The festivities were not as grand or as decorated as they would have been in normal circumstances, but the pictures and videos from the day chronicle events that encapsulated the meaning of what had been achieved. Rangers are champions.

"This team this year will be remembered, and rightly so, as a legendary team," Gough said. "They might not have the players of our team, might not have a Gascoigne, a Laudrup or a McCoist like we had, but this team will be remembered for what they have achieved and the way that they have achieved it.

"To do it with no crowds, it has been such a strange season for everyone and I don't think there will ever be a season like it. It has been a surreal season but you saw the outpouring of emotion over the weekend when the title was won and that had been pent up for so long by so many people.

"It has been a strange season all round, but I can only take my hat off to the players and Steven Gerrard for the fantastic job. It has been a marvellous achievement by everyone at Rangers."

The winning of 55 was always going to be special for Rangers but the circumstances in which it has been done are as extraordinary as the feat itself. This campaign – for all the highs and rushes that it has given supporters – will always be tinged with a sadness and sense of regret as fans were denied the chance to celebrate together.

Those that swarmed Edmiston Drive before and after the St Mirren match or that congregated in George Square over the weekend found themselves at the centre of a political storm. This wasn't just rival fans lining up to have a pop, this was large swathes of the media and the political establishment stepping forward in condemnation, with First Minister Nicola Sturgeon and her Deputy, John Swinney, particularly scathing about the actions of the thousands that defied lockdown regulations for the impromptu street parties.

"The behaviour of some fans has been an absolute disgrace and has undoubtedly cast a shadow over what should have been a special day for the team," Swinney said as the Scottish Government's daily Covid briefing became the platform for them to lambast Rangers and their supporters. "The success we have had in recent weeks in reducing case numbers is because so many people across Scotland have stuck to extremely tough rules, which are designed to stop the spread of the virus.

"To see so many people deliberately flouting these rules, with no regard to the safety of others, is shameful. Events like yesterday risk spreading the virus. And they show no respect at all for the millions of people across Scotland who have been sticking to the rules."

Given where Scotland was in terms of its fight against Coronavirus, those parties cannot be condoned or condemned. Yes, they shouldn't have happened, but it is understandable why so many came together and accepted the associated risks for those moments. After so long in isolation, Rangers fans were wholly united in spirit and many in person as football offered a mental and physical relief from the constraints of the previous year. Rangers are champions.

It was a situation where it became easy to criticise, but one support could empathise with Rangers. The links between Ibrox and Anfield had become stronger following Gerrard's appointment and Rangers fans would find themselves in a similar situation to their Reds counterparts as they were denied the chance to properly mark a sporting success that meant more than just a title being won.

A first Premier League crown in 30 years was secured in June 2020 for Liverpool. Like Rangers, their supporters had to watch on from home and cheer on another team and it was Chelsea's 2-1 victory against Manchester City that would finally get Jurgen Klopp's side over the line.

It had been a matter of when, not if, for some time. When it finally came, it was all worth the wait and a couple of thousand fans would head to Anfield to mark the occasion. In scenes that resembled those at Ibrox some months later, the crowd was good-natured and in high spirits as flags were waved and red flares and smoke plumes lit up the dark night.

A month later, the sky over Anfield crackled and popped to the sights and sounds of fireworks as a pyrotechnic display accompanied the trophy lift. Given the magnitude of the moment – one which football supporters could appreciate regardless of the colour of their scarf – it was a surreal occasion to watch as Klopp and his players partied in front of empty stands.

For Joe Blott, the chairman of Liverpool supporters' organisation Spirit of Shankly, they were times of mixed emotions. The sense of relief at ending a three-decade-long wait was palpable, but Reds fans have never been able to properly toast the historic success.

"It was incredibly difficult and I have certainly got a lot of empathy with the Rangers fans," Blott said. "We had two days, really. We won the league and there was that outpouring of emotion, but it felt weird at the time because we weren't at the ground and it was taken away from us, if you like, because it wasn't a match that we had won and that is always a strange feeling.

"Then we had the game against Chelsea when we were crowned Premier League champions for the first time in 30 years and that was really hard for the 54,000 usual match-going fans to not be part of that.

"We haven't had our city tour, which we would expect after winning the Premier League and the World Club Championship and Super Cup. Covid has had a real effect on Liverpool and the fans need to celebrate that to really get back to any kind of normality. That is not just getting back into the ground, it is celebrating with the team to mark what they achieved.

"It means just as much and in many ways it brings different memories because of the circumstances, as tragic as they were. It was a moment in time that gave people a relief from what was going on in the world outside. We will always remember it because 2020 was such a significant year for the world and to win the Premier League then will always stand out."

Given the seriousness of the public health crisis that was gripping the United Kingdom at the time, it was perfectly understandable why images and videos of supporters congregating in large numbers would provoke such outrage. Every excuse or argument that each fan could make to validate their actions is quickly countered by a tale of tragic loss or of personal sacrifice and suffering.

The gatherings at Anfield and Ibrox were always going to occur, though. Football can make rational people take irrational decisions and these clubs are not just a hobby for those that follow them, they are a way of life. Indeed, football provided the only sense of normality in times that were anything but and the release and relief from being able to watch their team cannot be underestimated.

Much of the criticism directed towards Rangers regarded their messaging to supporters and Sturgeon would express headline-grabbing fears that cases would surge, whilst appearing to suggest that fans who contracted Covid at title gatherings hadn't been honest with Test and Trace officials.

The First Minister had issued a cliché 'yellow card' to Scottish football earlier in the season and threatened a red if there were further rule breaches. To follow her example and to follow one banal line with another, this situation became an open goal for Sturgeon and those who had shown a disdain for football throughout the pandemic.

"Providing the club sends out the right message and the fans work closely with the authorities, there is only so much you can do," Blott said. "Who knows, if there were 2,000 there, that could have been 10,000 or 12,000 if those messages hadn't come out and maybe the majority listened to the advice.

"I know that we worked very closely with the relevant parties and urged supporters to stay at home and celebrate safely. We were saying not to gather in crowds, not to go to Anfield and it was a public health message.

"This wasn't about football fans, it was about public health and public safety. I think football clubs and football fans can be an easy target. What more can they do apart from statements from Steven Gerrard or the board or the fans' groups?

"Who knows, we might have prevented many more thousands from going because people made that choice. It was ten years without the league for Rangers and 30 years without it for Liverpool, so there were bound to be people who would celebrate in that manner.

"There is only so much you can do and unfortunately football fans get lumped together and people then call that out. In reality, it is human behaviour because people have been on beaches and in parks and wherever else at several points as well."

As politicians and commentators lined up to castigate Rangers, both as a club and a support, chairman Park would stand up for his board following criticism from Swinney, who had claimed the silence from the club had been 'deafening'. Park would point to comments from Gerrard in his press conferences urging supporters to behave responsibly, whilst highlighting the use of the Ibrox tannoy system in asking fans to disperse.

A timeline of meetings and correspondence was provided in an open letter as Rangers outlined efforts to engage with police and football authorities, broadcasters and the Scottish Government, in the build-up to the day when 55 was won.

"It is particularly disappointing that there has been a lack of acknowledgement from the Scottish Government to the wide range of efforts we undertook in recent weeks to limit public safety issues," Park wrote.

"It is also particularly disappointing that Mr Swinney has chosen to lambast Rangers, given the fact that we had proactively initiated engagement with Police Scotland, the SPFL, the Scottish Government as well as the local Member of Parliament. To brand us as 'disgraceful', is indeed a 'deep element of concern' for Rangers as we believe the narrative is unfair but crucially totally inaccurate."

Rangers fans have spent much of the last decade feeling under attack from all angles and they would again adopt a siege mentality as snipers lined up to take shots. There had to be a realisation that the gatherings were illegal and shouldn't have happened, but the coverage and condemnation would irk many as Rangers were used as a political football.

Warnings over a spike in Covid cases were spouted regularly, while there were suggestions that the Old Firm fixture at Parkhead later in March could be cancelled over fears that fans would congregate. It was a game that meant little and that hypothetical situation was more hyperbole than reality.

At the Covid press conference on 8 March, Swinney confirmed the total number of positive cases reported the previous day was 501. There was an increase of 26 people in hospital, taking that figure to 654, while 59 were in intensive care. Since the briefing the previous Friday, 13 deaths had been registered, which took the total under the Scottish Government's definition to 7,422.

On 6 April, Sturgeon reported that there were 259 new cases and 196 people were in hospital as no further deaths were confirmed. More than 2.5million people had received the first dose of a vaccine and the easing of restrictions that saw garden centres and hairdressers reopen continued as planned in the following days as Scotland made positive progress in the fight against Covid.

Politics, like football, can be a case of lies, damned lies and statistics at times, but the figures just didn't back up the doomsday predictions of a spike as a result of the Rangers title parties. That doesn't justify them happening, but the narrative at the time fed into the feeling from supporters that their actions had provided a useful distraction for a Government under pressure over their handling of the pandemic and the fall-out from the Alex Salmond trial.

A similar situation had unfolded in Liverpool some months earlier. Thousands would gather at Pier Head in the city and the morning after the night before saw a mammoth clean-up operation required as rubbish, laughing gas canisters and bottles lay strewn in the streets.

It was Liverpool supporters that found themselves cast as the villains and they were quickly condemned and criticised. It was easy to tarnish the reputation of the football club but the questions raised over the scenes were ones for society to answer.

"We worked closely during the year with the police, public health officials, the City Council and the football club and, like the Rangers situation, we had to put out messages telling fans not to go near the ground," Blott said. "This was before we won the league. We wanted people to stay away, it wasn't safe, and the fans adhered to that.

"We had a fantastic response to those messages and it is not easy telling football fans what to do. They are fellow citizens like everybody else but they stuck to it.

"When we won the league, there was an outpouring and you can't condone it nor condemn it, really. It just happened. We had conversations with the club and the relevant authorities and it was about managing it on the day.

"There were a couple of thousand around the ground and it was in high spirits. Yes, it shouldn't have happened. Yes, we were in the middle of lockdown. It was spontaneous. When we lifted the trophy, many people stayed away and there weren't a great deal of people in the city centre.

"There was one event at the Pier Head and that was an interesting one. It is on the banks of the Mersey and it is a big space. It was kind of a Facebook or social media gathering. The City Mayor called it out and said it was outrageous that the fans were doing this.

"Reality was, it was hard to see how many real Liverpool fans were there. It was a nice sunny day and people were there to be part of something that was taking place. There were people who clearly weren't football fans, never mind Liverpool fans, who were out for the day and had had enough of lockdown.

"We were asked to condemn that and it wasn't for us to do. I think Rangers – both the fans and the football club – have felt that as well.

"It is easy to round up football fans into a group, so you condemn football fans for breaking lockdown rules. Yet the previous weekend there were thousands on local beaches and parks. They were just citizens in that case but when it is football fans, they get a reputation and become an easy target."

Rangers may have found themselves at the centre of a political storm but the comment and the conjecture wouldn't take the shine off the celebrations. The support had been through too much together to allow their time to be taken by those who didn't understand why 55 was a shot in the arm that cured so many ills from the last decade.

Wherever and however they marked the title win, they did so with a sense of relief as much as pride. There were moments when they feared for the very existence of their club and in some ways winning or losing matches can seem inconsequential given the seriousness of the situation that Rangers previously found themselves in.

No fanbase has endured as much but they have emerged stronger and more united for the experience. There is no need to have a league table that ranks those who played their part in order, but each one of those who contributed can be proud of their endeavours.

Chris Graham became one of the public faces of the fight. On TV and radio, in newspapers and online, he was a driving force as groups united under the Union of Fans banner and later put their collective cash and goodwill behind Club 1872. Rangers are champions.

"There is a huge amount of satisfaction and at the end of the day this is what everybody did it for," Graham said. "It has been ten years and it is incredible to look back and consider everything that has happened in that period. I thought about it the other day and thought 'my God, I have spent ten years of my life doing this'. But a lot of people made a lot of sacrifices.

"Guys like Dave, Douglas Park, John Bennett, George Letham, George Taylor, all these guys put significant amounts of money in, and I don't think you can underestimate that. People maybe see it as a hobby that other people should pay for. It is incredible that the guys are willing to put their personal wealth in there and we are extremely lucky that they are.

"A lot of people gave up other things as well, there was a lot of time and effort put in, they gave up job opportunities and all sorts of things to make sure that it happened. They sacrificed time with kids and personal lives and there were loads of people that did that.

"I think it has been documented over the time and people will see who was involved and who did their best for the club. And it was all to reach the point where the club was back where it should be and it is back where it should be now.

"It doesn't matter whether we win every trophy, we just need to be back being Rangers and being competitive and having a team and a club that everyone can be proud of again. I think that is what this title signifies.

"It signifies that Rangers are back where they should be. To some degree, everyone can stand down at that point and say we can get back to enjoying title wins and enjoying the football. At least the club is back where it should be."

That position was secured courtesy of the win over St Mirren and Celtic's draw with United and those results sparked the celebrations. The party had started a couple of days previously, though, as Rangers left it late to beat Livingston at the Tony Macaroni Arena.

A crisp, cold evening in West Lothian burst into life when Gerrard confronted referee John Beaton at half-time and was subsequently sent off. In the 55th minute, fireworks exploded over the stadium and the festivities wouldn't prove to be premature.

Morelos had found himself at the centre of a diving controversy in the first half as Beaton booked him for going down under a challenge from Max Stryjek. The Colombian would have the defining say in the game as he netted an 87th-minute winner but it was Gerrard's words that were the most noteworthy.

A question about Morelos' mindset was brushed off with a quip about his striker dancing topless to 'Sweet Caroline' in the away dressing room but there was nothing light-hearted about his assessment of Beaton's performance. His comments would earn him a one-match suspension from the Scottish FA and he oversaw the win over St Mirren from the Directors' Box at Ibrox.

"I asked him for an explanation on why three people have missed a blatant stonewall penalty," Gerrard said after watching the second half from the stands as he received two yellow cards in a matter of seconds and was dismissed by Beaton.

"Not one. I'll go with one, we're all human, we all make mistakes. But I can't have three at the same time that are all looking at the incident.

"The linesman is looking straight at it with nothing in his way. The fourth official is looking straight at it with nothing in his way, because I was behind him and I could see it clear. And the referee is right on top of him.

"I'll go with a mistake from one of them but not three. It's not right, it's not fair. It's a stonewaller and it's bang out of order. I think I'm entitled to a conversation but obviously not."

The reaction from Gerrard at half-time was indicative of the fact that emotions were running high for Rangers. The title was so close and nothing was going to stop Gerrard and his players from achieving their dreams and realising those of long-suffering supporters.

The financial investment from so many, both before Gerrard's appointment and since he arrived at Ibrox, had been substantial. The support as a whole was fortunate to have those wealthy few who could contribute over and above but the input from individuals – whether it be through season tickets, merchandise or products from the Rangers Youth Development Company – had a collective impact.

Gerrard uses the phrase 'all-in' to define his mindset and lay out what he expects from his players. It applies to the fans, too, and Club 1872 director Laura Fawkes would reflect on the journey within 'The Journey'. Rangers are champions.

"It was an emotional commitment," Fawkes said. "I am not saying that prior to 2012 we didn't have that emotional commitment, but this was on a different scale and the level of belief that was required to do that was incredible. We went to a different level of belief, a different level of confidence in the club and a different level of emotional commitment that was unprecedented, not just for Rangers but in Scottish football.

"There has never been a story like the one we have just experienced. It definitely required a shift in mentality and it was painful at times. There was a real strength of spirit amongst the Rangers support.

"I think there is a sense of relief, but probably not to the level I expected. I think it is just more unbridled joy. And why shouldn't there be? This is a support that stuck with their club through the darkest of times, so we deserve it.

"We have been through enough, taken enough hits and we deserve this because, as a club and a support, it is not just on the park where we have been up against it and suffered and we have stood up to that and overcome that."

Title 55 feels like an end for Rangers. In many ways, that is true but the work at Ibrox can never stop if the club are to capitalise on their position of strength.

A fortnight after the title was won, Gerrard's side would travel to Parkhead as champions and a goalless draw was a somewhat low-key way in which to begin their reign. Given their exertions in the Europa League just a couple of days before and the emotional rollercoaster which Rangers had been riding, it was understandable that their performance was rather insipid as they ensured their unbeaten run continued in the Premiership.

It was only after that fixture that Gerrard, his staff and his players had a chance to take stock and to reflect but the magnitude of their feats would take some time to sink in. It may not be until they have left Ibrox that they realise just what their endeavours meant to so many.

At a club where the demands are incessant and the pressure is unrelenting, it is rare that successes can be savoured for too long. Once one trophy has been clinched, the focus immediately shifts onto the next challenge and the objective must be for Rangers to become serial winners in the coming years.

It is said that the first one is always the hardest to win. This league flag saw many players, and Gerrard himself, overcome that particular hurdle and the confidence gained from doing so will undoubtedly stand them in good stead going forward. Rangers are champions.

"When I was going for nine-in-a-row, I was going for my 18th trophy as captain of Rangers Football Club," Gough said. "For most of these players, it was the first trophy in their career, never mind at Rangers.

"It is only Allan McGregor and Steven Davis that had won a title with Rangers prior to this season and those two would have been a huge influence going down the stretch in terms of keeping players concentrated and focused on one game at a time.

"I have seen that has been the mantra this season and that was the mantra we had back in the day as well. You keep putting pressure on other teams and if you keep winning then they will fold and that is what happened. When you keep having to go and get a result, it becomes inevitable that you are not going to get it sometimes.

"Now they have that first one, I hope they go on and get many more. For Steven, it was the first trophy of his managerial career and it is hard to get over that hump whether you are a player or a manager.

"Hopefully 55 goes on and becomes 56 and 57 very quickly and I have seen Steven talking about that and about building on this. It is different when you are chasing in a championship compared to being the champions. It is a very different mindset and I am sure other teams will be gunning for Rangers next season."

With the Premiership race run and done, there was little at stake apart from bragging rights going into the Old Firm fixture. No meeting with Celtic can ever be described as trivial, of course, but it was the gestures before the game that carried greater meaning on this occasion.

Scott Brown, the Celtic captain, would show solidarity with Glen Kamara during the warm-up, while both sets of players stood united in their condemnation of the racist abuse the Finnish international had received just days previously against Sparta Prague.

The 2-0 victory for the Czechs proved inconsequential on the night as Kamara accused defender Ondrej Kudela of calling him a 'f****** monkey' as he approached him and uttered behind a cupped hand during a break in play late on at Ibrox. The reaction of Kamara, normally such an unassuming character, spoke volumes.

The images of Gerrard hugging him on the touchline were powerful, while Gerrard's press conference was evocative and footage would later emerge of him raising the issue with Slavia officials on the touchline. Rangers were united in denunciation as Slavia vehemently defended their player, repeatedly accusing Kamara of allegedly assaulting Kudela in the tunnel afterwards and highlighting, for reasons only known to themselves, the challenge from Kemar Roofe on keeper Ondrej Kolar that had seen him receive a straight red card and subsequently a four-match suspension.

The 2-0 defeat on the night would end Rangers' European campaign but that disappointment seemed irrelevant in context. Their efforts against Slavia – and the remarkable save from Allan

McGregor in the first leg – were to prove in vain but the same cannot be said for any time put towards fighting the scourge of racism.

Kamara was the individual who found himself at the centre of the storm but he was far from alone. The support of fans online far outweighed the trolls who sought to demean him with a torrent of hateful messages on social media.

"I didn't know how to feel to be honest, I was at a point where I was so angry I had tears in my eyes," Kamara said in his first interview – conducted exclusively with ITV's Scotland Correspondent Peter Smith – as the game rallied round him in his time of need. "I haven't felt like that in God knows how long. It was a really weird feeling.

"For that to happen, from a so-called fellow professional, it's crazy. It's something you don't expect in the game.

"Words can't explain how I felt. Hopefully I never have to feel that again. It was crazy really."

Kamara has always been a man who lets his football do the talking. He is pleasant to speak to, but he seeks to make headlines with his actions rather than his words.

In this instance, both were notable. His decision to speak out was brave yet necessary and his account of that evening was distressing to listen to directly as he recalled the abuse from Kudela and the aftermath of the incident.

"From the fans, the manager, the club, people I don't know. They've been really supportive and it's been great," Kamara said during an emotive interview with Smith, conducted inside the Ibrox dressing room a couple of weeks after the incident which shocked European football. "I've appreciated it all and I'm thankful for it.

"If I could go back to the game, to the time of the game, I would have walked off the pitch, 100 per cent. The manager was trying to get me off the pitch but it was like I was on my own and I couldn't hear anybody. I was just going through different emotions and I wasn't listening.

"This type of thing shouldn't be in the game. I don't know if in our lifetime we'll see it change. If I can make a change in some way, I'll do it."

That drive to eradicate racism was started a long time before this appalling set of circumstances and will go on for many years after it. Kamara would inadvertently become the reason the conversations were ramped up but this issue was bigger than just who said what or not.

It was one which would shine the spotlight on education, on sport and on social media and Rangers would later announce that their management and players would take a seven-day break from their online platforms, a gesture that would become widespread weeks later as clubs, associations and individuals sought to use their influence as a force for good. Connor Goldson had described the taking of a knee before matches as a 'token gesture' and Rangers would subsequently stand united as every effort was made to focus minds and transform mentalities.

Kamara would receive a three-match ban for the alleged altercation in the tunnel and Kudela was suspended for ten games following a UEFA investigation. It was a punishment that vindicated Kamara's stance but hardly one that would act as a deterrent for others and UEFA were roundly criticised for the leniency shown to Kudela as his sanction was ultimately measured in weeks rather than months. The punishment hardly fitted the crime.

Rangers had been at the forefront of that drive for equality for some time. In 2019, their Everyone Anyone campaign was launched to unite supporters of all faiths and none, of shared backgrounds and mixed beliefs. Whoever you are and wherever you are from, it was about the bond of being a Rangers fan.

The campaign launch was overseen by Stephen Kerr of

ChacePR. His association with Rangers started in the stands as a supporter and would later see him become a professional, helpful and valuable presence in the Rangers Press Office alongside Carol Patton and Donna Hannah for many years. After leaving the club, Kerr would work with Jim Traynor at Level5 PR and his efforts in raising monies, alongside director of operations Colin Stewart, for the Rangers Youth Development Fund were tireless and hugely significant to a generation of aspiring players.

His time on the Everyone Anyone campaign was important for a different reason, however. A series of committee meetings with representatives from the club and the Rangers Charity Foundation culminated in a launch at Ibrox as political figures from across the spectrum and supporters from every walk of life came together to promote the movement.

"The key messages of tolerance, respect, understanding, they resonate more than ever now and Rangers has to be seen to be a club open to all regardless of race, gender, ethnicity, religion or sexuality," Kerr said.

"The key thing for me was that it had to be authentic. It couldn't just be another marketing campaign with a polish or gloss. It had to mean something. All the fans in the campaign are not actors, they are actual supporters who have got stories to tell.

"They have all got a shared bond, a shared love for the football club and that is why it was so successful to start with, because they shared their memories of growing up as a Rangers fan and going through different eras, whether it was the Barcelona Bears, nine-in-a-row or the 'Banter Years'.

"They all had stories of learning about Rangers from their mum or dad or a relative or friend and being taken to games. It was great to hear.

"It was all about being a Rangers supporter first and foremost and that was one of the key successes right at the start. It is a club open to all and that is the way it should be."

The incident with Kamara, and the horrific abuse that Roofe would receive on social media, brought the issue of racism back on the news agenda once again. For those that live it and suffer it, the scourge of discrimination had never gone away, though, and club captain James Tavernier would reveal that every black player in the Rangers squad had been targeted because of the colour of their skin at some point in the season.

Rangers cannot influence opinions or prejudices in other countries or within opposition supports, but the unity shown at Ibrox and amongst their followers was inspiring and offered hope for the future. It is sad that the vocal minority shout as loudly to this day, but the majority will eventually silence those who seek to spread hate and cause division.

"It is a shared bond and we are all in it together," Kerr said. "Previous campaigns like Pride over Prejudice and Follow with Pride were more anti-sectarianism messages but this was celebrating what it was like to be a Rangers supporter from different backgrounds.

"It wasn't just 'don't sing this song' or 'don't engage in this kind of behaviour' when that should be a given. This was a more positive campaign to celebrate the club and the message that everyone is welcome.

"It is a great title and it should never be forgotten that Rangers is about the supporters. The people that are in charge are the custodians at any one time, but the supporters are the one constant. The fact that they were telling the same stories but from so many different backgrounds was inspiring in many ways."

The launch of the Everyone Anyone campaign was a stride forward from Rangers and the club cannot allow steps backwards to be taken in the coming years. There are moments in every season that are defining in a football sense, and the abuse of Kamara felt significant in the battle against racism as the game and the country sought to find a concerted way in which to ensure we live in a more open and accepting society.

If there is one positive to come from a dreadful situation in the following years, it will be that this is seen as a point from which real progress is made. Time will tell if that is the case and the black players at Ibrox and in dressing rooms across the country will be the ultimate judges.

"We are better together than divided and it is absolutely outrageous that in this day and age we are still talking about incidents of racism and sectarianism," Kerr said. "You look at the rise in internet trolling and the abuse that people are suffering online as well unfortunately.

"The incident with Glen was really shocking. He is a very mild-mannered man and clearly something has gone on there which is completely unacceptable.

"It was great to see his team-mates all supporting him, the manager spoke very well after the game and the supporters, to a man and woman, came together to support him and call it out. It was absolutely disgraceful and it really has to be stamped out, there is no place for it in society, never mind sport or football. The 'Rangers Family' is a well-worn phrase but it certainly rallied around Glen on that occasion and quite rightly too."

The show of support from Celtic preceded a 1-1 draw that was notable only for the fact that Morelos would score his first Old Firm goal. Somewhat fittingly, it was also his 55th league strike for Rangers as Gerrard's side maintained their unbeaten Premiership run.

The break offered after the derby was welcome for Rangers. March had been historic and emotional, yet also physically and mentally draining. As with most times at Ibrox, it was certainly never dull as the title was won and celebrated amidst a political whirlwind before a remarkable Europa League run came to an end in acrimonious circumstances.

The Premiership race was over and The Journey had been completed. Of all the words said and written, three meant everything. Rangers are champions.

ELEVEN

THE TOAST is to Absent Friends. It is to those that were loved but are now lost, those that were part of the Rangers Family yet did not see the club, their club, get back to where it belonged.

Amid the celebrations and the sense of achievement as 55 was won and cherished, there were feelings of sadness for many. This title win will be the most significant that generations of supporters ever savour but their thoughts were with relatives, friends and former players as they remembered the fans and the heroes who didn't see Rangers rise again.

The period between the day that the Premiership was won and the afternoon when the silverware was taken into the Ibrox Trophy Room was strange for Rangers. The euphoria of March would return in May, yet April was largely a month of disappointment as the Scottish Cup campaign came to a premature end and Steven Gerrard and his players squandered the opportunity to add to their medal collection.

As always at Ibrox, a sense of perspective can be hard to find. The defeat to St Johnstone in the quarter-finals was one of the real low points of the campaign, and of Gerrard's tenure, but it would not detract from the significance of what had already been achieved. The season would not end with another trophy, but it had still provided supporters with the ultimate high as Rangers accomplished the feat they had been working towards for a decade.

The trials and tribulations of those years put immense strain on a support that would overcome challenges like no other fanbase had ever faced up to. Rangers is, and always will be, a way of life for those that follow the club and its health and its fortunes shape how they lead their personal and professional lives.

Friendships have been formed and partners have been found through a mutual love of Rangers and the stories told and memories made at home or away, in victory or defeat, last a lifetime. As managers are hailed or criticised, players revered or heckled, the bonds between individuals are strengthened as Rangers defines moods and shapes outlooks.

Those connections may be broken in death, but they are never completely fractured and a love for Rangers is the link that binds many together. In these times of celebration, thoughts naturally turn to those who would tragically not see their club's finest moment.

The 'Rangers Family' phrase may be a well-used one, but it does encapsulate the feelings that supporters have for players who live their dreams and pull on that famous blue jersey. Many would never meet their heroes, but they feel as if they know them and they care for them in times of triumph or of hardship.

The days and weeks after the title was won and after the trophy was lifted gave fans a chance to reflect and to remember. There will be moments that are lost in the mists of time, but the protagonists from their personal and collective Rangers stories will never be forgotten.

For Colin Stewart, the director of operations at the Rangers Youth Development Company, those connections are ones of friendship rather than just sporting adulation. His position is a labour of love not a chore, a hobby more than a job. He works for the club he loves.

In 2015, he would assume control of the Rangers Former Players Benevolent Fund following the deaths of Sandy Jardine and Colin Jackson and his efforts alongside John Greig, the Greatest Ever Ranger, and Barcelona Bear Peter McCloy are tireless. By that stage, his club had emerged from the most tumultuous period in its history and Stewart had overcome his own adversity as he fought a battle with cancer that could have cost him his life.

His personal tale is an inspiring one and there are few at the club who deserve to savour this title victory more than a man who has given two decades of service to Rangers and who epitomises the class and dignity one should expect from a key figure at Ibrox. Stewart would cherish the moment that Rangers were crowned champions, yet in celebration there was recognition for those that he cheered as a supporter and would later work with and for.

"One of my favourite banners that the fans put out is the 'Absent Friends' banner," Stewart said. "I love to see that out at Ibrox and it is a banner that means so much to so many.

"I immediately thought of Sandy when the league was won and the guys that saw Rangers go down the leagues but didn't see us win the Premiership. They were in my thoughts.

"Guys like Sandy and Colin, Bobby Brown, Big Tam Forsyth, Fernando Ricksen of course, and David Hagen more recently. They didn't get to see Rangers get back to where they are now and didn't get to see 55 and it is something that myself, Peter and John talk a lot about.

"Peter knew Bobby well and talks of the 'goalkeepers' union'. He met Bobby a few times at various functions and they would always talk about their respective eras and John will tell me stories about Big Tam.

"Not having them around for these celebrations and these good times is very sad. But I like to think they are looking down and watching it with a smile on their faces. At the Fund, it is something that we always talk about and it is very sad that these guys are not here to see it. All of the former players, and many other people, are very much in our thoughts right now."

The death of Jardine in April 2014 would rock Rangers as a club and a support. He had announced his cancer diagnosis two years earlier, just months after Ally McCoist's side started their Third Division campaign and set off on the long, difficult road to recovery.

As a player, Jardine was a classy, skilful defender and a man who represented Rangers and Scotland in the right way. He would make more than 1,000 professional appearances and, at the age of 37, he won the Scottish Football Writers' Association Player of the Year award, becoming only the second man after Greig to collect the prize on more than one occasion.

His influence cannot be solely measured in titles or accolades but his part in the European Cup Winners' Cup success of 1972 and in the trebles won under the guidance of Jock Wallace in 1976 and 1978 ensured his place in Ibrox folklore. At Tynecastle, he would earn that SFWA award whilst working as an assistant to manager and friend Alex MacDonald and Jardine is revered in his native Edinburgh as well as his adopted Glasgow.

That fact was never clearer than when he unfurled the Third Division flag at the start of Rangers' League One campaign. His appearances around Ibrox and Auchenhowie had become less frequent by the summer of 2013 but he would take the acclaim of a capacity crowd ahead of the opening fixture of the campaign against Brechin.

Just weeks after his death, the Govan Stand at Ibrox was renamed in his honour as a lasting tribute to a man who gave the best years of his career and his life to Rangers, while a bronze bust was later placed on the Marble Staircase. Jardine would go above and beyond the call of duty and he was a stalwart, a pillar of support to those around him even in ill-health.

There is nobody that benefitted more from Jardine's time and compassion than McCoist and he would dedicate the League One title to his friend and confidant as Rangers beat Stranraer at Ibrox just days after Jardine lost his battle with liver cancer. The second stage of 'The Journey' had been completed, but the club had lost a giant of a man.

McCoist and Jardine had been through the toughest of times side-by-side at Ibrox and one of their last acts together was to film an 'in conversation with' style interview. The hour-long production for RangersTV is an insightful yet emotional watch even today and is worth the time of any supporter as two Ibrox greats share tales that transcend the generations and speak with such fondness about a club that stands the test of time.

"Sandy was phenomenal for me to tell you the truth," McCoist said as he paid tribute to a man who, like him, didn't do walking away during Rangers' darkest days. "He used to come up into the office at Murray Park and we would have a cup of tea and a right good moan at each other!

"We would say 'how the f*** have we got ourselves into this mess?!' But, in all seriousness, he was brilliant for me, absolutely brilliant. I owe him so much.

"Obviously I had people like Walter Smith that wasn't at the club any longer that I could phone, but Sandy was there on a daily basis and he was a tower of strength at the football club.

"That wasn't just for me, that was for everyone and I'm thinking about the girls in the marketing department, thinking about Iona, Claire and Allison, about Carol and Stephen in the

Press Office. Sandy was there for everybody, absolutely everybody from the tea lady right up to the players and the management.

"I thought about him myself and often do. That wasn't just when the boys won the league after Celtic drew up at Tannadice, I have thought about him on numerous occasions, numerous occasions. I can't believe this season is seven years since he passed away, that is staggering, it really is.

"I think it is natural that in times of great joy, in times of such an outpouring of emotion and celebration, that there is pause for reflection as well. I think it is absolutely only right that a lot of people did that with Sandy and that will continue for many years to come."

It was indicative of the standing with which Jardine was held amongst the Rangers support that tributes and messages appeared online in the hours and days after the Premiership was won in early March. Seven years after his untimely passing, he was at the forefront of thoughts once again.

Jardine had always been a man to lead from the front. He would oversee the Rangers Fans Fighting Fund when it was launched in the aftermath of administration and later stood on the steps of Hampden as supporters protested at punishments handed down to the club by a Scottish FA judicial panel.

Around 7,000 fans would march to the National Stadium on that day and Jardine was front and centre as an inspiring and respected figure. It was a time of uncertainty and of anger and the animosity that was nurtured between Rangers and those that sought to punish and demean the club lasts to this day. Fans now, as they did then, stand up for their club and that unity has not been more prevalent than in these times of jubilation that title 55 has sparked.

"When Rangers were in trouble all those years ago, Sandy was there leading the way and he was crucial to keeping the club alive, that is for sure," Derek Johnstone, a former team-mate of

Jardine that was friendly with the defender long after they ended their respective playing careers, said. "Sandy kept everyone in the know and gave them hope and we all remember that great picture of him walking to Hampden with thousands of Rangers fans behind him.

"He absolutely loved the club. He and Greigy were big Hearts fans, but once you go through those front doors at Ibrox, you become a Rangers man and that is what happened to Sandy.

"There was no leadership at that time and everyone was just in shock at what was happening. Someone had to take stock and lead from the front and that person was Sandy Jardine. He was someone that the fans hugely respected and he was there 24/7. If he was needed, he was there.

"There are so many people that will be remembered for the part that they played during those dark days – everyone from the likes of Ally McCoist to Dave King and the Three Bears – and the fans will always be thankful for their efforts. Sandy Jardine has to be right up there with the lot of them.

"He was there through thick and thin, trying to help the punters through what was happening and giving them a figure to rally behind. Rangers owe him a massive, massive debt for that. He was a fantastic player and a wonderful ambassador for the club."

The moment that Jardine unfurled the Third Division flag at Ibrox was one of the most poignant of Rangers' time in the lower echelons of Scottish football. Now, the Premiership flag will flutter from the roof of the stand that bears his name after a first title success in a decade.

Rangers had to wait a year longer than that between titles before their triumph in 1975 and that famous afternoon at Easter Road summed up Jardine as a player and a person. A header from Colin Stein would earn Wallace's side the point they needed to be champions and Jardine elected to come off the park in the closing stages to allow Greig to take to the field and be with his team-mates when the final whistle was blown. It was a gesture that was the mark of the man.

He was serenaded as 'Sandy in royal blue' and the part that he played in Rangers' fight for survival will forever be appreciated. Few have given more to the club as a player; even fewer have contributed as much as a person.

"He could handle any situation and he would do it in a way befitting Rangers Football Club," Johnstone said. "He was a great speaker, he was always immaculate with the shirt and tie on and he carried himself like a Ranger.

"He deserved to have his name on the Govan Stand and I am sure his family and friends will be very, very proud when they see the league flag flying above the Sandy Jardine Stand. What a fitting tribute to a wonderful man.

"He was at Ibrox right until the very end. He could easily have said that he wasn't well, that he wanted to spend some time at home. He was there until the very end and every Rangers fan should be proud and appreciative of what Sandy Jardine did for this football club. They will never forget him.

"As a player, he was everything you could ask for in a professional and a team-mate. You never read about Sandy Jardine on the front of any newspapers or heard about him on the radio or television for anything other than his football.

"He was the consummate professional and if everyone played and behaved like Sandy we would have a far better game. He had a real class about him and it is sad that he wasn't with us to see Rangers take their place at the top of Scottish football once again."

The legacy that Jardine has left behind is a profound one. Those that he helped, consoled or encouraged during Rangers' troubles will never forget his influence, while those that saw him in a fine and successful team will long revere him as one of the true Ibrox greats.

The players that he played with and those that followed in his illustrious footsteps owe him a debt of gratitude, too. He was one of four legendary figures that formed the Benevolent Fund to support players from before, during and after their time, providing medical and financial assistance if required.

Stewart would join Greig and McCloy as trustees of the Fund and now helps the very men that he supported from the terraces. He recalls a story with a member of the Barcelona Bears when a response of 'ach, I'm sore. Knees, ankles, hips, you name it . . .' greeted an enquiry into their wellbeing. A tale of playing the second half of a match with a broken ankle after a quick painkilling injection in the dressing room followed and those days of patching players up and sending them out – at a time when it was deemed a 'man's game' in a machismo manner – are now catching up with those who didn't earn the financial rewards of their contemporaries for their fine efforts at Ibrox.

"John came to see me one day, which he had done many times before, and we sat and chatted for half an hour and had a cup of tea," Stewart said. "He said 'you are probably wondering why I am sitting here?' and I said I thought he was just here for the tea!

"The Former Players Benevolent Fund was started by Sandy, Colin, Peter and John and it had been launched initially to look after the interests of players pre-Souness.

"Those players just didn't earn enough money that they could retire on. John asked if I would do him the honour of looking after the Benevolent Fund. It was an honour for me.

"I am now looking after the interests of players who I watched and who were heroes, and it is a privilege to be able to help the guys out. Every time the phone goes and it is maybe one of the Barcelona players, it is an honour to help them out whenever we can.

"There was no hesitation from me when John asked. Prior to

that, Colin Jackson and his good wife Pam, they looked after the Fund and I am privileged to have taken that on now."

The money donated by supporters and assistance provided is a source of relief to those who require it, yet there are many for whom the goodwill is sadly not enough in times of illness. Some would lead full and fulfilling lives, whilst others saw their time cruelly cut short and were taken too soon.

Former keeper Brown passed away in January 2020, aged 96. He was part of the first treble-winning side in 1948 and kept 109 clean sheets in a Rangers career of almost 300 outings, including a run of 179 consecutive appearances over a six-year period.

He was an Ibrox icon and a national treasure. In 1967, Brown would lead Scotland to the momentous 3-2 victory over England at Wembley as his side became unofficial world champions and legends of our game.

Just months after the loss of Brown, Forsyth died, aged 71. He is remembered by DJ as 'a gentleman off the park and a colossus on it' and is most famous for his winning goal – scored from just inches out and with the studs of his boots – against Celtic at Hampden in the Scottish Cup final of 1973.

As a player, 'Jaws' as he was affectionately known, seemed invincible at times and his death would hit team-mates and a generation of supporters hard. These legends may pass, but their names and deeds will live forever.

That is certainly the case in the tragic story of Fernando Ricksen. The tributes that followed in the days after his death in September 2019 spoke volumes of his character as a player and a person. Ricksen was unique, inspiring and had a resolve that was evident on and off the park, in sickness and in health.

His battle against Motor Neurone Disease was certainly not futile and the money raised in his name ensured his final years were not in vain as he showed a remarkable bravery and defiance in the fight with such a horrible and debilitating disease. Ricksen was a hero of Helicopter Sunday and cup final successes, but the fund-raising matches held in his honour would surely have carried just as much significance for the Dutchman as he sought to inspire those sadly suffering a similar fate.

When a member of the Rangers Family passes away, there is an individual and collective grief amongst the support. In times of celebration, it is only natural that they come to the forefront of minds once again.

The last decade has been arduous for fans to live through and each will have their own tales of worry or hardship from along the way. Stewart is no different in that regard.

His work with the RYDC has seen him hand over cheques for more than £9million to the Rangers Academy as funds are invested directly into the next generation of up-and-coming talents. As Rangers' business model evolves, the importance of producing their own players will increase and every pound earned and spent is worthy.

Stewart is one of the few who have been with Rangers every step of the way along the road to recovery. He recalls his fears over whether McCoist would even be able to field a team in that first match against Brechin after looking out over the training pitches at Auchenhowie and seeing only kids and a couple of experienced pros. The scene today is very different.

Funds from the relaunched Rangers Pools have been used to enhance the facilities behind the blue crested gates on the outskirts of Milngavie and at Ibrox as, after years of neglect under the previous regime, the custodians of Rangers have cared for the club on and off the park, as is their duty.

He would steadfastly refuse to hand over cash from his reserves during the final days before regime change and he would never meet the likes of James and Sandy Easdale or Derek Llambias and his conversations with Craig Whyte were brief.

"I only met Craig Whyte twice," Stewart said. "I remember

sitting for the first time with Craig and I thought to myself 'I have never sat with a billionaire before'. Before the second meeting, I realised I still hadn't."

Stewart would lock the doors to his office to ensure he and his staff were kept isolated from those that supporters had real concerns over. At other stages, he would take his laptop home to work away from Ibrox for a week and return to a voicemail full of missed calls from those that were running Rangers.

They are days that supporters hope will never be repeated. For those that lived through them, they act as a reminder and a warning, while signifying just where Rangers have come from to reach a position of strength that so many would sadly never experience.

"I got very emotional when the title was won and there are not many of us at the club from those days and who have gone through the whole good to bad and back to good again," Stewart said. "It has been a strange time, that is for sure.

"I can remember meeting Craig Whyte and after that I refused to meet any of the others. I refused to meet Charles Green. I was invited many times by his PA to go round there but I just saw through things and I thought 'I am not doing it'.

"I never met the Easdales. I just refused point-blank to meet any of them from then on. To see us back where we are now means so much and from the moment that Dave King, John Gilligan and Paul Murray came in, I knew that Rangers were safe again.

"Emotional is probably the best way to describe it. I am just a fan like the rest of the support and I shared those emotions with them when we were saved. To then see us win it, I always hoped but it was difficult to see when it would happen at times.

"When you go from where we were to what we have now, watching us compete in Europe as well as we are and beating top teams to get to the last 16 of a European competition, it is remarkable.

"It has been a whole mixture of feelings along the way. It has certainly been a rollercoaster of emotions to go from where we were then to where we are now. But it is great. I am very proud and very pleased."

Stewart is fortunate enough to have stayed on the ride until the very end. Many staff would pay the price for cost-cutting measures at different stages of Rangers' recovery and those changes would be felt around the club. The team, the stadium and the badge make Rangers special, but the people and the history make it unique.

That first sight of Ibrox as you approach by car or by foot still takes the breath away, as does the moment that the pitch comes into view as those final few steps are climbed. It is clear in the mind, a recollection that will, much like the affection for the club, never fade once love has struck.

Jamie McEwen can credit his grandfather, Gordon, for introducing him to a sporting institution and a way of life and the famous Champions League nights with Porto and Villarreal in Alex McLeish's reign remain vivid memories. Gordon worked for the club as a chauffeur and tickets for the hospitality suites in the Govan Stand were a perk that Jamie would get to benefit from.

The family is steeped in Rangers. Gordon was a young acquaintance and team-mate of Walter Smith at Bishopbriggs Amateurs and he was the cousin of Gilligan. Also on the family tree is the name of John Lindsay, who spent five years at Ibrox before moving to Everton in 1951.

As a child, Jamie was told of the stories of yesteryear. As a teenager, he would live through the most turbulent period in Rangers' history. While he did so, his grandfather battled the disease that would eventually take his life before he could savour the ultimate title triumph.

"He had breast cancer before, which was unusual for a man, in 2010/11 and he did well to recover through that," McEwen said. "Then in August 2018 he got told that it had come back. The first question for most people that day would have been 'how long do I have to live?' But his question was 'will I get to see Rangers win the title?'

"That didn't transpire but I remembered that when we did win it. That was his first question. It was a bit left-field but funny at the same time as well!

"Whatever was going to happen was going to happen so he was as well thinking positively and he did so with a sense of humour. I think it threw the doctor that was telling him right enough!"

The last wish that Gordon had wouldn't be granted unfortunately. Even the football gods didn't have it within their capabilities and his death brought a premature end to a long personal and professional association with the club. He had, at least, seen Rangers back in the hands of the people who would eventually restore it to its place at the top of Scottish football.

He would chauffeur Gilligan, King and Murray around the time of their EGM win in 2015, the free service a thank you and the least he could do for their efforts in rescuing his club. A couple of years later, he struck up a friendship with the man that preceded Steven Gerrard as manager as he helped Pedro Caixinha during his brief and ill-fated tenure.

An initial expectation that the Portuguese would require his services for a couple of weeks proved wide of the mark and Caixinha and his staff were regular customers. When Jamie was receiving treatment on a knee injury from physiotherapist Stevie Walker, Caixinha would always ask for his grandparents whenever the two met in the Auchenhowie corridors.

The night of the defeat to Progres Niederkorn in the Europa League will go down as the most ignominious in Rangers' history. For Jamie, it was memorable for another reason.

Caixinha was effectively done as manager that evening after the 2-0 loss at the Stade Josy Barthel. Hours earlier, he had come up trumps for two supporters within a couple of thousand strong contingent that had travelled not knowing what embarrassment would await them.

"Our first away journey together without parents was Luxembourg," McEwen said. "I got a ticket through the Travel Club but my mate didn't have a season ticket and didn't get an away end ticket.

"I asked if there was any way my grandad could ask one of the staff if he could get me a ticket and they said to Pedro and Pedro got back to him saying there would be a ticket at the collection point for us.

"I went and got mine and there were two queues, one for fans and one for officials. The fans queue was massive and I met my pal and went to the officials one. They asked who the tickets were under and we said Pedro Caixinha and they all looked at each other and went 'aye right, no chance!'

"They checked the name David Williamson and sure enough there was a ticket for him. Everyone was just looking at us! It is funny looking back on it and all these things are part of the journey that has taken us to the title."

Such tales offer confirmation of the view that Caixinha was indeed a decent man. He was never a Rangers manager, though, and those months under him were some of the most difficult for supporters to stomach during the last decade.

The appointment of Gerrard would change the course of history. In December 2018, Rangers would beat Celtic for the first time in 13 encounters. It was historic, it was poignant.

"My grandad had witnessed so much dross since 2012 right through to 2018 but he was starting to see an improvement when Gerrard came in," McEwen said. "Anyone with a brain could see that was going to be a turning point for Rangers. He wanted to see Rangers win the league again but wouldn't get the chance unfortunately.

"When he started to get ill, that is when Rangers started to progress after Gerrard came in. He was in Marie Curie at the time and his last game was when we beat Celtic for the first time in the league since 2012. It was the Ryan Jack game and that was the last goal that he ever saw. "That was very fitting for him after everything that he had seen in the years before that and the goal that beat Celtic again was the last one that he saw. He wouldn't see us win the title again but I know he would have been delighted and so proud this season."

There will be many families who share similarly heart-breaking yet warming tales. It is why title 55 is as sentimental to the support as a whole and why this campaign, no matter the failures that preceded and followed the Premiership-clinching weekend, will be remembered as reverently.

Murray and Gilligan have spoken of the importance of this achievement in terms of giving the current generation a success to feel part of and that cannot be underestimated. The flickering love of Rangers will never burn out, but this season ensures it shines brighter than ever before.

It is a victory that means different things to different people. Whatever emotions it inspires or feelings it provokes, each fan will think of those lost along the way and look forward to future triumphs alongside those with whom they share a special bond.

"I am only 23 but when you put it into context it is the most important title in my time, especially after everything that could have happened to the club," McEwen said. "We might never have risen to the top again so when we got back up the aim had to be to win it. My fear was that we would be living off past glories, that we would have the big fanbase but have nothing to show for it going forward.

"It was just a relief when we won it. It made it better for me that it was this year and that we got 55 in the same year that we stopped ten-in-a-row. It has been a long journey and we have got there in the end.

"It is hard to explain but it is just so important after everything that we have been through over the last ten years. The new board came in in 2015 but there is still a six-year period from then to actually rising to win the league and that is a long time for Rangers.

"The only honours there were the Championship and the Petrofac Cup. When I was growing up, I was used to Rangers winning one or two trophies a year so to go ten years without a major title was hard, but it makes it even more rewarding."

The weeks after the Premiership was won allowed supporters an opportunity to regroup and to take stock. League matches with Hibernian and St Johnstone ultimately mattered little apart from the fact that the results – a 2-1 home victory and 1-1 draw at McDiarmid Park respectively – kept the unbeaten league run ticking over. In the end, Scottish Cup successes against Cove Rangers and Celtic were futile as St Johnstone won a remarkable quarter-final tie to ensure Gerrard would have only the one medal to show for his efforts at the end of his third term in charge.

That one, of course, was the most important one for Rangers. There was something of a vacuum between the two significant days in the Premiership and supporters were unaccustomed to such a hiatus, especially given that so many other league wins in recent memory had come in far more dramatic circumstances.

There was rightly a sense of profound annoyance that Rangers had missed out on a double, or even a treble, this term but 55 was all that really mattered. That hadn't just been the ambition since August, that was the target that the last ten years had been geared towards achieving.

The bitterness and anger of the early days of the fight were now gone. Whatever else happened in this season, fans should remember just what has been accomplished and why this one is simply the best, better than all the rest.

"Yes is the quick answer," Craig Houston, the founder of the Sons of Struth, said when asked if it was all worth it to win title 55. "I have been fortunate to have lived through trebles, nine-in-a-row, last day title deciders, but this is bigger, and possibly bigger than the sum of all the other titles I have been fortunate to witness as a fan.

"That is for two things. The amount of effort that the fans put in to get us to this point should never be forgotten and there are people that helped us through the journey that aren't here to see the end of it. We will raise a glass for them. It is bigger than any of those triumphs for what it means to the club and the support.

"When we were protesting against the board, we always said that we were here before you, we will be here after you and be here forever. This is the icing on the cake to prove to ourselves and the rest of the world that Rangers are back.

"We are back to normal. This is the end of that journey and it is the outcome that we all wanted. Even in the dark days of 2013 and 2014 when things were really tough for everybody, that was the driver.

"It was to get us back to winning leagues and this is years of work, of pain, of stress. It is years of being arrested, of being sued for £200,000 and having lies told about you.

"It is all of that. When the final whistle went on that league-winning game, it was a feeling of it all being worth it."

Those emotions would not be felt again until the last day of the campaign. Ibrox lay empty for the final time in an unusual season as a title party like no other took place on the pitch and a handful of directors and staff watched on.

Had events on the last weekend in April been different, those same scenes could have been replicated at Hampden a month later. Once again, Rangers had blown their big chance, though, and there was an even greater sense of grievance amongst supporters as the Scottish Cup bid ended in improbable, preposterous even, circumstances in the final game of the month.

The path to the National Stadium had looked clear for Rangers after a Steven Davis overhead kick and own goal from Jonjoe Kenny earned Gerrard's side a third Old Firm victory of the season. Within a week, the champions had fallen at the next hurdle.

The build-up to derby day had been dominated by the reaction to comments from John Kennedy, the interim Celtic manager, as he sought to give his side a much-needed confidence boost after an abject campaign. His assertion that, on their day, Celtic could claim to be the best team in Scotland drew widespread reaction and defender Borna Barisic would provide a statement that many supporters agreed with.

"I didn't hear the comments but I read the interview beforehand and I think that is the biggest joke I heard this year," Croatian internationalist Barisic said at a press conference on the eve of the Scottish Cup tie. "They didn't win against us in three games and we are 20 points in front of them, so it is disrespectful a little bit to us. That's my comment on that.

"You need to be in life always realistic. If someone is better and if someone is 20 points in front of you, you just don't talk like that. It is disrespectful for all the things we do this season.

"It is not only from him [Kennedy]. I know a lot of people talking about Celtic's situation with Covid and all of these things. It's like we've lost five games or we are just five points in front of them.

"We are 20 points clear in front of them, we didn't lose a game this year. It is disrespectful to talk about anyone and changes. I am talking about this season. That's it."

The following day, the champions did their talking on the pitch. Gerrard would eulogise about the endeavour, heart and desire of his players in the aftermath of the win over Celtic. It was a victory that consolidated the shift in the balance of power across Glasgow and Rangers today are a very different prospect from the side that beat Celtic for the first time in a long time three years previously, courtesy of that Jack strike.

They had shown they had the mark of champions in the Premiership, but that wasn't the case in the cups. Seeing Celtic knocked out of the Betfred Cup and then losing to St Mirren was bad enough, but overcoming Kennedy's side themselves and going on to be eliminated by St Johnstone was a cause of real angst at Ibrox.

"Listen, we won't shy away from the importance of the game," Gerrard said. "It became a priority as soon as the league was done and we were out of Europe.

"We'll take the responsibility for that and the reality is we need to be better in cup competitions. We're getting to this stage too many times and getting stung – for example, St Mirren in the League Cup – in the final moments of games. Four days ago [against St Johnstone] we haven't managed the game well enough as a team and we paid for that, two points were taken away.

"That's a challenge for me to improve on cup competitions and get a group that's capable of being better and giving our fans what they deserve, which is more trophies – not just one out of nine. That's not good enough."

Given how unrelenting Rangers had been in their pursuit of the Premiership over the course of the campaign, the two failures in the cup competitions were hard to fathom. Of all the nights to produce such abject performances, Rangers picked the two worst ones of the season and they would pay the price on both occasions.

The defeat to Callum Davidson's side was up there with the most staggering of Gerrard's tenure. James Tavernier thought he had won it with a header in the 116th minute but Saints keeper Zander Clark was left unmarked from a corner and Chris Kane converted with the final kick of two hours of action.

It was one of those nights for Rangers and Gerrard. Indeed, it was one of those nights for St Johnstone and Clark and the keeper would emerge as the hero as he saved from Tavernier and Kemar Roofe in the shoot-out to send the Saints through to the last four.

The challenge for Rangers after wrapping up the league title was to prove that they could be serial winners and add trophy after trophy to the Ibrox honours list. The ability to do just that is what separates good Rangers sides from great ones and former manager McLeish knows that as well as anyone.

His first season at Ibrox saw him win the League Cup and Scottish Cup before he completed the treble the following term. Another League Cup was won in 2005 ahead of that unforgettable afternoon on Helicopter Sunday, but the barren years live with a manager as much as the glorious ones.

"On paper, Rangers should have won at least one of the cup competitions this season and should have progressed a lot further than they have done at various stages over the last three years," McLeish said. "They had their chances against St Johnstone but they were just not clinical enough in front of goal and Steven, his staff and the players would have had a sleepless night on the Sunday, that's for sure.

"Rangers haven't progressed beyond the quarter-finals in the Scottish Cup and only have the one League Cup final appearance in three seasons under Steven and we all know that the demands at Ibrox are such that having a record like that will be questioned. But you have to look at the building process that has gone on over the last three years and the improvements that Rangers have made since Steven and his staff came in.

"This season, it looked like everything was right. The recruitment was excellent, the title was won in style and you would have thought that the door was open for them to do a treble or a double.

"It is a missed opportunity and Steven will be thinking that as well. Speaking from experience, I know what it is like to be at Rangers when you don't win and you don't add to your trophy haul and you do feel that weight of expectation from the support. Steven will rue the St Johnstone result for a while and he will know that they should have added at least one more trophy."

That quarter-final defeat at Ibrox ensured Rangers would only have three more fixtures to play before this momentous season would come to an end. There would be no fairytale ending at Hampden but the story of triumph and glory had already been written.

The cup results were clearly a black mark on their record but it would be ridiculous to say that the campaign was anything other than a success for Gerrard and his players. He may only have had the one medal round his neck, but it was by far and away the most important one as he celebrated for the first time as a manager.

"The Premiership title was the main ambition for Rangers this season and they won that so emphatically," McLeish said. "To win the league for the first time in a decade was a huge achievement for Rangers.

"But Steven would have gone into the summer thinking 'I should have had a couple of trophies this season'. That is not being disrespectful to anyone else, it is just acknowledging that he could have had a couple of medals. He did, though, get the most important one and that is the one that the Rangers support will cherish right now.

"Going forward, there will be that expectation that Rangers win as much as possible. When they win one, they want to go and win the next one and the next one and I know the disappointment that he will be feeling having not done that this season."

Given the myriad pressures and factors involved in life at Rangers, it can often be difficult to find context. In terms of this campaign, it will be noted that 55 supersedes all. The title was the non-negotiable but there is no doubt that other honours should have been won.

The fact that the demands were as lofty and the disappointment as deep served as confirmation that normality had returned to Rangers. This is a club where one victory is not enough and it is that demand that has fuelled recent improvements and will continue to power their drive for success.

The support have never dropped their standards. Once again, they are aligned with those across the club. Rangers are back where they belong.

"I still strongly believe that our demise was down to greed and the club being under the stewardship of people who didn't have Rangers' interests at heart," Houston said. "That was the case until 2015 when we managed to get a board of people who support Rangers.

"People said to me after the EGM that Rangers fans now owned Rangers Football Club and the majority of the shares today are held by Rangers fans. It is our own destiny now. We can't blame Craig Whyte or Charles Green or the Easdales anymore.

"It is in our own hands. We might not agree all the time, we might fall out from time to time, but it is Rangers fans that steer the ship now.

"We have managed to steer the ship back to the latter stages of Europe and to a momentous 55th title. The emotions are through the roof from a personal point of view and for every fan that did something, anything, to get us back here. We all deserve a medal."

The walls and corridors of Ibrox are adorned with the trinkets and trophies that catalogue Rangers' greatest accomplishments. The deeds of Gerrard and his players will now take their rightful place alongside those of their illustrious predecessors, those whose history they have now added to.

The closing weeks of the campaign were a time of reflection and of contemplation. As supporters remembered those who started the journey but didn't finish it, they crowned new champions and hailed modern-day heroes.

Though times had been hard, they had followed near and far and 55 marks a beginning as well as an end. Nobody appreciates the past more than McCoist, but he knows the future is where the focus must be now for Rangers.

"I think it is fair to say that it will never be forgotten what the club has gone through, and nor should it be forgotten what the club has gone through," McCoist said. "But, at the same time, the most important thing is that you have to look forward and look to the future and that is the same with most organisations, not just sport.

"It has been a fantastic season in the league and we now have the chance to look forward to the next step, which is the Champions League and looking to retain that Premiership title.

"That is what great clubs do and great organisations do, they never forget the past but it is more important to look to the future. Rangers will continue to remember what has gone on, and so they should, but they will look forward now and look to that next title and next trophy."

The last ten years had produced a concoction of feelings for those with an emotional investment in Rangers and a lifelong bond with their fellow fan. Loved ones were lost but friendships were made, tears of sadness were followed by those of celebration.

To forget the individuals and their efforts would do them a disservice and the heroes of yesterday should be held as dear as the ones of here and now. In victory and defeat, Rangers stand united once again, ready to strive for that next achievement.

This was a time to toast the greatest story in Rangers' history. It was just as important to remember those who had helped write the previous illustrious chapters. Here's to Absent Friends.

TWELVE

THIS IS not the end, this is only the beginning. The message from Steven Gerrard had evolved from 'let's go' to 'let's go again'. Now it is 'let's go for more'.

At a club where the pressures are as relentless and the demands as incessant, there can be a tendency to look forward too quickly and to think of the future rather than live the moment. That balance is one that Rangers must now strike as they seek to mark the achievements of here and now but strive for the next one.

There will come a time when Rangers must regroup and refocus for the upcoming challenges and there are plenty of goals to achieve as Gerrard tries to finally succeed in the domestic cups, retain his Premiership crown and make an even more profound impact in European competition. Even when attentions turn, these joyous, historic moments will never be forgotten.

Title 55 means more than any other for Rangers, and perhaps more than the sum of all the others. This has been their season, and Saturday, 15 May was their day.

There has been a sense throughout this campaign that it was just meant to be for Gerrard and his players, for the club and their supporters. The fact that the Premiership was won over the weekend that was six years since regime change was poignant. A decade to the day after their last league triumph – as Walter Smith's side were crowned at Rugby Park and coronated at Ibrox – the blue flag would fly high once again.

The time in between those two moments had been labelled as 'The Journey'. When captain James Tavernier raised the trophy above his head, Rangers had reached their destination.

The images and videos from those celebrations will be iconic. They would be cherished in the days and weeks after the Ibrox party, but in another decade's time they will be looked at just as fondly as any that chart the glorious, illustrious history of Scotland's most decorated club.

"That moment was significant for so many reasons," Willie Vass, a photographer and the co-author of *Glasgow Rangers: The Journey: Mission Accomplished*, said. "When that trophy was lifted, it was for the staff that lost their jobs along the way, the real Rangers people who were the backbone of the club for so many years but are no longer there because of cutbacks and shenanigans.

"There are so many that should have been there to see that moment but weren't. It was for them. Look at the people that Ally McCoist had to try and keep in a job when he didn't take a wage. Laura Tarbet, for example, was secretary to managers from Willie Waddell to McCoist and you think of the security staff, the kitchen staff, the ground staff, that all lost their jobs because of what happened to Rangers.

"There are so many. The trophy lift and the title was for them as well as the fans. That is why this meant as much to everyone associated with Rangers and every Rangers supporter."

Rangers had counted down to that moment for 69 days. There had, of course, been huge disappointments in between the two cherished dates, but their final three fixtures of the campaign had shown just why they were champions as Celtic, Livingston and Aberdeen were brushed aside with the ruthlessness that had been the hallmark of the season.

On the final day, a Joe Lewis own goal, brace from Kemar Roofe and late Jermain Defoe strike would earn a 4-0 victory and the win that took Rangers through the 100 points marker for the first time. Gerrard's side were invincibles.

They had arrived at Ibrox amidst scenes that were reminiscent of those in March. A jubilant crowd gathered on Edmiston Drive and flags fluttered through the mainly blue and red smoke that filled the air.

The songs of celebration were sporadically interrupted by the whistles and bangs of fireworks and a banner which proclaimed '55 times the kings of Scotland' was hung adjacent to the front door. Friends were reunited and families gathered as fans of several generations marked a date that will be imprinted in minds like the name of Rangers engraved on the trophy.

Each goal that Rangers scored was greeted with a roar from outside. Gerrard, his staff and his players would get the chance to celebrate once their job was done, but the party was in full flow before, during and after a fixture that earned the champions a spot in the record books. Their place in the hearts of the fans had already been enshrined as they joined heroes of yesteryear.

Vass would start his career on the same day that the Souness Revolution began at Easter Road in 1986 and this title win saw another prolonged wait for success come to a glorious end. After hopping over the fence with a folding chair and his camera to get pitchside, he knew he had to 'act the game' and 'look the part' in an attempt to convince those around him that he was a full-time snapper.

The lifelong Rangers fan is now into his fourth decade of

capturing every high and low that his club have enjoyed or endured. His images tell the story of a past that is illustrious and chequered, but nobody can look into the future.

"I watched Celtic being dominant then falling away, Rangers winning nine-in-a-row, then Celtic getting nine," Vass said. "This season, it is just vindication for Rangers and the Rangers fans. You knew that Rangers would come back. It is vindication for the last ten years.

"Rangers were not going to lie down and disappear, they were always going to come back stronger, and perhaps stronger than before. The backing of the fans, the size of the club, Rangers weren't going to be down for long and if it hadn't been this season then it would have happened soon.

"This might start a new era of dominance of Scottish football for Rangers or it might start a new cycle where they win for a couple of seasons. Celtic have had the benefit of European money for so long but Rangers now have that and if that is invested wisely then there is no reason why they can't continue to win domestic trophies. Who knows? It is an open-ended book, so who knows what the next chapter will be?"

The Premiership title means different things to different people. For Gerrard, it was a momentous feat and his first as a manager, while his players would earn the rewards that their efforts so richly deserve. There will be an understanding at Ibrox why it is as significant to the club, but many will probably not realise the true sense of their achievement for some time to come.

There are those for whom the meaning of the moment needed no explanation and former chairman Dave King is one such figure. King may not have been at Ibrox to see Rangers finish what he had started, but the sense of a chapter being closed wasn't lost on a man who has become one of the most symbolic figures in Rangers' history.

"As you know, we tried for a number of years and I see this as the culmination of that," King said. "I came into the club and was, as I have said often, an unwilling investor because I really felt that the local Glasgow and Scottish community should have been doing what I ended up doing. Irrespective of that, I chose to get involved and even though there were the naysayers, etc, that is just part of being in Glasgow.

"I would regard this as the culmination of everything that I tried to do with the club in terms of bringing it back and making it the number one club in Scotland again. I really, genuinely, believe this will not be a one-off.

"Steven is absolutely committed, he is not going anywhere, and with Steven around for the next three or four years I really think that we will go on to dominate Scottish football and start to make a meaningful impact in the Champions League and operate at a level above where Scottish clubs have been for the last nine years.

"This is probably more of a culmination for me because I asked the supporters to back me to try and get the club back. For me, it is a culmination, but for Steven it is a beginning and part of a process to get Rangers there, keep Rangers there and progress in Europe and that will stand us, as a club, in good stead. We will continue to invest and improve the squad and support Steven.

"It is a great time to be a Rangers supporter. We have had terrible times for so many years but it is just lovely to be in such a great moment and time as a Rangers supporter. I am loving it at the moment."

King was not the only one. The Ibrox stands may have been empty, but fans were inside in spirit as they remained locked out in body and a campaign that started under the dark cloud of Coronavirus would end with Glasgow still gripped by lockdown restrictions.

There will come a day when Gerrard and his players will get to hear the Ibrox roar once again. When they do, they will be left in no doubt just what impact so few have had on so many during a historic season.

When King met Gerrard that afternoon of Rangers' Old Firm defeat three years earlier, he would speak of missing the 'buzz' that he experienced as a player. On the day that he was appointed as manager, it was clear that the lure of having that rush once again was a key factor in his decision to move from Liverpool to Glasgow.

There will only ever be one club that is within Gerrard's soul and his DNA but Rangers are now in his heart. That affection and understanding is mutual. There will always be a natural draw of Anfield for Gerrard, but Ibrox is not just a stop off on a coaching journey. Ibrox is home.

"The one thing I have said to him, which is quite ironic in a sense, is that I am a huge Liverpool fan and I have Kenny Dalglish as one of my closest personal friends, but he is also a Celtic legend," King said. "And the other one of the two greatest players in Liverpool's history will be a Rangers legend.

"I have made it very clear to him, and I don't have to because Steven understands this, the importance to Rangers Football Club, of what he and his team are doing and how this will cement his legacy with Rangers.

"I am absolutely convinced that Steven will continue with us and what I can say is that Steven is absolutely committed to staying with Rangers and winning further titles. What Steven will not do is leave Rangers on the back of one title and go to Derby or something like that. That is not what he is going to do because there is no upside for him doing that.

"To go to a club where he would moderately fail is not what he wants to do. He wants to win with Rangers, take Rangers into the Champions League and then in three or four years' time when Jurgen Klopp steps down, be ready for Liverpool.

"I see the beauty of the situation with Steven is that no matter how well he does with us, I think from his point of view winning this first league is not enough. He wants to cement it, he wants to repeat it and I think it is only with repetition that he will be satisfied.

"His record in Europe is excellent and I think he would like to have a better go at the Champions League than Celtic have done and then say that he had done three titles out of four or four-in-a-row and then that would be a nice time to move on to Liverpool."

That prospect of a return to Merseyside has always been around any conversation about Gerrard. He was asked about that likelihood on his first day at Rangers and his endeavours this season will do nothing to dampen the talk about when, not if, he will succeed Klopp as Liverpool manager.

The attraction for both parties is clear. Time will tell what the future holds for Gerrard but those who once chanted his name on The Kop have kept a close eye on his fortunes in Govan.

"Steven Gerrard is the ultimate legend at Liverpool, so wherever he is Liverpool fans are going to follow him," Joe Blott, chairman of the Spirit of Shankly, said. "It has drawn attention to Rangers and their title bid. He is an absolute legend, so people are going to follow him wherever he goes and whatever he does.

"He could have gone to MK Dons or other clubs in previous years and when he went to Rangers I think some people raised their eyebrows and there is always that view of Scottish football that it is not as good as others. It is as good as it is and he can only manage with what he has got and beat what is in front of him.

"He picked up a club that was low on confidence, Celtic were going for eight championships on the bounce and it was a huge challenge. It was set up for him to fail, really. I think Liverpool fans have watched him grow and they will be pleased for Steven to get his title."

Had league flag 55 not been delivered this term, then Rangers and Gerrard would have had some serious thinking to do about the way forward. From the dark days at the end of his second season, he has shone brightly throughout his third and he has now guided Rangers to the ultimate achievement.

His name and stature alone would surely not have been enough to get him the top job at Anfield but he now seems destined to add to his Reds legacy at some point in the future. Before he does so, he has unfinished business at Ibrox and new goals will be set as Gerrard seeks to become a serial winner in the coming years.

That trait is in his make-up and was one of the reasons why Rangers appointed him in 2018. Gerrard the manager is very different to Gerrard the midfielder, but he is still the same man with the same motivations.

"The level of maturity, the sense of determination, is clear," Blott said. "He is so driven and he comes across incredibly powerfully and people see that.

"A lot of feedback I see is people saying he is fantastic when he does an interview. He says what he means to say, he doesn't use anecdotes and clichés, he talks about the match he has just seen.

"What we see there is the footballer that we had for all those years, the one that was driven, that pulled Liverpool through. In some games, he won the game on his own because the other ten around him weren't performing well enough.

"You can see that he does that with Rangers as well. He does it in a hugely positive way, he clearly motivates the players incredibly and he has demonstrated what a really great leader he is. I think Liverpool fans have been silently, or maybe loudly in some cases, celebrating that Steven has done a fantastic job up there and they will continue to watch his progress with a keen eye."

Those observations about Gerrard's manner and messages are not new, yet they are the essence of why he is so impressive as a character. He is not merely a coach or a manager, he is a leader.

He would conduct his final press conference of the season with Tavernier by his side. In between them sat the Premiership trophy and Gerrard would frequently glance to his right, giving the silverware and the red, white and blue ribbons adoring looks whilst speaking of his pride at the achievement and ensuring his players received due credit and prominence.

Gerrard's first medal at Liverpool came two decades ago as Gérard Houllier's side lifted the Worthington Cup after a penalty shoot-out victory over Birmingham City. He was a Champions League winner five years later and the ninth medal of his career – coming in the Carling Cup in February 2012, a month that Rangers fans know all too well – was his last at Liverpool.

"I've got a lot of experience," Gerrard said. "I've been a professional since I was 17 years of age.

"Sometimes these moments pass you by when you're younger. But I won't let another one of these moments ever pass me by again. What you have to sacrifice for moments like this family-wise on a daily basis – getting up really early, working late at night, sleeping through the night with stuff on your mind . . .

"I wanted to enjoy this moment because it's been a long time since I've smelled this success and the champagne. I absolutely stink right now. It feels really good and I want more of it.

"I'm as hungry as anyone. It's in my DNA to go on and fight for more. That's what I've tried to instil in my players since day one. It's about getting their mentality into the right place to win and I believe I can do that."

Those days as a captain at Liverpool saw Gerrard stand front and centre in good times and in bad. As a manager, he seemed eager to take a step back and let others come to the fore.

He would pick up his medal and then embrace chairman Douglas Park, vice-chairman John Bennett and John Greig before walking in front of the podium to join his backroom team as Connor Goldson and Tavernier, last but by no means least, stepped forward and walked into Ibrox folklore.

Confetti cannons blasted ticker tape into the air and bursts of flames erupted as champagne was sprayed and players recorded the moment for posterity on mobile phones. This was the first occasion of its kind for many of Gerrard's squad and the man who had experienced it on the biggest stage of all would offer advice to those that had to savour every second.

"It is very different," Gerrard said when asked about the comparison between winning as a player and a manager. "It is a different career for me, a different place, a different role and responsibility. Today was about getting the result done and then just really enjoying the moment and soaking it up.

"James, I know what he has been through, I have lived with him for three years and I have educated myself on previous years before I came in. These are good people, these are good lads. Even when we have gone close and had a wobble and a setback, it hasn't been through a lack of effort. There is no ego in the dressing room.

"Led by him, they are a good group of lads and I am so proud of them. I am delighted for them because I'm not sure they realise how big this is but they will do in time.

"It is only really now that I appreciate what I won as a player. The message to the players talking to them after the game was to reflect, soak it in now and enjoy every single second of it."

There are two players that Gerrard would not need to relay that message to. Allan McGregor and Steven Davis had been there and done that earlier in their careers, and now they had 55 shirts to go with the latest medals on their CVs.

The influence of the most experienced professionals within the Ibrox squad was decisive throughout the campaign and, alongside Tavernier and Goldson, they would make the four-man shortlist for the Scottish Football Writers' Association Player of the Year award. There were compelling cases for each given their levels of performance and consistency over the course of the season, but it was Davis – who had become the most capped player in British football with his 126th appearance for Northern Ireland in March – that collected the prize. Tavernier took the award from PFA Scotland, completing a double for Rangers as Gerrard was named Manager of the Year by his fellow professionals.

"We have so many guys who could have won," Davis said. "The problem is that it is so difficult to pick one because of the season we have had. There are a number of players including ones who have not even been nominated.

"It's been such a strong season as a group and as individuals. I wouldn't like to be making that decision. I think Greegsy [McGregor] has been outstanding and I have a great relationship with him. I'm just thankful I've been chosen.

"You set out to have as strong a season as possible and bring your attributes to the team. I am absolutely delighted to be recognised for your efforts over the course of a long, hard season and especially given the season we've had, the performances we've put in and the consistency that we've shown. It's very special."

The fourth league medal of his career will surely be the one that Davis holds dearest. He had been an integral part of Smith's side during his first stint at Ibrox and his second will be prolonged for another 12 months after he agreed an extension to his contract that will see him be an influential part of Rangers' title defence.

At 36, Davis was as good as ever this season. His overhead kick against Celtic was the headline moment of the campaign, but it has been his consistency that has marked him out throughout a wonderful term as he controlled proceedings from the middle of the park.

He had faced criticisms over his levels when he returned to Glasgow from Southampton in January 2019 but he has strolled through this season with an elegance and style. His class is permanent.

"He deserves huge praise from me personally," Davis said of Gerrard as he reflected on his time under a man he played against for club and country. "When you are setting up a team you recognise the attributes that individuals have and try to find a system that works for them.

"The way we play in midfield and the role I am asked to play certainly suits my attributes and gives me the platform to perform to my best level and show what I can do.

"I thoroughly enjoy playing in that role, the way we are set up and the players I have around me allows me to show my best qualities so the manager and his coaching staff have to take huge credit for that and of course just giving me that belief as well. There's nothing more that a player can ask for than the manager's trust. You've got to gain that, but whenever you have that it's a great feeling."

The endeavours and achievements of Gerrard's side this term have earned them a unique place in Rangers' history. There is an affection from supporters that is deeper rooted than just sporting success, though, and this team is more likeable, more trustworthy, than many that pulled on the shirt during the barren times of the 'Banter Years'.

Fans may not have been able to witness their glories in person, but they relate to this side and have a bond with them. Title 55 is a triumph that has been won by a handful of individuals but that will be remembered by generations as Gerrard has succeeded where too many before him failed.

Stuart McCall would never get the chance to challenge for a league flag during his time as manager. He was the man who would oversee the start of the recovery in the weeks after regime change as he picked up the pieces following the departures of McCoist and Kenny McDowall. Neither McCall or King, nor

Paul Murray or John Gilligan, would be at Ibrox for the crowning moment but each had played their own part in the process that led Rangers to that point.

From those difficult days six years earlier, it was a matter of when Rangers would be champions again. Their time had come.

"Listen, we are going to enjoy it and we – the supporters, the players, the staff – deserve to enjoy it," McCall said. "The club has gone through a journey and at times it was so depressing. But now they have this title.

"They sold more than 40,000 season tickets in the Third Division. It was hard at times and no supporters deserve it more because they have stuck with the club through thick and thin and the ups and downs.

"Going down to the Third Division was hard enough and the journey back wasn't without its difficulties, but this season and the title coming back now is a reward for everyone that has been involved, but most of all for the supporters.

"Even when they have been back in the top division, they had to see their biggest rivals winning and being successful and playing in the Champions League. So this one just means everything and all the perseverance of everyone who has been involved, right from Dave, John and Paul, to now has paid off.

"It was a journey to get back through the leagues, that was started by Coisty and his staff and the supporters have been there every step of the way. Nobody could have foreseen this at the start of the season. I was hopeful that Rangers would win the league but it is incredible to do it as comfortably.

"The performances and the results, to be unbeaten for so long, everything about the season has been terrific. Rangers have been very impressive and they deserve everything they get."

This historic success has seen the history books rewritten. The tally of 102 points is Rangers' highest ever total, while a British record was set as just 13 goals – courtesy of 26 clean sheets –

were conceded as Gerrard's side eclipsed the achievement of Jose Mourinho's Chelsea side that won the Premier League in season 2004/05.

It may seem a strange suggestion to make, but the campaign could easily have been better for Rangers and the points dropped and defeats suffered will still irritate today. Those negatives are engulfed by the euphoria of 55, though, and Gerrard's side have nothing to apologise for to the supporters that backed them from afar this term.

A minority section of the fanbase would unfortunately let themselves down and tarnish the club's reputation, however, as the celebrations turned sour at George Square. It will be for the justice system to deal with the fall-out from the various incidents that erupted on the Saturday evening but the court of public opinion cast a harsh and unfair collective judgement.

The criticism for gathering in such huge numbers was always going to arrive, especially coming so soon after Nicola Sturgeon, the First Minister, had announced that Glasgow would be remaining in Level Three restrictions following isolated Covid outbreaks in the city. Such condemnation was also selective, though, and other sporting and societal crowds – both in the days preceding and following Rangers' celebrations – wouldn't attract the same headlines or levels of comment.

On the Friday night before trophy day, the Union Bears had organised an eye-catching pyrotechnic display as the banks of the River Clyde were filled with smoke and bathed in a bright red glow. Just hours later, thousands would bouncy in unison on the Squinty Bridge on their march from Ibrox to George Square and those celebrations – like they had been on Edmiston Drive – were good-natured and evocative as fans shared unique moments together.

The actions of the mindless minority later in the evening would not dampen the spirits or tarnish the memories of the thousands who revelled peacefully. Advice from the Government and Police Scotland, and a request from Rangers, to stay at home was always going to fall on deaf ears and it was completely understandable why so many congregated despite the ongoing Covid regulations.

The ills of society would fall at Rangers' door once again. The colour of your shirt is irrelevant when you choose to indulge in anti-social or criminal behaviour and the club cannot be held accountable for the misdeeds of those that follow it or attach themselves to it.

Anyone that was surprised by the reaction in certain quarters clearly hadn't been paying attention for quite some time and Sturgeon would say she was 'utterly disgusted by the Rangers fans who rampaged through the city' in a series of Tweets the afternoon following the night before.

Acknowledgements that it was a minority were lost amidst her condemnation of the 'violence and vandalism' and 'vile anti-Catholic prejudice' as Sturgeon urged Rangers to reflect on what more can be done to tackle such behaviour. Rangers were under fire from Holyrood once again and the censure from Hampden quickly arrived as Scottish FA president Rod Petrie claimed the scenes were an 'abomination not a celebration' that 'brought embarrassment to the national game'. The SPFL were also scathing in their criticisms of the small percentage that sullied Rangers' name with their moronic behaviour.

This was not the first time that football supporters had been lumped together and tarred with the same brush. It was perfectly possible to condemn the conduct of the few whilst empathising with the many, but agendas would not allow for such positions to be held as Rangers found themselves at the centre of the storm once again.

The scenes that caused such anger and that drew such criticism were not for Rangers or their supporters to call out. The scarf those involved wore was as relevant as the political party they voted for or the company that they worked for, but it is easier for some in the public eye to castigate the collective rather than offer solutions to Scotland's myriad ills.

Rangers had requested that 10,000 supporters be granted entry to Ibrox on trophy day and in the subsequent days. It was a move designed to reduce the need for fans to gather at the stadium but one which was rejected by the Government. Rangers had sought to be pro-active, but found themselves on the back foot in the days that followed their Premiership coronation.

"Winning our 55th league title in our 150th year was a historic day for Rangers Football Club," a statement read. "The support from millions of our fans across the world has been incredible.

"The achievement by Steven Gerrard and his team has received plaudits from across the football family, including recognition by sports writers, opposition players and managers.

"We are grateful to Scottish Government officials, Glasgow City Council and Police Scotland for the constructive engagement in the lead up to the weekend's game. We worked closely with the authorities for two weeks before Saturday's match to ensure a consistency of message.

"Sadly, a small minority of people behaved inappropriately and in a manner not reflective of our support. Some of the scenes were unacceptable and have besmirched the good name of Rangers Football Club. These so-called 'fans' should reflect upon the values and ethos of our club, and consider the damage this does to the reputation of the club. We will continue to engage with authorities as required."

The actions of the minority simply cannot be brushed aside or condoned. It should not be used to denigrate and demonise the majority, however, and those that enjoyed such times of jubilation will never allow the mindless to spoil their memories.

No matter how hard those that lined up to take shots at the support tried, their comment and their conjecture wouldn't take the shine off the day. Fans had waited too long, had endured too much, for that to happen.

The achievements of Gerrard's side deserved to be celebrated and cherished. Whether that was on the streets of towns or cities or in pubs or homes, that is what Rangers supporters did on a day that meant more than just a game.

"It was ten years to the day since we last experienced league success," Steven Clifford of the Four Lads Had A Dream blog said. "Everything that happened to the club in that time meant that number 55 had become a symbol for everyone, a symbol of hope and encouragement.

"We knew that when it did come that there would be a massive outpouring of emotion and gatherings and, on the whole, it was a brilliant celebration. It was a pity that the fans couldn't be in the stadium, that is obviously something that everyone has missed. Some of the games this season, Ibrox would have been rocking and it would have been fantastic to be at.

"That has been tough. But, if you had said to people at the start of the season this is how it would pan out, we would all have gladly accepted it. The celebrations were, on the whole, fantastic for the club and hopefully it is the start of more for everyone."

In many regards, that Saturday afternoon felt like the end of an era. In others, it felt like the beginning of a new one for Rangers. This has, after all, been a season of varying and contrasting emotions from the first goal that Ryan Kent scored at Aberdeen to the final one that Defoe netted against the Dons.

There is no doubt that title 55 marks the end of a chapter in Rangers' history, yet it is also an achievement from which the club must build in the coming seasons. It never can and never will be considered anything other than a hugely significant moment, but extra value can be found in it if Gerrard can truly use it as the foundations to build upon.

"I think the final step in the journey for Rangers fans will be hearing the Champions League music at Ibrox," Clifford said. "When that happens, I think a lot of people will close the book on the last ten years. For me personally, trophy day almost did that.

"I would have liked the season to have panned out differently and to have won the Scottish Cup, but in terms of what the team have done in Europe and the league, everything has built towards this. It has been a fantastic achievement to do it in the style in which they have done it. In such a pressure year, it has been exceptional.

"It came out of nowhere. It is not as if we could have said after Hamilton last season that it was OK because we would comfortably be where we are at this moment. It is an incredible achievement. It has been a cumulation of the ten years emotionally for the support."

As fans revelled off the park, Gerrard's side were typically ruthless on it. He had urged Rangers to leave a legacy this season and their final three fixtures of the campaign ensured they did just that.

The 3-0 win at Livingston just days previously was controlled and comfortable as Tavernier, Kent and Ianis Hagi got the goals. It was their other game in the month – the 4-1 victory over Celtic – that really emphasised Rangers' superiority, though, as a fourth Old Firm win of the campaign was secured.

It was style and substance for Rangers. Roofe would net twice, Morelos got another derby goal and Defoe was emotional at scoring his first in the fixture. Rangers had been on the end of so many demoralising defeats against Celtic and there was a sense that this one was retribution, of sorts, for the years where they were outplayed and outclassed.

The balance of power had shifted across Glasgow. That process had been seismic, but Gerrard's reign has always been more evolution than revolution. In this campaign of many challenges, Rangers had fared better in the new normal than those around them.

"I think this season they have been good at mixing it up, not changing the style completely but just mixing and matching players and making sure they have the right relationships in the right areas of the park for who they are up against in each game," Jordan Campbell of The Athletic said.

"Last year it felt like everything was in front of the opposition but this season they have been trying the ball over the top, turning people and making them turn away from the game and that, to me, has helped them break down the teams that in the first couple of years they might have come unstuck against.

"Now they are moving them a lot more freely and they seem a lot more patient this year. I don't know if that is to do with the lack of crowd and the fans getting on top of them. Thinking back to the second season post the winter break, that Hamilton game was absolutely toxic towards the end and the players looked stressed playing.

"People like James Tavernier, who usually plays quite freely, you could see the nerves getting to him, the same with Connor Goldson. I think that has probably helped them this season and even when the pressure has been on they have been able to play their game.

"Across the board you have seen the best-coached teams being able to play their game, whereas the teams that are relying on those spurts of 15 minutes and the crowds to get them going haven't fared as well. You can see the ones that don't rely on possession or that fuel to fire them up, it is more premeditated and considered."

There have been many hurdles that have been placed in Rangers' way along the road to redemption and glory but the final one, the most important one, has now been cleared as the Premiership title has been lifted. The next obstacle will soon come into view.

The transformation in Gerrard's side in every aspect has been remarkable. A year on from the lowest points of his reign, he would earn the achievement that he had been working towards from day one. As he raised the trophy on the park and posed for pictures in the dressing room and the Thornton Suite afterwards, he would bask in the glory of what had been accomplished.

The dynamic is now different for Rangers. They are champions rather than challengers and Murray has seen this situation on many occasions, both as a fan and a director. There has been a changing of the guard, but Rangers' focus cannot alter now as attentions turn to the next success.

"It is a bit like the Souness situation when he came in and won that first championship after so many years, and in some ways the first trophy is the most difficult to win," Murray said. "You have got to get over those mental and physical barriers and the players in that squad have now won a championship.

"They have won so they can draw on those experiences and I think having done it so comprehensively must give the players so much confidence. It will be interesting when the crowds come back and we see whether they can put that together with the crowds there. You know as well as I do that the crowd at Ibrox can be very demanding and it is a tough environment to play in.

"You would hope that the confidence we have from winning this championship would give us the mental strength as well as the physical strength to go and play in that environment. It is a great foundation.

"I think the player recruitment is something that has been really good and if we can build on the foundations that are there then that should bode well. There are no guarantees with player recruitment but it is a very professional setup in place with Ross Wilson and the rest of the team. I think the future is bright."

Rangers can approach those impending challenges with a self-belief and swagger, and they will do so undaunted by what lies ahead. This side is one that fears no foe.

This summer will see the latest round of changes to Gerrard's squad. Some 55 icons may depart, but their exits create opportunities for new heroes to be born and the transfer window will shape ambitions for Gerrard's fourth campaign at Ibrox.

Rangers will naturally keep one eye on events across the city to see how Celtic deal with their summer overhaul but events at Parkhead will not be Gerrard's focus. They never have been and his only concern will be improving on what he has as Rangers stride forward into a brighter future.

"I don't see major changes," Campbell said. "But you can look at small things and see how they have evolved, even things like the full-backs when one goes up and one stays or not playing a flat three in midfield as often to try and free them up. I think they are playing with more freedom this year.

"The Champions League money would be transformative and if they can bring in the calibre of player to take it up a level then I am sure they will do well in that tournament. No matter who they are up against, whether it be Porto, Braga or Benfica, you never think they are going to get a hiding. They might lose by a goal but it never seems that the game is going to run away from them.

"When they are struggling in games, like they were away to Benfica, they just reverted back to something that they had been working on for three years because they knew it worked for them. When you have that buy-in from the players, it is difficult to go wrong when you have experiences as a group and you know what works against that level of opposition.

"Going forward it will come down to what they do in the transfer market and whether they have to sell a couple of their players, especially the ones at the ages where they have real value and they need to cash in on them. That is a big thing in terms of how they replace those players and that is where Ross Wilson will come in as well."

Rangers had already started planning for next season back in January when Jack Simpson and Scott Wright were brought in ahead of schedule and Nnamdi Ofoborh, the Bournemouth midfielder, signed a pre-contract deal. In early May, KV Oostende striker Fashion Sakala became the latest piece of the Gerrard jigsaw to be put into place as Rangers refused to rest on their laurels.

The role of Wilson, the sporting director at Ibrox, will be crucial going forward. He had rejected a return to the Scottish game in 2017 before Mark Allen was appointed to oversee Rangers' football operations but he finds himself in the right place at the right time today.

Murray had been one of those on the board who was keen to bring Wilson to Ibrox. He had admired his work at Falkirk many years before and his mentor, Alex Smith, would speak highly of his endeavours. When Rangers appointed Mark Warburton as manager in 2015, Wilson was one of those who provided a reference to the board as the former Brentford boss was brought in ahead of the Championship campaign.

Gerrard may be the dominating figure at Ibrox, but he is far from a one-man band. The job is too diverse and time consuming for a single person to effectively run Rangers in a football sense and his relationship with Wilson – like those the Scot had with the likes of Mauricio Pochettino, Ronald Koeman and Ralph Hasenhüttl at St Mary's – will continue to develop as Rangers progress on and off the park.

"I think the days of the manager being the one person that does everything are gone," Murray said. "It is just impossible now with the size of football clubs and all the media aspects, the relentless number of matches and the professional level you have got to get to in sports science and all the support functions.

"The first team always has to be the focus because what happens on the pitch with the first team drives the whole football club and the success then drives the commercial aspect. You have to focus on the first team but put all these support mechanisms in place. If you can keep the manager focused on doing that, Ross in his position as sporting director manages all those other areas.

"For example, in player recruitment, if Steven and his staff want a left-back with certain attributes, Ross is keeping all of that information logged, through the scouting network, as to the kind of players that might be available. He might say there are five players available, lay out their characteristics and then it is up to the manager and the staff to narrow that down.

"There is so much work that is done behind the scenes now and it is keeping information updated and refreshed so that you are taking decisions with the best possible knowledge. That is absolutely a full-time job and that is why you need someone like Ross in that position to support the manager."

The financial backing of so many has been imperative for Rangers since regime change and the successes that are savoured today would not have been achieved without the selflessness of those that put their personal wealth into their club. To them, their fellow Rangers fan owes a debt of gratitude.

Rangers cannot rely on such generosity forevermore, however. In time, the business must become self-sustaining and self-fulfilling and that is the platform that Gerrard has provided over the last three years as he has assembled a squad that has value on the park and on the balance sheet.

This team will not be broken up and the component parts flogged on the cheap. When Gerrard was asked about possible departures after the Aberdeen game, he joked that any suitors had to 'bring an army with them' if they wanted to take any of his key men away from him.

When the moment and the money is right, there will be departures from Ibrox. It is all part of the blueprint, though, and there will be no need to go back to the drawing board for Rangers.

"When I was on the board the first time and Alastair Johnston took over as chairman after David Murray stepped down, we operated the club in the last two years of my first stint, which was 2009 to 2011, on a break-even model," Murray said.

"You have got your domestic matches that you can guarantee and your cup games and you run your operation on those foreseeable and guaranteed revenues and then we always saw the European runs as being an investment fund to put into the infrastructure or to buy players.

"I think that model is the model, I have always said that, and from what I gather that is what the board are moving towards. Obviously Europe will be a big part of that and if you then have a player trading model, that can complement those funds as well.

"We shouldn't be ashamed of trading players, we shouldn't say 'well, Rangers don't sell players'. We should be proud if we bring a player through the processes and then sell them on because that is showing that you are doing something right. We have made real assets out of most of the squad and developed them into players who can play at a really high level."

No matter who goes and who stays this summer and in the subsequent transfer windows, the ambitions for Rangers are clear. The names may change, but the goals do not, and they have a title to defend, cups to win and a European campaign to prepare for.

So much of the last decade has been spent looking at the past and analysing events that were outwith Rangers' control. Now they have a chance to shape their own destiny.

"It has to be a success from which we build in the coming years," Clifford said. "This is Rangers. We can't stand still and we can't rest on our laurels. It is not a case of 'we have won the league, now everything is fine'.

"We have to continue to build and the great thing about this management team is that they continue to strive for better and we want to dominate. This needs to become a regular occurrence.

"We want the league title to be at Ibrox next season and we want cups to join it. In order to do that, we have to keep pushing on. It doesn't matter what anyone else does, it will always be about striving and pushing on and always be about Rangers."

That is certainly the case for Gerrard and there is a clear, sincere pride in his players and affection for the club when he speaks. His legacy can now be enhanced after he joined the iconic figures he has often referenced so fondly as a title-winning manager.

Gerrard had missed the surge of adrenaline coursing through him, missed the pressure that only life under the spotlight can elicit. He is a legend in Liverpool and now a god in Glasgow. It was almost written in the stars for him to feel that excitement at Ibrox and Gerrard now, finally, has a league medal in his collection.

"Right up there, because I love winning," Gerrard said when asked where this success ranked in terms of his career. "That is my drive, that is my buzz, that is what I get out of bed for in the morning. My family will always be number one in my life, football will be number two. I have still got drive and hunger to achieve more.

"My playing days were different, it was a different club and I am really proud of my playing days. Now it is a different journey and this is the first one, I hope it is the first of many.

"I will continue to sacrifice and grow and learn and push myself and the group that I am here representing to achieve success. That is my draw, that is my buzz."

Title 55 is a marker post on Gerrard's journey. For Rangers, it signifies the end of one and the beginning of another. It is a triumph the likes of which has never been seen before, one which will never be surpassed in terms of the story or the significance.

It was as challenging as it was compelling personally and professionally. Never has a moment in Rangers' history meant as much, never has there been those levels of pride in the club, in your club, in our club, than the day when Rangers got back to where they belonged.

Some gave more financially, but all gave some emotionally. This title is for each and every one of them, for those that loved and lost, those that feared and fought, and the message of 'Rangers then, Rangers now, Rangers forever' acts as a reminder as much as a motivation.

The past will never be forgotten, but it is time to look forward. This title may never be surpassed, but it will certainly be added to by Scotland's most successful club.

Rangers welcome the chase. Rangers are Ready. Rangers are Going for 56.

ACKNOWLEDGEMENTS

THE STORY OF Rangers' fall and rise and the pursuit of title 55 has dominated my life personally and professionally for the last decade. The Premiership success in 2021 felt like the culmination for the club and there was a sense of a chapter being closed for me as well.

I am privileged to have had the opportunity to witness such a historic achievement in person and this book is a proud moment in a career that has offered me so many opportunities and allowed me to make countless acquaintances and friends.

The list of people that I owe thanks to is lengthy, but none are as important as my parents, Stephen and Jacqueline. For their love, encouragement and guidance, I will be forever grateful and I wouldn't be where I am today without them.

To close friends and my family – to Jonathan and Iain, to Russell and Blair and especially to Lyndsay – a heartfelt thank you for your support. I am fortunate to have had you all close during this time and I couldn't have done it without you.

The 2020/21 season was not without its issues, but those moments of celebration will forever live in the memory. I know they will have meant as much to every supporter as they did to me as Rangers returned to the top of Scottish football.

It has been an honour to chart the story of the campaign and of 'The Journey' and my appreciation in that regard begins with Peter Burns of Polaris Publishing for giving me the opportunity to write my first book. Having this work to commemorate 55 is a privilege I will hold dear.

That achievement would not have been possible without Dave King and my thanks to him extend far beyond writing the foreword to this book. He – alongside Paul Murray and John Gilligan – saved our club and every Rangers fan should hold those three and those that followed them in the highest regard.

The insight and opinions offered by respected press colleagues has been invaluable throughout the writing of this book, as have the contributions from staff, managers, players and observers from near and far. To each one, and to the many others who gave up their time to assist me and support me throughout, I owe a sincere thank you.

It may seem somewhat clichéd to use the phrase 'living the dream' but my role as Senior Rangers Writer with the Herald and Times Group is one which allows me to do just that. The job and the industry may be ever-changing and bring increasing challenges, but I never take my position for granted and I am lucky to have the friendship and faith of so many colleagues, both past and present.

My only regret in journalism is that I wasn't able to embark on my career a decade or more earlier and to experience the game and the business at a time of even greater opportunity and excitement. I have been fortunate to work through such a unique period in history, though, and these days will forever be cherished and forever belong to Rangers. Here's to 56.